Andrew Emery is the author of *The Book of Hip-Hop Cover Art* and comic memoir *Wiggaz With Attitude: My Life as a Failed White Rapper*. The founding editor of cult rap magazine *Fat Lace*, he was contributing editor to *Hip-Hop Connection* for 15 years and has written for dozens of publications on music, street culture, sport and even sleep paralysis.

He discovered hip-hop in 1984, and it changed his life. He has since failed to be a breakdancer, rapper, DJ, croupier and video shop manager, but did manage to succeed at interviewing his personal hero, Chuck D of Public Enemy. He is not the Andrew Emery who wrote a book about Bournemouth Seafront. He pays the bills as a copywriter and lives in Leeds with his wife, stepchildren and other animals.

First published by Velocity Press 2024

velocitypress.uk

Printed and bound in Great Britain by Clays Ltd, Elcograf S.p.A.

Cover design
Rich Firth
richfirth.com

Typesetting
Paul Baillie-Lane
pblpublishing.co.uk

ISBN: 9781913231507

WRITE LINES

ADVENTURES IN RAP JOURNALISM

ANDREW EMERY

For Emma, forever

CONTENTS

FOREWORD

Whole careers can pivot on the flimsiest of axes. Would the six-year-old Bow Wow become a rap star were he not pulled onstage at a Snoop Dogg show in Columbus? Would Will Smith become the Fresh Prince of Bel-Air had he not bumped into Benny Medina in Universal Studios' parking lot? Would 50 Cent have become richer than his wildest dreams had he not survived nine drive-by bullets outside his grandma's house? Here's another: would Andrew Emery have become one of rap's greatest journalists had he not crashed and burned, again and again, in his attempts to become Leeds' premier league emcee?

If you read Andrew's brilliantly scathing first memoir, 2017's *Wiggaz with Attitude*, you'll know first-hand the pratfalls and frustrations involved trying to get a foot in the door of the UK's nascent rap industry. There's every chance he felt the journalistic jig was up before it had even started, when *Hip-Hop Connection* (*HHC*), the UK's only monthly rap magazine, rejected his first submission in late 1995.

That may have held true had Andrew's sample reviews not entered my orbit. Finding writers in those days was all about looking for diamonds in the rough. And just as we'd listen to every single record or demo that came through the door, we'd try and read (and sometimes re-read) everything sent to the magazine. While deputy editor Stephen Worthy initially passed on Andrew's reviews, I felt differently. I don't recall being blown away by his words, I just knew he had that indefinable *je ne sais quoi*.

The publishing landscape, at the time, was radically different to now and *HHC* had already explored multiple directions when I took the editorial reins in late 1993. Born from dark pre-internet days where info-starved music fans resorted to calling up answerphones such as British Telecom's *Dial-a-Disc* for their kicks, *Hip-Hop Connection*'s first life was one such line whereby a pre-BBC Dave 'Dangerous' Pearce relayed the latest rap news at a premium rate. The line's owners, Music Maker Publishers, responded to its surprise success with a one-off print title edited by Chris Hunt in late 1988.

After a second successful one-off, the *Smash Hits*-styled mag went monthly the following year, when I first joined the team (after graduating from cut-and-paste fanzine *White Lie*). Briefly helmed by the late Michael Leonard in the early 90s, whose hardy embrace of UK hip-hop was gruffly rewarded with dwindling sales, Chris and I played comeback kids and rebooted the franchise in 1992, before Chris shifted his allegiance to football journalism.

My vision was a bit different to his or Michael's. Although we were saddled with a glossy format and a restricted number of pages – 48 to start with, but I soon pushed against that – my prime concern was to find fresh, untapped writing and photography talents. I wanted *HHC* to be as vital and critical as the weekly music press (*NME*, *Melody Maker*, *Sounds*) I grew up reading. So far there had been a tendency to treat rappers with kid gloves, to not call them out on their indiscretions or let them get off lightly with releases clearly not up to snuff. For rap journalism to progress, it needed stronger voices, harder opinions, but also more humour and irreverence – the qualities Flavor Flav brought to Public Enemy to stop them sounding like an unrelieved lecture.

It was an ambitious remit, given the slightness of our set up – Stephen, production editor Jill Carter and me in a large, very empty office that we grandly dubbed the Tower of Power, amid the fenland wilds of Ely (officially a city, effectively a small market town to the north of

Cambridge). That locational challenge was compounded by more basic logistics – no email, no internet, no mobiles – everything was organised by landline or fax, interviews often taking place via leaps of faith, especially when working to hip-hop time, perpetually three or four hours later than GMT.

To borrow a footballing analogy, *HHC* was very much a feeder club, the Southampton of magazines. We grew adept at scouting talent – the likes of Ekow Eshun, Angus Batey, Frank Broughton, Danny Eccleston and Ted Kessler all got their critical first ink in the title. But we had the tiniest of budgets and simply couldn't compete when the Man Uniteds and Liverpools swept in waving bigger chequebooks. The whole process would have to start over again.

There was another difficult equation at play too: while most of our most hip-hop savvy contributors were perhaps not the best writers, our best writers were not the most hip-hop savvy either. If Stephen was the first to truly bust that myth – his early contributions led Chuck D to name him one of his favourite writers in 1997's *Fight the Power: Rap, Race and Reality* – from the moment Andrew got his eye teeth in, he blasted it to smithereens.

It was clear from Andrew's first feature in April 1996 – a percipient double page spread on the demise of female rappers – that he was far from a diamond in the rough and already the finished article. Savvy, opinionated, steeped in hard-won hip-hop knowledge but, beyond all that, able to express it in sparkling prose with an acute grasp of comic timing, he was the dream ticket, a box-to-box Diego Maradona on an unstoppable course to the very top of the game. I often spent hours finessing other writer's work for the printed page, I barely had to lift a finger with Andrew's (the rare correction, here or there, sometimes felt like butchery).

He underlined his greatness when Stephen left for pastures new and the powers that be declined to replace him, becoming *HHC*'s most important writer during a turbulent period of change. Whipsmart, prolific and forever bursting with ideas, it's hard to single out individual pieces as Andrew never dropped his standards, but insightful cover features on the rap's newest popstars the Fugees and grimy ruminations with RZA's horrorcore pioneers Gravediggaz both stick out.

There was a memorable occasion, in 1997, when a joint Jay-Z and Foxy Brown interview got pulled at the 11th hour. Given a few desultory minutes with a far from forthcoming Jay-Z, Andrew didn't blink, writing a detailed cover story exposé of Moët-guzzling, Versace-wearing playa rappers and Jay-Z's role within that beyond his bleated protest: "I'm doing a job." It peaked as he updated Chuck D's description of hip-hop as being the 'black *CNN*' into "the black *You've Been Framed* – strictly for the camera, full of comic pitfalls, farcical behaviour and role-playing."

Andrew also led the vanguard as hip-hop roads forked at the end of the decade, championing Rawkus and the legion of spiky independent labels putting out material most majors wouldn't touch and certainly didn't get. That decision wasn't just aesthetic.

It marked a sea change in rap magazine publishing. Up until that point *HHC* had largely survived on making its own connections – with artists, labels, managers, graffiti artists and so on. But just as the Puff Daddy-led lowest common denominator R&B/rap fusions started to exert a stranglehold on the charts, hip-hop became a much more corporate and PR-driven beast, obsessed with appealing to the biggest possible audience, often to the detriment of its core demographic. Where once artists would give their time to the magazine unbidden, now we had to beg sulky intermediaries for a few crumbs from the table.

It didn't help that we were tossed around like seals amid the clueless killer whales at Future Publishing, who bought the magazine as part of a job lot, before being thrown to the sharks at Ministry of Sound (wild machinations that probably deserve a book of their own). When *HHC* went independent in the early 00s, bloodied but unbowed, Andrew kept the faith, despite being in great demand elsewhere. A crucial ally, brilliant contributing editor, and forever shrewd columnist, he also brought in other talents – DJ Yoda, Mike Lewis, DJ Greenpeace, Rob Pursey – that buttressed *HHC*'s infrastructure.

Most *HHC* readers will be aware how high he raised the bar for hip-hop journalism, up and beyond the UK, and it's not an overstatement to say he inspired a whole new generation to arm themselves with a pen. Pin-sharp, cultured, and inspired contributors such as Phillip Mlynar, James McNally, Richard Watson, Adam Anonymous and Hugh Leask all came up reading Andrew's work and aspired to scale the same dizzy heights.

Equally, Andrew's writing never plateaued. Some of his most insight-ful and storied pieces came in the late 00s. That was when the dream team of contributors I'd envisaged in the mid-90s finally coalesced, and *HHC* became the wise and authoritative magazine I'd always hoped for. No matter that it came at a price – every dark force was working against run-ning an independent print title at the time – we had made it, collectively, on our own terms, snatched unlikely victory from the jaws of defeat.

A confession. I'm writing this foreword having only seen the cover of *Write Lines*, having not read a single word. That may be a folly – it could be that Andrew disses my cats, slams my slinky 5-a-side skills, even asks for his picture of Eddie Large and the UK's largest ever steak and kidney pie back – but as a true chronicler of the world's most rest-lessly inventive music form, I implicitly trust him to do an honest job. I don't need to read *Write Lines* to know it will be brilliant. Can't wait to get stuck in though.

Andy Cowan
Editor, *Hip-Hop Connection* 1994-2009
Author of *B-Side: A Flipsided History of Pop* (Headpress, 2023)

PROLOGUE

In the movies, the drive from JFK airport into Manhattan is romantic. It's all magic-hour light, a couple looking cool in the back of a sleek, sporty car, the window wound down to let the wind work its wonders on the Hollywood hair. That skyline heaves into view just as the serried lights start to come on, bathing the island in promise.

It's somewhat different when there are five of you crammed into the back of a cab. Hot, clammy and pasty from an eight-hour flight, which took off at an unpopular and unpleasant hour, mostly because that was the cheapest option. The five are operating on a mixture of too much airline wine and too little cabin sleep. The jet lag will come and sap their energy later. There's no elan about them right now, no smooth, friction-less glide into the city of dreams.

Instead, there's the usual choke of traffic as you skirt Corona, Queens. Generally speaking, it's an unprepossessing route, although perhaps not the valley of ashes described by Nick Carraway in *The Great Gatsby*. The glacial progress is enlivened, however, by the unfamiliar billboard signs – there's no T. J. Eckleburg here, but this quintet of Americophiles still scan the skies for brands they've only heard of through the lyrics of the music they adore.

Maybe that's the idea. Get them deflated by the suburbs and, when they round that corner and the peaks of Manhattan appear, they'll soar. And it works. You do. Even without the romance of the big screen, that promise is still intact. New York is a place of possibilities for five friends armed with cameras, Dictaphones and suitcases carefully under-packed to leave space for the inevitable record and sneaker shopping. It's the city where hip-hop was born and that's enough in itself to lure them 3,459 miles across the sky.

They're hardly prepared for what's going to hit them. They'll share beds, five of them in a single hotel room. They'll share colds and late nights, big diner breakfasts and street cart hot dogs on the go. They'll meet their heroes. They'll break bread and beers with rap legends. They'll hop from downtown to uptown in cabs and on the subway, back over to Queens, Brooklyn, then back to Manhattan again, in search of the next story. They'll get lost, and in doing so they'll find the very best places. They'll let a rapper sleep in their bath, and receive death threats from rivals. They'll have the time of their young lives.

1: THE SAGA BEGINS

The rap career? Yeah, that didn't happen. Like it doesn't for so many. Today, the world is full of labels dropping limited-edition releases on splatter vinyl of dusty 1990s demos that never saw the light of day. Some from artists you know, some from artists you've never heard of. As of yet, no-one is beating a path to the door of myself, or my former partners-in-rhyme Dan Greenpeace and DJ Countdown, to release our demos[1]. Nor am I expecting them to.

I'd made peace with my failure as a rapper long before I wrote *Wiggaz With Attitude*, but it was still hugely cathartic in that book to explore in excruciating detail the missteps, the mishaps and the misappropriation that constituted the stillborn recording careers of Prehistoric Ages, PA Posse, Progressive Agenda and yours truly, SCAM the Solo Prophet.

There are much better artists than me that also never got to have their moment to shine. And there are, believe it or not, people with less talent than me that actually got to prosper, release records and make videos. I'm at peace with that too.

Spend any time around the music industry – and as you'll discover as you read on, I spent a metric shit-ton of time around the music industry – and you'll realise the combination of idiocy, venality and

---

1 My children were very amused to see one of my old demo tapes, complete with a photocopied black and white picture of me when I still had cheekbones, in Leeds Museum's very good *50 Years of Kulture* exhibition. There were also numeros photos of me with the PA Posse, looking not at all like a man on the cusp of rap stardom.

selfishness that lies at the core of much of the decision making about music careers.

"Nobody knows anything," said the screenwriter William Goldman about the movie world, but it applies equally accurately to the 'wet your finger and put it in the air to see which way the wind is blowing' approach that dominates many of the boardrooms, desks and ping-pong table-infested break-out areas of record labels, radio stations, PR companies and more.

Don't get it twisted. I'm not saying they were wrong to not take a punt on me and my posse. That was one thing they most definitely got right. But I saw and heard enough over my time as a music writer to know that it's hard to swim upstream against the torrent of bullshit that is the music industry.

It has tossed aside many who have deserved better, and promoted countless who deserved less. And that makes it, of course, just like any other industry inside capitalism. Many people know and appreciate that, but lots of the people inside it, from the 9 to 5ers to the mavens to the label heads who got lucky with one artist and rode that to the moon, pretend that they're different. They like to think that they're 'creative' and therefore kinder. That they're not 'the man' and are in fact down with the kids. That they're somehow special[2].

Trust me, the music industry is no different from content creation, from oil rigs, from outsourcing companies. It has good people, bad people, clever people, idiots, psychopaths, legends, geniuses and total

---

2 Keeping it 100, as we said until 2021 in the hip-hop world, there are good people in the industry who know their stuff – they're rare, but they exist. Hey, this is the first footnote. Of many. Numerous people who read *Wiggaz* said they loved the footnotes. A few people said they liked them but they were a bit long and they didn't like the ones that went over a few pages as they had to go back. Hey, it's not 4D chess, use a bookmark. However, I have a publisher this time and he wants shorter footnotes, so I'll do my best to obey.

idiots spread throughout it. It's about profit, and it can curdle the spirit of even the most optimistic soul. It only seems different because it's music, and music is good, right?

Damn, this is a bleak start. Didn't the blurbs for this book say something about the writer being funny? Do I get to do this over like Woody Allen at the beginning of *Manhattan*? Rest assured, it's not all like this. It's mostly light hearted. Promise.

Wiggaz With Attitude was all about my attempts to forge a rap career despite a lack of talent. That quest was entirely fuelled by my admiration and passion for rap music, and that was also the major theme – how this single, wonderful genre of music transformed my life completely. Friends, family, work, holidays, clothes, the way I talk – all of these were sculpted by hip-hop. They are to this day. I'm a man who used to set his alarm to 8.08am because it referred to the sounds of the Roland TR-808 Rhythm Composer that underpinned so many of my favourite 80s rap songs. Well, at least I did until I had to commute and get up earlier.

The other thing I tried to do with *Wiggaz* was tell the story of the generation of UK rap fans who came up in the 1980s when this music wasn't cemented into the world's consciousness. When it was still seen as a fad and we had to fight for its recognition. Such is the ridiculous ubiquity of hip-hop today – the adverts, the radio shows, the slang, the sheer number of people engaged with it – that it almost seems as if we were making that up. We weren't. It really was like that. I wanted to tell the story of those who tuned their radios into John Peel's show in the hope of hearing three rap tracks in three hours. Who stuffed tissue into tapes to record those tracks. Who swapped them hungrily in the playground. For the rap fans who didn't have it easy, who couldn't access it all at the click of mouse. Who couldn't go into Uniqlo and see a dozen different T-shirt designs harking back to rap's golden age. Not every story has to be about those Bronx pioneers who somehow created this joyful noise – that tale is already out there in myriad forms. It's also time to tell other stories than those of artists and producers, labels and moguls. The fans deserve to be counted too.

It's not for me to judge whether or not the mission of my last book was a success, but I was buoyed by the response I had from people who said the book really resonated with them. That they felt part of their personal story had been told – their generation had got its due. For a writer who has toiled away and isn't going to make any real money from the book, that's sheer joy. So, how about that difficult second album?

The challenge for this book is that it doesn't have that arc. This story is about hip-hop after it's already a success. It's not a book about personal failure either. There are calamities along the way – fights, beefs, mistakes, moments of sheer idiocy, bits of writing that I genuinely regret – but it's really about me finding something that I think I'm actually pretty good at. It's about being a rap writer.

There are plenty of books full of really good hip-hop writing[3] but, to my knowledge, none about what it's actually like to do it. To try and make a living out of it. To be the person on the other side of the Dictaphone. To go home after meeting your hero/an artist you can't stand/ someone you're completely indifferent to, and to turn that experience into words that some people will actually enjoy reading.

Wiggaz chronicled our failure to make it as a rap group, but what came out of that period, the people we met, the places we went, is that

---

3 Strangely, for someone who is obsessed with hip-hop, I don't read many books about it. Maybe I don't want my view of it tarnished or maybe I feel like anything I don't know my equally obsessive friends will fill me in on. Most likely, it's because I've always been a voracious reader of fiction, and my pile of unread books hasn't numbered fewer than a couple of hundred books in decades. You can only take so much in. However, amongst the ones I have read, I can unreservedly recommend *The Big Payback* by Dan Charnas, Jeff Chang's *Can't Stop, Won't Stop* and Brian Coleman's *Check the Technique*. Most rap autobiographies are ghost written and not all that interesting, but Jerry Heller's *Ruthless* is a breathlessly entertaining read and definitely my desert island rap book just because it makes zero attempts to be worthy.

we – Dan Greenpeace and I – were still eager to carve out our little niche in hip-hop regardless. Like our happy times making tracks in bedrooms and studios, we were to do a lot of this together, along with other amazing colleagues and friends. We did our own thing too. If we couldn't be hip-hop stars, we could still do something within this music that dominated our lives and thoughts. We could still count for something.

So maybe that's the arc – we'll see. But one thing is for sure, there are some stories you need to hear.

2: WRITING SLAPS

There is no music, and never has been, that says as much as hip-hop[1]. Even when the message is irrelevant, muted, unclear or unpleasant, there's usually a lot of information being shared. Great NSFW stories by Slick Rick, ongoing narratives about the drug trade by Berner or Clipse, relationships, street knowledge, tales of sex and love, black history by all manner of rappers – even rappers who can't tell a story all that well are all, somehow and in some way, part of the art of storytelling. This isn't to say that only hip-hop can convey a story – clearly that would be a nonsense assertion – but it's the sheer weight of information and content in rap lyrics that impresses. What other genre could consider 4 x 32-bar verses as suitable for a cheery lead single?

I've always felt – and this might just be pure self-justification, but bear with me – that a music that conveys that much material is a very rich one to write about. Let's take Public Enemy's *Rebel Without a Pause* as an example. For many, it's one of hip-hop's best ever records. For me, it's the absolute, undisputed best. Chuck D delivers dozens of dizzying rhymes, densely packed with strong messages, hidden meaning and obscure references. You can spend hours analysing it as you would T.S. Eliot's *The Wasteland*, only it's actually nice to spend time with and the

---

1 There is much joy to be found in the brevity of a lot of music and whole genres such as jazz can convey a lot of emotion and subtext without lyrics but, you know, I'm being literal.

artist isn't just trying to show off[2]. There's something new to tease out on every listen.

Yet it doesn't end there. You also have the music underpinning it. The hotpot of at least half-a-dozen samples, and The Bomb Squad's uniquely collaborative approach to putting them together. It's a soup of sound that, even when you know all the samples that are in it, as you easily can these days courtesy of the Internet, you still don't understand how they marshalled them into something so funky. Making a soup that complicated isn't that easy. My dad used to talk about his amazing soup invention that was mixing a Heinz beef soup with a chicken noodle one. He wanted to pitch it to them. I tried this invention once – it was not a good soup. It tasted exactly like what I've just described, and in no culinary culture can that be a good thing. Throwing a set of diverse ingredients together and the result being genius is the preserve of the very best chefs… and The Bomb Squad.

After that, you've got the context of Public Enemy themselves, how they injected an urgent, intellectual black nationalism into a music genre that is, at the exact same time, content to release records about women with big arses and brand new dances. You've got their paramilitary styling. The clowning of Flavor Flav next to the po-faced genius of Chuck D. The strange role occupied by Professor Griff and the S1Ws. Terminator X speaking with his hands but somehow already dreaming of his future as an ostrich farmer[3].

Beyond all of those things, you've just got the good, guttural feeling of a record you instinctively love. The musical X factor that, even if all

---

2 F.R. Leavis, your job is safe.

3 Terminator X – aka Norman Rogers – released one solo album. Its title, *Terminator X & The Valley of the Jeep Beets* suggests two things. Either he couldn't spell 'beats', or he was thinking about being a farmer with a jeep full of actual beets. And possibly the odd turnip. With an ostrich riding shotgun.

the above wasn't true, if all that complexity didn't exist, would still make you love it.

Who doesn't want the job of trying to unpick some of that? To dive deep into the motivations, the conflicting personalities, where those ideas originated, how aware they were in the studio that they were creating truly timeless music. What was the process where they tried to marry those samples together? What ideas did they reject? What was the first draft of Chuck D's lyrics? What is it that Professor Griff does again? Okay, whatever you say mate. The question really is: why doesn't everyone want to be a hip-hop writer?

My passion for hip-hop writing began long before I'd even thought about being a rap writer myself. I loved those early writers who were doing my beloved music the honour of taking it seriously in print. Before the hip-hop monthlies arrived on the planet, I'd shuffle into WH Smith to flick through the pages of *Record Mirror*. They'd interview the latest breakthrough rap stars at a time when there wasn't much coverage in papers or magazines, but that wasn't the really good stuff. Instead, I was almost hypnotised by the writing of James Hamilton.

Hamilton was born during World War Two, and was a DJ from the 1960s through to his death in 1996. He was one of the first mobile DJs, using the excellent name Doctor Soul, but is mostly remembered as a champion of disco mixing and as the man who introduced BPMs to writing about music. In other words, he was the DJs friend and perhaps one of the most important pioneers in that essential job. I say 'mostly remembered' because what adherents of *Record Mirror* – even me when I couldn't actually afford to buy a copy – really loved about the man was his style of writing. He would cram vivid adjectives of what a record actually sounded like, along with quick facts, into capsules that were dazzlingly erudite and always accurate. An example:

> *"With the "Los Angeles, gang capital of the nation" documentary quote introed, violently churning Chuck D guesting 'Endangered Species (Tales From The Darkside) (Remix)' (108bpm), similarly churning 'The Product' (110½bpm), street confrontation introed then sampled breaks weaving 'Jackin' For Beats' (104¼bpm), languidly but chillingly narrated 'Dead Homiez' (84¼bpm), jolting romantic 'Get Off My Dick And Tell Yo Bitch To Come Here (Remix)' (97¼bpm), and respects due namechecking 'I Gotta Say What Up!!!' (88¼bpm). Radio jocks will need to be good tape reversing splicers before they can air any of it, as usual!"*

That is, obviously, Ice Cube's *Kill at Will* EP. Written about like that – even despite the jarring editorial policy of not hyphenating any of it – who wouldn't want to hear it? The great thing about Hamilton's writing about singles was that, when I was reading them in the early to mid-80s, I didn't know what any of them sounded like as I didn't have the budget to buy them, but I wanted to, and he transmitted the propulsive feeling of them brilliantly. Being too young to go to clubs, too skint to go to record shops and living in a country where hip-hop was rarely on radio or television, the next best thing was reading James Hamilton.

Over the years, I've admired many music reviewers, some of whom can craft prose beautifully, but Hamilton's dense way of handling sonic and thematic description has not been improved upon. Can you imagine how much music he listened to? Also, that 'jolting romantic' for *Get Off My Dick…* is low-key genius.

An inescapable part of the UK music landscape in the 80s and 90s were the 'inkies' – most notably *New Musical Express* and *Melody Maker*. To be utterly fair to them, you'd have to say their coverage of hip-hop was patchy, inconsistent and often wilfully ignorant. I can say this with certainty about the *NME*, because I read it weekly for about 20 years. I'd buy a copy every Wednesday and read it cover to cover, whether on the bus to school or between lessons in the 6th form common room.. While I was telling people in real life that only hip-hop mattered, I was devouring articles about indie also-rans just because I liked the journos who were writing about them. It's the same principle I apply to books. I might not like wars, nuclear bombs or spy assassinations, but good writing about them is still compelling, and *NME* had some really good writers.

I'm not talking about the iconic but overrated Parsons/Burchill era, but the late 80s and early 90s. You'd tap into the *NME* for deep knowledge, outrageous subjectivity, a mixture of levity and bookwormish attention to detail. In other words, the ideal music publication. The fact that many of their writers expressed a distaste for hip-hop didn't bother me – in fact, it probably influenced my own future 'fuck all of you over there' approach to writing. No, my ire was reserved for those writers who simply got stuff wrong.

In the *NME* and *Melody Maker*, that was endemic[4] and screamed out that they should be using specialists. Dates were wrong, facts were way off, quotes misattributed, the whole point missed. A writer saying that an album is an artist's second when it's their fourth might not seem like a big deal, but if you know that's wrong when you're reading it, it breaks the spell. If they don't know that, what else are they getting wrong? Why don't they know that – they're full-time music writers? Age and experience have subsequently taught me that you can't possibly know everything, and music research was notably harder in the pre-Internet era but, still, fuck those guys.

It wasn't all bad. There were great features on some of rap's early stars, a piece about the Juice Crew tour of the UK that I stuck to my bedroom wall next to the NFL posters and Samantha Fox calendar, an in-depth

---

4 *Melody Maker*'s rap coverage improved immeasurably when they hired Neil Kulkarni in the mid-90s.

piece on the mighty Just Ice. But then you'd go months at a time without mention of what, to me, was the most exciting music genre to ever exist.

What was really clear was that hip-hop was getting big enough not just to merit weekly coverage in *NME*, or its own section in *Record Mirror*, but its own, dedicated magazine. Yet there wasn't one. The shelves of the library or bookshops weren't much help, either. The first proper book about hip-hop was David Toop's *The Rap Attack: African Jive to New York Hip-Hop*, which came out in 1984. Toop is a musician rather than a writer, but he still does an admirable job of doing what many people have been trying to do since – establish a lineage from earlier black music through to hip-hop. He treats the genre with respect and admiration, and captures some of the threat of it too.

I guess it wasn't a complete piece of piss being a rap writer early on. You didn't have a lot to work with. Obviously, the early days would have been a gift to someone who could immerse themselves in those block parties and gigs, but hip-hop at that time was by its very nature bitty, choppy and incoherent.

That didn't change for a while – look at hip-hop albums in the 1980s for example. Today, albums sprawl over 20 tracks and are somewhat redundantly called 'projects'. There was a period in the 2000s when everything seemed to be a mixtape and the difference between them and actual albums was blurred and indistinct. The era of clearly delineated albums that were coherent and cohesive probably lasted from 1987 to the early 2000s, with just the odd few afterwards and a couple before. What you got to write about in the mid-1980s often didn't feel very serious, especially when it came to LPs. It was, without any doubt, a 12"-led genre back then.

If you, as a critic, wanted to critique an album in the 1980s, there wasn't much to go on. Often, they were just a cash in, a hastily assembled collection of the singles with some filler and an instrumental or two. The approach to what was actually on an album often still lacked ambition right up to the end of the 1980s – it was very often a box-ticking exercise. There'd be a political song, a love song, a track about partying, a fast brag rap to show off some skills, a hip-house song to appeal to some spurious crossover market, maybe a track to showcase the DJs skills. It never felt organic, natural or heartfelt, but like a contractual obligation, designed to appeal to numerous demographics at once.

As a writer about hip-hop albums you wouldn't know any different, but perhaps you'd grown up on albums by Kate Bush, Marvin Gaye, Steely Dan or Stevie Wonder when an album felt like a statement. It all added up to something that was more than just an assemblage of songs. If you had, hip-hop albums, while possibly containing some real gems, could feel a little empty in comparison. It wasn't until around 1987, the early days of the soon-to-come Golden Era, that hip-hop albums began to feel like an event.

Without wanting to be unfair to Doug E. Fresh, he's a good case in point. He's a wonderful artist with a slew of indisputably brilliant 12"s and, to this day, I can enjoy his 1986 *Oh! My God* album very much indeed. However, it has only nine tracks, two of which are DJ interludes, one clocking in at just over two minutes, the other around 40 seconds. That leaves seven songs. Four of those came out on 12"s, including the huge hit *The Show*. So there are three tracks left, one of which is a pretty regrettable anti-abortion song. As I say, I love this album in many ways, but there's no disputing that it's thin fare for both a listener and a critic to get to grips with.

So, where were we supposed to get our regular hip-hop fix?

You might have thought that by the late 1980s, the answer might have been America, but it wasn't so. In fact, the world's first hip-hop monthly was born in the UK. *Hip-Hop Connection* would have peaks and troughs. It would have different publishers and editors. It would be thin, it would be fat. It would have CDs on the cover. It would have Mariah Carey on the cover. But, when the dust settles, let's put our cards

13

on the table. For all the heft of *The Source*'s reputation, *XXL*'s self-belief, *Vibe*'s access, *ego trip*'s iconoclasm, for all of the plucky competitors and the behemoths with bigger budgets, there's only one publication that truly nailed it for a consistent period. I don't really want to die on any hill, yet I will stand on the top of this particular hill and push you back down it. *Hip-Hop Connection* is the greatest rap magazine of all time.

3: GOD CONNECTIONS

Hip-Hop Connection wasn't always the greatest rap magazine. It grew out of a phone line. That 'connection' was there from the very beginning when you were encouraged to dial up a premium-rate 0898 phone line and kick some of your rhymes, after listening to the one judged to be the best from the previous week. The phone line was hosted by the pre-recorded voice of Radio 1 DJ Dave Pearce. It was a wheeze to make some cash from the growing market of rap fans. It was so successful that the company that ran it – Popular Publications – thought they should have a go at making a magazine out of it, and thus a legend was born.

The first issue of *Hip-Hop Connection*, popularly known as *HHC*, arrived on shelves in July 1988. At this time, I was 15, living in Leeds, and I can still remember the little thrill I got when I spotted it on the shelves of WH Smith. Salt N Pepa, Public Enemy and Run DMC were on the cover, along with the UK's own leading star Derek B. I bought it instantly and sat on a bench outside the shop reading it. For someone starved of up-to-date hip hop info, it was heaven sent. It was packed with interviews, reviews, opinion pieces and wonderful photos taken by future legend Normski. I was already taking note of the writer's names – Simon Trask, Simon Dine, Malu Halasa. The latter would become my favourite hip-hop writer at the time, and in the first issue she's already opining about whether or not independent hip-hop has a future[1], a debate that has never gone away.

Chris Hunt was the editor, and in the early issues he steers a neat line between featuring all the big US stars and giving plenty of shine to homegrown acts as well. The first issue alone finds room not just for Derek B, but also the Wee Papa Girl Rappers, Monie Love and the Demon Boyz. There's also space in the first issue for an early opinion that perhaps hasn't aged brilliantly. Apparently, Eric B & Rakim's *Follow the Leader* is, "not a great album, but a grower."

The second issue – one that I stalked the shelves of Smiths for – saw the writing team expand and KRS ONE grace the cover. There's graffiti, there's London's Overlord X who I've heard on John Peel. Hannah Ford takes us on a guide to hip-hop fashion shopping in London, starting off at the legendary 4 Star General. And, in only the 2nd issue, mind, we find the worst and least accurate album review that *HHC* would ever publish, with Lee Holding delivering a kicking to Ultramagnetic MC's *Critical Beatdown*.

It took until April 1989 for the magazine to go monthly – a year's subscription then costing a bargain £10! – with an issue that had no reviews but debuted the *Gangsta Limpin* column from David Klein. Funkenklein, as he was better known, went on to write the same column for *The Source* and *The Bomb*, but started dropping his stateside news and gossip in *HHC* first. It's only issue 3, but *HHC* is already a must read, and is inevitably receiving letters from moaning readers complaining that their area of the UK isn't getting enough coverage. Public Enemy's Chuck D is more impressed, commenting, "You English

---

1 Malu Halasa burned briefly but brightly within the pages of HHC, and is fondly remembered by early readers. The Oklahoma native would go on to become a prolific writer and editor behind such important publications as *Syria Speaks: Arts and Culture From the Frontline* (Saqi, 2014). Who knew we'd still be having these exact same debates about hip-hop's survival several decades later?

kids do a better job of covering rap than anyone in my country." Tell it like it is, Chuck.

I don't want to write a complete issue by issue history of *HHC* – that's probably best left to someone who edited it – but that first year deserves close scrutiny. Looking back at those slightly yellowed issues, you can see a magazine really finding its feet. By May, the *Connections* column was in place, inviting readers to place free adverts to meet and correspond with other rap fans[2]. In August, a free LL Cool J flexi disc was on the cover (it isn't very good) and the month after, *Demo Blaster* was born, a regular feature where the magazine reviewed demo tapes submitted by readers. For the first instalment, UK rapper MC Duke was joined by a record label A&R man to run the rule over them. The very same month, we found an entry in the *Connections* page by yours truly, albeit with my name misspelt as 'Andy Emey aka Scam'.

I think I wrote to *Connections* a couple of times, and it opened up a whole world of pen friends. I'd get dozens of hand-written replies and before long I was trading tapes with people all across the UK. It even led to me writing lyrics for an Irish rap group who'd send me their beats on the cassette to write to. It became an unsung part of what *HHC* did. It didn't just carry interviews and news, it linked and grew the hip-hop community in the UK at a time when it was disjointed and disparate. It helped to break down the regional barriers between scenes.

Malu Halasa further cemented herself as my writing hero with a provocative regular column called *Science – Malu Halasa's Revenge*. It focussed forensically on racism, and was forthright and fiery. An early classic was a passionate back and forth with Harry Allen – Public Enemy's 'Media Assassin', about Professor Griff, rap and religion. By

---

2 Lee Holding is also back in this issue with another great take that has aged as well as milk left on a radiator. *Road to the Riches* is "a rather disappointing debut for Kool and Polo". Good ear, Lee.

the end of 1989, Ekow Eshun[3] is contributing and a man called Andy Cowan has joined the *HHC* team as production and news editor.

By the close of 1989, the first issues of US rap magazine *The Source* were being brought back over from New York by visitors. It started as a newsletter in 1988, put out by David Mays in Boston, but by 1989 it was a regular magazine. It was more up to date than *HHC*, it had better access and it would go on to become arguably the most important hip-hop magazine ever. And, for a while, the best. But copies of it were scant until it got proper distribution a couple of years later, so for now we UK fans turned to *HHC* for our monthly dose of all things hip-hop.

Shock, horror – Malu Halasa departs the pages of *HHC* in 1990. Yet huzzah, for we now have posters on the back, which are rapidly cut off and blu-tacked to our bedroom walls. The March issue featured a letter from future contributor, future friend of mine and subject of a whole chapter in this book, Pete Cashmore. He's already showing an early gift for pugilistic writing. Also of note, a month later, was a letter from one 'King Lou-E' of Oxford, who just so happens to be Louis Theroux[4]. A couple of months later, *HHC* published stacks of reader's letters taking a pop at King Lou-E's opinions. Another major departure followed in October, with Chris Hunt vacating the editor's chair and Michael Leonard taking over, assisted by Alex Constantinides.

I'm not a fan of this short-lived era of *HHC*. The magazine felt a bit testy and mean spirited. The writing wasn't as good, with the exception of the arrival of the estimable Angus Batey, who'd go on to become a major contributor for nigh-on two decades. By August of 1992, Chris Hunt was

---

3 Ekow Eshun didn't write much for HHC and soon faded into obscurity. Oh, wait. No, he became the first black editor of a major UK magazine (*Arena*) and also became director of the Institute of Contemporary Arts in London. He now chairs the group who decide what goes on that fourth plinth in Trafalgar Square, which is something you can't say for old tin-eared Lee Holding.

4 Confirmed to me by Mr Theroux himself, over a Soho pint back in the mists of time.

back in the editor's chair, and that man Andy Cowan was now the Deputy. Under their reign, the magazine became much more professional, with a higher quality of writing and much more insight into politics and the state of rap. In other words, it had reacted to the gauntlet thrown down by *The Source*, which was doing that sort of thing very well in 1992/3.

Then, Hunt having steadied the ship, he handed over the editor's pen and visor to Andy Cowan. His first issue landed in January, 1994, and he will go on to edit *Hip-Hop Connection* for the remainder of its long life. But we're getting ahead of ourselves.

It's now the mid-1990s and hip-hop is firmly established in the culture. The late 80's Golden Era has paved the way for a time of restless creativity, of good music coming from every corner of the globe. Those of us who remember the times when it was taking its first baby steps in the UK are now watching it as a grown up, surefooted, cocky and with absolutely zero chance of fizzling out. We're also seeing moral panics as rappers become controversial and take on the political establishment. Much of this plays out in the US, but thanks to the growing number of rap magazines, we're across all of it.

The Source is now known as the 'bible of hip-hop', but, truth be told, its existence didn't really threaten *HHC*. They really had non-overlapping magisteria, with the US counterpart at the front line of political debate, breaking new acts and pretty cutting edge. *HHC*, on the other hand, reflected more of what hip-hop culture was like in the UK, with local scenes getting plenty of notice, pages of graffiti from every corner of the British Isles and in-depth pieces on homegrown heroes who couldn't even dream of getting a single column inch in a US magazine. If you only read *The Source* in the 1990's, you'd be forgiven for thinking that the only rapper the UK had ever produced was Monie Love – and she'd been transplanted to the US.

What *HHC* did during its choppy, often troubled time as the UK's largest rap monthly, is hold up a mirror to our domestic scene, with all its passion and failings. It carried adverts for the brands we wore – Troop, SPX, British Knights – and showed the streets we lived on. It acted as a sponge for the spite of rappers who felt they should get more space in its pages, grace the cover, and get better reviews. In reality, it gave them more support than they could ever hope to get anywhere else.

It wasn't perfect, but then not a single hip-hop magazine ever has been. They've all had blind spots, aspects of hip-hop they either ignored or handled badly. Terrible writers mingled in with the good and the great. Questionable design decisions. Columns and opinions that have dated terribly. Yet what *HHC* always had, which is something that probably can't be said for many other magazines in the rap space, is integrity.

If you've bought this book already knowing who I am, you'll probably already be aware that I'd go on to write for *Hip-Hop Connection*. If you've no idea who I am, sorry for the spoiler, but I go on to write for *Hip-Hop Connection*. That will, of course, colour my opinions of it. No doubt about it, I'm biased. I'm sure everyone who wrote for *The Source*, *Vibe* or *Rap Pages* thinks they were on the best rap magazine of all time, too. However, there's one major difference – they're wrong and I'm right.

4: SLEEPING WITH THE NME

While never having a clear idea of what my future career would ever be – in my early teens I was still convinced of the delusion that I could actually make it as a rapper – I always loved writing. From primary school onwards I exceeded the word count on every single English project with relish. I had an imagination then that I wish I could recapture now. I'd get an assignment from a teacher, largely ignore the constraints set and would turn in, for example, a seven-page piece of fiction inspired by the 12 1/2p Buytonic Boy strip from *Whizzer & Chips*. I was always restlessly scribbling stories and poems. If I wrote one at my Grandad Ramshaw's house, he'd preserve it for posterity or, occasionally, send it to a local newspaper or community publication where it often got included. They must have been slow news weeks, but I was very proud nevertheless.

Much of that energy was redirected into writing lyrics and devising fictional rap groups once I discovered hip-hop. Schoolwork aside, I was no longer writing creatively for pleasure. It's almost like I only had so many words to use, and exhausted them all on rhymes. It was only when I went to University in 1992 and stopped dreaming of rap stardom that I began to write once again.

It wasn't fiction, however. In 6th form I was never without a copy of the *NME*, transferring its ink to my fingers. I was getting into *The Guardian* and would go through a phase of reading Andreas Whittam Smith's *The Independent* cover to cover. I wasn't thinking of becoming a journalist, but I was becoming increasingly familiar with the tempo of newspaper and magazine writing. My school friend Simone Ivatts was involved in publishing a fanzine called *Sawtooth*, and despite the fact that it was largely about the Riot Grrrl scene, she let me have a go at some hip-hop reviews in there. It was a thrill to hold a physical copy afterwards and that feisty zine planted a seed that would grow some years later.

My first regular writing gig was for the Nottingham Trent University newspaper *Platform*. I'd had a couple of letters published, unfunny in-jokes written with my housemate Christian O'Connell, of future radio and TV fame. I managed to leverage that into a meeting with the editor[1] and started contributing regularly. I covered a 'Blind Date' event at the University union bar and ended up blagging myself a date with the female contestant. I wrote an obituary of Labour leader John Smith (I'm still pleased with my headline 'Fanfare for the Commons Man') and then started a weekly TV column called 'Eye on the Box'.

They're a little faded, but I still have all these cuttings filed away. There's not much merit in them – laboured jokes, endless digs at the BBC adaptation of *Middlemarch* – but the likes of Garry Bushell built a successful career out of little more. They're filed away with a few pieces from my sole outlet in Leeds, a short-lived indie magazine called *Blag*. Again, I did a few hip-hop reviews and some TV stuff – an appreciation of the underrated Timothy Spall vehicle *Frank Stubbs Promotes*, I recall. I kept up the *Platform* column for all three years at

---

1 Editing *Platform* was a paid position open to graduates of the University. The idea was that you graduated and then, if you wanted to, you could campaign for election to editor of *Platform*, a job you could do for one year. I did indeed run for election to edit it, and placed last out of three. I sobbed openly on the night this unfolded, and I don't think I've quite processed this trauma yet, which is why this is tucked away as a footnote and not in the main body of the book. In conclusion: bastards.

uni, even during that difficult time when I was kicked off campus for saying something unkind to the Sheriff of Nottingham[2].

I didn't really have a plan B beyond *Platform*. I was convinced I was going to edit it, and that that would be a passport to journalism either back in Leeds or in London. Almost without noticing it, with no real intent, it seemed that I'd decided that I wanted to be a writer. As many people know, there's a huge difference between wanting to do something and actually being able to do it and life had other plans for me at that time.

I graduated, and headed back to the attic at my mum's house in Beeston, Leeds. I didn't have a clue what I was going to do, but I needed cash and wanted to contribute some board money for my mum. I started applying for proper jobs, shelving the dreams of journalism for the time being.

One job I wasn't dreaming about? Personal Assistant to the Principal of a further education college, but that's the job that came knocking. The principal, Graham Binks, could have had his pick of able PA's that could perhaps do shorthand or type a reasonable amount of words per minute. I could do neither of those. But Graham wanted a graduate, and so I started my first proper job, in the town of Morley, for a salary of £9,900 per annum.

While I did okay in the role, there's no doubting that I was the archetypal 'frustrated writer' at this time. I'd go home after a day of taking minutes and making coffee, and relax by poring over *NME*, *Hip-Hop Connection*, *The Source* and my sister Susan's copy of *Empire* magazine, wanting to write for all of them at the same time. I applied for a few local writing jobs, and got nothing but rejections. My *Platform* cuttings simply weren't cutting it when it came to applying for roles in London, either.

---

2 You'll have to buy *Wiggaz With Attitude* for that story. You can only recycle so much material.

At one point I thought of becoming a teacher. At another of knuckling down and becoming the best damn PA I could be[3]. Neither took. The college – Joseph Priestley, with several sites across Leeds – created the role of 'House Journalist', which was swiftly taken by another man fresh to the world of work, John Mullen. A Cambridge graduate with a first class English degree, John was a great fit for the role, and we soon became firm friends, allies who delighted in laughing at the silly internal politics of the college, while sharing a love of music, Manchester United and writing. John was already contributing to Jonathan King's *Tip Sheet*, and would go on to become an excellent magazine writer and then a notable TV producer. Joseph Priestley College couldn't really contain his ambition at that time, and he was gone within months.

My boss finally took note of my frustrations in my present role and moved me into the House Journalist position. At last! Of course, there's a world of difference between sitting at a desk being paid hundreds of pounds to write about TV or hip-hop and covering the thrilling events at a further education college in Leeds. There wasn't a whole lot of journalism to be done. I was mostly helping out the marketing department, and putting out a monthly in-house newsletter. I gave that a revamp, retitled it *Oxygen* (big up all my Joseph Priestley fans) and added a splash of colour. My personal obsessions bled into it, and before long I was dropping in musical references and interviewing staff members for a 'favourite book' column. One of my bosses, an endlessly sardonic man called Ian Carass[4], who was Clerk

---

3 I got sent to Bath for a two-day 'PA to the Principal' training event. Of the 70 or so delegates, I was the only male. I was an object of great curiosity on day one. Day two? No idea, as I blew it off to explore Bath. My heart wasn't in being a PA as much as it was still in the PA Posse.

4 I bought two cheap suits from Burtons when I got the Personal Assistant job. I wore one on the first day, the other on my second. Carass: "How many bloody suits have you got?"

to the Corporation, questioned the need for such 'flippant' content, but I was not to be deterred. There was only so much fun one could glean from writing about the launch of a new Social Care course at the Alec Beevers Centre.

And then that came crashing down. It turned out that there was a massive black hole in the college's finances. Graham Binks was quickly ushered out of the door and there were a number of redundancies. The role of House Journalist was deemed inessential – I couldn't really agree more – and after just over a year at Joseph Priestley, I was on the dole. The upside? I had time on my hands, I had 'journalist' on my CV and, within weeks, I had my first material printed in a weekly music newspaper that I'd avidly read for years – yes, the *NME*.

It was almost too good to be true. I wrote a handful of hip-hop single reviews in what I hoped was the perfect combination of my personal style (which, let's be honest, I hadn't really developed at that point) and a tone that was *NME*-friendly. A little bit snarky, knowledgeable but not arcane. I typed them out – the Internet was only just kicking in at this point, and like most people I didn't have a computer at home – and sent them off to King's Reach Tower with a covering letter. I didn't hear a thing back.

What did happen, however, is that I went to the corner shop on a Wednesday shortly after, following a ritual that had been established back when I first started reading it as a 6th former. I bought the *NME* and a bag of beef-flavoured Space Raiders and walked home to read it cover to cover, putting aside the snub of them not replying to me. It was still a great read back then, even if there was scant hip-hop content in there. I loved their writers, from the bolshy gonzo rants of Steven Wells – Swells, as he was known – to the more considered approach of Steve Lamacq, Andrew Collins, Andrew Harrison and Stuart Maconie, although many of them had moved on by the mid-90s. They had a small section – hardly even a page some weeks – called Vibes, edited by Ben Willmott, that covered dance music and, occasionally, hip-hop.

I turned to that page to see if there was a small interview with a rapper there, or some reviews, and was shocked to see my own words – and my own name – there in print.

Of the five or six reviews I'd submitted, they'd used three. They hadn't really changed anything, and they'd spelled my name correctly. I was in the bloody *NME*. I was straight on the phone to all my friends, telling them to buy a copy. I bought about five more. I didn't even think about the fact that I was going to be paid, until a cheque from IPC Publishing arrived on my mum's doormat a few weeks later.

I held this cheque up to the light like I'd discovered the Holy Grail. I wanted to frame it, a souvenir of my first ever paid writing. Of course, I was so skint as a result of being made redundant that the cheque – which was for a total of something like £4.46 – had to go straight in the bank. This was it – this was the start of a beautiful career. I was going to write for the *NME*. Except I wasn't, not really.

There's a great scene in Jonathan Coe's novel *The Rotters Club* where Doug Anderton, who has submitted some of his school writing to the *NME*, gets an invitation to 'pop in' when he's next in London. He takes them up on it and arrives to find the office pretty much empty. No editor, none of the storied 70's writing gang he'd hoped to find. They don't know who he is. It didn't quite go like that for me, but there's a world of difference between getting a handful of reviews published and shifting into a staff position or getting regular commissions to interview rappers. While I had more reviews published over the next year or two, it was only ever pocket change. My pitches to Ben Willmott for interviews got short shrift.

I was going to have to go in a different direction. It was time to approach *HHC*. By the mid-90s, it seemed to be in a strong place under Andy Cowan's editorship. You could read Nihal Arthanayake reviewing the singles. A new, somewhat controversial column called *Wassup? With Colonel Taylor* was helping to fill the letters page. Spencer Kansa was writing his *Media Assassin* column and, once more, Pete Cashmore was a frequent correspondent to the editor, stirring up shit. Stephen Worthy had become the Deputy Editor in March of 1994 and it was to him that I wrote at the end of 1995. I sent some photocopied cuttings, my *NME* bits, and a few ideas for features. After a couple of weeks, I got a polite 'thanks but no thanks'. This I was not expecting.

I'd been reading *HHC* for seven years by then. I felt that I knew the tone, I felt that I was an adequate writer and, most of all, I felt that I knew more about hip-hop than all of their other writers. Yep, I was that full of myself. In my teens and into my late 20's, I had an amazing recall for lyrics. I could listen to a new track a couple of times and all the pieces would slot into place. I also loved tracing the artists – reading the liner notes to see who worked on what, so I could hunt down more of their work. By 1995, I believed I'd built up a store of knowledge that would prove utterly useless if I didn't get to write about it. My brain felt fit to burst with all the hip-hop trivia and opinions washing around in there. Stephen's rejection of my approaches was a severe blow.

I doubled down. I sent some more ideas and some more cuttings. But this time, I went straight to the organ grinder, not the monkey[5]. I got a phone call from Andy Cowan a few days later. I was expecting either broad London tones or a smattering of hip-hop slang from the *HHC* head honcho. I couldn't have been more wrong. The husky, breathy tones that greeted me were the first inkling I had that Andy wasn't like most hip-hop fans. He was the Whispering Bob Harris of the rap publishing world, a gentle bloke who never dressed hip-hop, but whose sense of style was more in fitting with the *Melody Maker*

---

5 The actually lovely Stephen Worthy is now a friend who I see from time to time at publishing events and reunions. He went on to do very good things at the likes of *NME* and *Loaded*. I always take delight in reminding him of his attempts to kill my career before it even started. He takes this stoically in the way that people do when they've heard the same joke 80 times before.

world, proof of a cultural hinterland that went well beyond Run DMC and Public Enemy. Andy proved more receptive than Stephen Worthy had, and asked me to put together one of the features I'd pitched, a piece about the demise of female rappers. There it is in the April 1996 issue – a double page spread with my name on it. I felt like I'd broken down some invisible barrier. I was now a feature writer for one of my favourite magazines, something like an insider in the hip-hop world. RuPaul voice: Don't fuck it up.

5: MY WRITES

Does writing articles about hip-hop give you the same visceral thrill as writing rap lyrics and then performing them? I'm no neuroscientist – no, really – but it seems to come from a similar part of the brain. Dashing off a sentence that you're proud of, that really says what you were wanting to say, seems, for me at least, to operate at a similar level of joy to finding the perfect rhyme. Equally, you know when it's not right. When you deliver a half-rhyme, or you feel there's a better way to keep the verse flowing, you scratch out the lyrics and revise. Writing doesn't differ. You work at it like a sculptor with a block of marble. Occasionally you get it so wrong that you have to get on to that quarry in Wales and order some new stone. And they don't have any because they're filming a new episode of *Doctor Who* there.

Sometimes you absolutely can't get it right. You can't find the payoff line or you fail to make yourself clear. When you see that in print, your heart sinks a little. Especially if, after the magazine has gone to print or the blog page has gone live, you have the journalistic equivalent of esprit d'escalier, the staircase wit when you think of the witty rejoinder after the time has passed. That happens a lot. And it must happen to rappers – there are some truly terrible lyrics out there in the world of music that their creators must regret. Sometimes, as a fan, you can fill in the blanks for them. Why didn't they use that rhyme instead? Still, who wants advice from a failed rapper?

Writers tend to operate, mostly, in a vacuum. You get your brief, you write your piece, you send it off and, days or weeks later, it appears in print or online. It might have been rewritten, edited to within an inch of its life, or it may be completely untouched. It will have a headline and a 'sell' that you had nothing to do with. Rarely, an editor will be in touch to ask for revisions. Usually, they just make them – that's their prerogative.

Even rarer – you get a note of appreciation, saying how good it is, how you've smashed it. That, by and large, is the bubble you operate in. Okay, there might be a reader's letter published in the magazine that refers to your piece, or some online comments, but it's generally a feed-back-free zone. This is why most writers, quietly in the vast majority of cases, have to give themselves a pat on the back. Which takes us back to the start of this chapter. That moment when you hit the target or nail the bullseye, you allow yourself to think that you might just be a good writer. That you may have some real insight into this whole thing. It's a fleeting feeling, but it delivers the feel-good chemicals in a way that hitting that punchline in a rhyme with precision does[1].

I was getting used to that bubble, although the reality of having become a writer for *HHC* took a while to sink in. The editor liked my piece and wanted to hear more ideas from me. He'd add me to the review team and I could expect to get promos in the post. Great – so when are you going to fly me to New York to interview every rapper in the history of ever?

In fact, it was a slow burn. I sent a deluge of ideas for 'state of the culture' pieces, but Andy, wisely, decided to bring me along slowly. He didn't have any writers based in Leeds, so wanted to focus on my local scene too. In May, 1996, I submitted a review of a DJ set by hip-hop

---

1 I remember, on a couple of occasions, dropping in a new punchline in the studio with the PA Posse, something I'd prepared and hadn't told them about. If you landed it, you could see the nods of appreciation, or the laughs if it was a zinger. It was a rare thing for a rapper as lumpen as me, and therefore even more treasured.

Afrika Bambaataa at Headz Club. This night, based in the now defunct Cockpit nightclub, was an instalment of a regular event promoted by Richard Watson and George Evelyn – the latter better known as Night-mares on Wax. George had started out on the Leeds hip-hop scene in the early 1980s as a breakdancer, and had gone on to experience musi-cal success beyond rap, but he always kept his toe in it. He regularly DJ'd at legendary Leeds club The Warehouse, and would drop hip-hop bangers galore before the evening explored other areas of dance music.

Headz Club – and Funky Mule, another night Richard and George ran – straddled the worlds of hip-hop and what came to be known as trip hop. So while they'd bring over a hip-hop stalwart like Bambaataa, they were also a stop for the first Mo' Wax tour and hosted one of the very earliest UK gigs for DJ Shadow. My friend and former partner in rhyme Dan Greenpeace was one of the resident DJs, alongside Wayne Sealey and others. On this particular night, I was accompanied by notable Leeds photographer Richard Moran, a mate I played 5-a-side with who had agreed to take some pictures for *HHC*. Bambaataa did his usual thing of playing his own records, some of the stuff he sampled and then, without any kind of mixing or segue, some AC/DC. Later, there was a chance for some on-stage freestyling. I'd shelved my aspirations as a rapper, but some local guys got up there, as did Tricky, whose debut album *Maxin-quaye* had been released to acclaim the year before. He hogged the mic, refusing to pass it along to all the other waiting rappers, and got heartily booed as a result. Leeds, innit? My piece summed all this up, but I was already chafing against the limits of writing about live shows.

I turned in my first album reviews and, let's be honest, I wasn't exactly being sent A-list stuff. Albums by Suspekt, Without Warning, MC Ren's *Da Villain In Black*. I was itching for something bigger, but didn't know what it would be.

There's a four-month gap between my first ever feature for *Hip-Hop Connection* and the first letter slagging me off. There I am, all bright and eager in April 1996, proud of my first feature. And there I am, in August of the same year, reading a letter on the *Bite Back* page saying, "Andrew Emery is a complete wanker."

Is it better to be hated than loved? Is being ignored worse than either? Once the Internet was invented, and articles were published with below-the-line sections for comments, it became very easy for writers to get instant feedback on what people thought of their work. Guess what? People still think this is a good idea. It never is and never was. Letters pages weren't much better.

To be honest, I loved it when there was a letter praising something I'd written, and loved it just as much when someone has taken the time to write a letter calling me a prick, buy a stamp and post it so the editor could then choose whether or not to publish it. One of the things I hated about a lot of hip-hop writing – and still do – is blandness, a sitting-on-the-fence approach to opinion, especially when it comes to reviews. The news section of a magazine is where you go for the opinion-free facts about what's coming out, who's signed to what label and who has dissed so and so. The rest of the magazine should be dedicated to sifting through that, analysing it, applying subjectivity. Someone writing in with praise or bile was for me a sign that I was doing something right.

That's not the same as writing to provoke, although there is some overlap. My verbal contract as a hip-hop journalist was very simple – they were paying for my voice, knowledge and my opinions, plus lots of other little things like hitting deadlines, being pleasant to deal with, respecting the process and all the many facets that make up being a writer. They weren't paying for me to espouse a view they had, or one that reflected some reader consensus. As most hip-hop writing was so boring, I was always bound to spark some reaction, whether positive or negative, by being opinionated and very firm in those opinions[2].

---

2 'No shit' echo my friends and family simultaneously.

In years to come, someone told me that I had the harshest reputation of all the *HHC* reviewing staff. When I was passionate and keen about something, I went all out to let people know, but they also felt that I was too unkind to many albums and artists. I took exception to this, while simultaneously knowing there was a grain of truth in it[3]. I decided to put this to the test. I grabbed all my issues of *Hip-Hop Connection*, drew out a list of all the writers in that time and decided to tabulate the average mark they gave albums. My aim was to prove that there were numerous writers less generous at handing out stars than me. Surely Tom Dartnell, who rarely had a kind word to say for major label hip-hop, was the meanest of all? Surely somebody else was getting sent loads of dross to slag off? It turns out the grain of truth was actually a whole paddy field of truth. My statistical analysis – there was no fiddling with the figures here – showed that of all *HHC* writers with at least 10 published reviews, I gave the lowest marks out of 5. Bah. I regret nothing.

I personally liked to read reviews I disagreed with purely because of the brio of the writers. I also loved that *HHC* had the back of the UK scene from its debut issue on to the last, even when many of the readers bristled at US artists on the cover or the artists themselves bleated about negative coverage.

The latter is an issue for scribes around the world, of course. We aren't the truth-telling journalists losing our lives to Mexican drug cartels, we know that. We're not Carole Cadwalladr exposing the blighted politics of 21st century Britain. But we did get our share of threats. The hip-hop generation I grew up in loved talking about freedom of speech and seized every opportunity to say the unsayable

---

3 From a 1996 review of 15-year-old rapper A+'s debut album *The Latch-Key Kid*: "In the escalating battle for pre-pubescent rap eminence, it can only be a matter of time before some misguided svengali brings us the world's first rapping foetus." I think 2 stars was quite generous, in retrospect.

in rhyme form. But woe betide you should exercise the same rights when writing about them.

The UK rapper Chester P of Bury Crew and Task Force said some pretty idiotic things about me on the Internet after a bad review in the pages of *HHC*. Don't get me wrong, if someone got something wrong about me, I wouldn't let it lie, but he didn't take a few things into account. One – I didn't write the review. Two – he was probably mistaking me (Andrew Emery) for the editor (Andy Cowan). Three – Andy Cowan didn't write the review either. Four – Adam Anonymous wrote the review. Five – Three out of five seems a generous review to me, to be honest. Six – I'd interviewed Chester P before over a few pints in Soho's The Lyric with my man AJ from Hardnoise for a feature in a top-shelf magazine. You're fucking welcome.

Look at his Wikipedia entry (and, after doing so, consider who might have written it), and it says, "*From the Ashes* in 2008, which was largely a hit with the Task Force fan base, despite receiving a mixed review (3 out of 5) from UK hip-hop magazine, *Hip-Hop Connection* (as Chester had previously ripped the magazine on *MFTC 2*)."

The implication here is that the magazine gave a mixed review to the Task Force album because he'd made comments about it on his *Music From the Corner 2* project. This would be something I never witnessed in all my time at *HHC* – an edict to diss an album because of some perceived beef. We didn't review by committee – we were all given the opportunity to be right or wrong and put our name to it. If an artist got salty, so be it. Looked at another way, our lack of access to the biggest US rap names insured us, somewhat, from retribution. We took the same approach to UK stuff, even if it was slightly riskier. It's why *HHC* was fearless in the freedom of its opinions, and another reason why it's the best hip-hop magazine ever.

By autumn of 1996, the editor started to trust me more – or didn't have the strength to resist my ceaseless pitching of features and ideas.

I got invited down to London to interview Sadat X, formerly of Brand Nubian, and spent time chatting to him at a rather chintzy hotel about going solo and his really very good *Wild Cowboys* album. The £80 I got for the piece barely offset the cost of the train journey down, but that wasn't the point. I was getting to sit face to face with people I'd long admired and ask them questions that I'd thought of. This was what I'd wanted, and it didn't disappoint.

Part of me had worried that for all my confidence, all my years of study, I wouldn't be up to the job. That I'd get found out. Instead, I was revelling in it. I'd found a clear writing voice quite quickly, and was encouraged by Andy Cowan to continue with it. He was happy for me to stack my copy with jokes, but also indulgent when I decided to be a bit more fiery, or pompous, or whatever mood struck when I started writing. He also trusted me enough to send me on my first writing trip. It wasn't New York – it was that well-known hip-hop hotbed Brussels. But it was something I'd never done before, a thrill all in itself. I dusted off my passport.

6: TRAVEL JAM

'm playing chess with Anthony Kiedis from the Red Hot Chili Peppers. I'm not particularly starstruck, because I was never a fan of the group – and won't become one even when I live with a woman in the future who plays their music for 25 hours every day. In fact, that makes me even less of a fan. But nevertheless, I'm playing chess with Anthony Kiedis from the Red Hot Chili Peppers, and I'm beating him.

It's my first ever paid writing trip. I've been sent abroad on an interviewing job, something so exciting to me that I think it's opening the door to a future of globetrotting writing trips. Maybe I'll play draughts with Thom Yorke in Barcelona. I could be taking on LL Cool J at backgammon in New York – although I'd have to learn the rules first. Sadly, these trips never come to pass. Not many do. Writing for an underground hip-hop mag with a small budget doesn't come with many perks, so make the most of them when you can.

I'm with Richard Reyes, one of the stable of freelance photographers who work for *Hip-Hop Connection*, and he's brought along a friend whose name I can't remember, but I do recall him being about 18 feet tall.

The job is to interview House of Pain, who've moved on from their huge hit *Jump Around* to that difficult second album (not really that difficult in truth – it's better than the first, despite the absence of an iconic single). They're playing Rock Werchter, a legendary music festival in Belgium, and if the interview comes off and is half decent, it's going to be the cover story. My first ever.

The record label has arranged a return Eurostar ticket to Brussels, but after that, we're on our own. We don't have a hotel room, but we're there for two nights. We spend the first day doing what any self-respecting professional writer/photographer team does – drinking in the Grand Place in Brussels. We look at the Manneken Pis – it is, as the guide books have promised, the statue of a small boy urinating. We drink beers that are served in the kind of apparatus normally found in chemistry class when you have to do titrating. We then have to make our way to Leuven.

Leuven's most famous contribution to society is Stella Artois, and the festival takes place just down the road from the brewery. The 1996 festival is notable for two things – it's the first time it has taken place over two days, and it's the first time that Radiohead ever performed *Paranoid Android* live. Scratch that, it's notable for three things – it's where I beat Anthony Kiedis from the Red Hot Chili Peppers at chess while he was waiting to go on stage. Fancy a game of Rummikub, Taylor Swift?

We have real trouble getting into the festival. There has been a paperwork cock-up. This was my first press trip, so it was all new to me, but it was only the first of many times that I'd go somewhere I'd been told to go and the person at the record label hadn't done their job. Journalists were past masters at still managing to blag their way into events when their name wasn't put down as promised / was misspelt / security were intent on being maximum dicks. Mobile phones didn't really exist then, so instead of calling up someone at the label or the press office, we just have to gesticulate a lot. Photographer Richard turns out to be much more of a diplomat than me, and by the time he's finished the Potsdam-level negotiations, we've actually been upgraded. We're no longer just backstage to do an interview, we've got access to absolutely all areas, and he's got his giraffe-like mate in as well.

Backstage at Rock Werchter is like a little village, with musicians mingling, a smattering of journalists and PRs, and some truly excellent hospitality staff. While playing the aforementioned game of chess, I'm constantly offered beers and sandwiches. This is the absolute life. Kiedis, licking his wounds from losing in about 40 moves[1], slinks off (okay, he goes to perform to a huge and adoring crowd).

We take a wander, and end up speaking to loads of musicians while we kill time waiting for Everlast, Danny Boy and DJ Lethal to be ready for our chat. I wander up to Radiohead, sidle up to Massive Attack and blunder in to interrupt an Afghan Whigs band meeting. Greg Dulli is very gracious about it. I get quotes about House of Pain from all of them – always be thinking of a sidebar[2].

Our 'Access All Areas including secret sections of society, US government bunkers and the changing room from Mr Benn' press pass means we can literally wander onto the stage when some of the acts are performing. We do just that during the Chili Peppers set (meh) and the House of Pain shows (suffice to say, people do 'Jump Around' when instructed to do so). It's only after we leave that I realise the missed opportunities. While I was thinking about playing Cluedo with Aretha Franklin, I missed performances by some of the greatest ever artists – and numerous personal favourites. David Bowie was playing! Bjork was there! I missed The Chemical Brothers, Neil Young & Crazy Horse, Rage Against the Machine and Pulp. But at least I got free sandwiches, triumphed at chess against the figurehead of a bizarrely overpraised band and that's really all that matters.

The interview? It was as standard as they come. House of Pain had been on stage and the adrenaline was curdling inside Everlast, so he

---

1 I'll be honest, when it comes to chess, I'm no Boris Spassky. I played a few games for my cub scout team in the early 1980s. This isn't *The Queen's Gambit*.

2 More on sidebars later on – oh, the anticipation – but for the uninitiated, they're just the bits and bobs that go alongside the main article. They're often called box-outs and they're usually a chance to highlight something special, use a particularly good quote or, always a fallback with rappers, get them to run through their album track by track.

wasn't all sweetness and light. But it was fine. The joy of this trip wasn't in asking questions about the guests on the 2nd album, but in the fun we had milling around with pop stars who didn't have a clue who we were. And we overstayed our welcome so long that by the time we got back to Brussels, we couldn't get a room for the night. Instead, we stayed up in all-night bars, drinking fierce and fruity Belgian beers until the sun came up, the trains started running and we could enjoy our hangovers in the Channel Tunnel, replete with stories to share.

How do you top that trip? You don't, really. I'd go all over the world to interview rappers, but I never, truly had a paid trip like that again, although I imagine *NME* writers who covered festivals regularly lived like that the whole time. That kind of freebie was standard for certain magazines and certain writers, but writing for a niche genre magazine doesn't get you flown around the world all that much.

I'm not complaining. There are some future trips in the offing[3]. If I concentrate and sit very still, I can still capture some of the excitement 20-something me felt about that adventure. The sense of a new world opening up to me. And then, at the end of the day, I'd go home. To my mum's house in a not particularly lovely bit of South Leeds. And to the video shop where I'd got a job as a supervisor so that I could at least contribute to the household.

The economics of niche journalism can be quite harsh. As I've mentioned already, *HHC* paid around 5p per word. For a 1,500-word interview where you might stay up until 4am to do a phone interview with a rapper somewhere in America, then transcribe it, then turn it into a piece that people would enjoy reading, you'd get £80. It's not like this is in the distant mists of time and that if you run it through a calculator

---

3 I got flown to Puerto Rico to interview Missy Elliott, including two nights in the Ritz-Carlton. But that was much more constrained, closely organised and, notably, I really managed to fuck that one up. That's coming up later.

that allows for inflation, that ends up being a lot of money. It never was. It certainly helped, and like many contributors I soon made peace with the paltry sums on offer because we were still getting paid to write about hip-hop, and that was quite a platform to have. But it did mean I needed a regular job to pay board, buy records, go out and buy clothes, have a pint with friends.

I was now in my mid-20s, and many of my friends from uni had gone on to proper careers. Ollie was working in sales. Geordie 'ran' a pub. Chiv was selling booze to students. Tom either made pork pies or worked in a bra factory. Or both. My former rap group buddies Dan and Barrie had both moved to London for jobs. I'd not only lost mine and replaced a bit of it with writing and a bit of it with working in a video shop, but I was also losing friends to other cities.

The video shop didn't help matters. On the plus side, it was only a few hundred yards from my house, and... no, that's it, that was the entirety of the plus side. I wrote about it in my last book, so I'll be brief here: One of the junior members of staff showed me a picture of her dead baby on my first night on the job. She later sexually harassed me. The manager was sacked for stealing[4] and I got dragged into testifying. I got offered the job of manager, but said no as I thought that would lock me into working there and I'd never get to be a proper writer. I did write a piece for a video shop industry magazine about growing up in one in the early 1980s and how the 90's compared, but that was unpaid so didn't help much either. I felt like I was treading water, and if I did that much longer, I was going to run out of energy and drown..

The only thing keeping me going was the work for *HHC*. As the leaves fell from the trees that autumn, I was sitting up late, long after my mum was in bed, to interview Nine, Yo-Yo and others. I spoke to Xzibit for the first time. He teased the possibility of a Golden State Clique

---

4 For stealing big bottles of pop. What a thing to lose your job for.

album with fellow west coast stars Ras Kass and Saafir – something that would never come to pass.

Dan had an idea for a column, and I put him in touch with Andy Cowan. He too entered the *HHC* fold, joining me there until the end of the magazine's life – the PA posse might not have set the rap world alight, but we'd found our place in print. Dan's *Independent's Day* column would be an important one, a place where he could shed light on the growing indie rap scene, from one-track obscurities to people who'd go on to shape hip-hop. It was so good that *The Source* ripped the idea off completely and launched their own column with the exact same title. It wasn't anywhere near as good.

Around the same time, I wrote a think piece about how rappers were obsessed with the 'New World Order', using quotes I'd got from Wise Intelligent of Poor Righteous Teachers and De La Soul. The piece prompted an almighty fax from the Universal Zulu Nation in New York, multiple pages sent through (again, can someone hurry up and invent email) attempting to refute my point and then, as the fax went on to bang on about conspiracies and how we should only drink distilled water, it completely proved my point. Andy Cowan posted it to me in its entirety, amused at what I'd provoked.

Getting this fax through the post did three things. First, it amused me. Here was a mighty and legendary hip-hop organisation[5] getting all upset over something written by me in a UK hip-hop mag. Secondly, it thrilled me. Here was a mighty and legendary hip-hop organisation getting all upset over something written by me in a UK hip-hop mag.

---

5 The Universal Zulu Nation was born out of the New York gang The Black Spades in the late 70's. By the 80's it was a pro hip-hop organisation overseen by Afrika Bambaataa. With chapters all over the world it was widely regarded as a positive thing, but the fax they sent me displayed some truly troubling beliefs and the group adopted many elements of other fringe groups as it developed. Bam stepped down after allegations of sexual abuse tarnished his previously untouchable reputation.

Wow. And thirdly, it helped water a seed that was already germinating. I could write about this fax, poke more fun at this esteemed but po-faced group, and the perfect forum would be a magazine of my own. It was an idea I'd been kicking around for a few months with Dan and our friend Mike Lewis for an independent rap mag. A game-changer in hip-hop publishing, or so we thought. We had some ideas, we had the name, we had boundless enthusiasm. We also had a budget of about three pounds.

7: APPOINTMENT AT THE FAT CLINIC

Why launch your own hip-hop magazine, when there's already a long-established one with proper distribution that pays you for interviewing artists you love? It's a good question[1]. Andy Cowan is the most affable, amenable and accommodating editor I've ever worked for, but even he would surely baulk at some of the ideas we had lined up for the publication we had planned – *Fat Lace*. After all, he was trying to actually sell copies, establish a position on the shelves and stay in a job. What we wanted to do was the niche of the niche.

If you want to be a millionaire in publishing, start out as a billionaire. We never launched *Fat Lace* to be rich – who would get rich from making jokes about Basement Khemist[2] and Kukoo Da Baga Bonez[3]? – but to do something no-one else had done before. A hip-hop magazine that didn't just focus on the new, but also talked about our favourite artists of the past.

At that stage, nobody was doing that. Probably because the hip-hop nostalgia market wasn't yet a thing – now we're firmly in an era when

---

1 It's also a question you didn't ask, but writers love to do this stuff where they ask a question as if everyone is lining up to ask it. I'm just joining in.

2 I think if I write a footnote about every rap group I mention in the book I'll try the patience of both the reader and the publisher. Google exists.

3 Honestly, even if I was happy to write a footnote about every rapper, I wouldn't bother to do one on Kukoo.

documentaries, publications and more embrace the past and retell those legendary stories in ways both novel and tedious. *The Source* had done a really good issue with the holy original trinity of hip-hop on the cover – Bam, Flash and Kool Herc – but it was a one-off. We wanted to write about both the new school, the old school and the future school. To interview Aaron Fuchs about his legendary 80s label Tuff City while indie darling J-Zone would tell us all about his favourite TV shows.

We also didn't want to be boring or worthy. Passion was a given, but we wanted to be funny too. There were other hip-hop fanzines out there in the world, and some really good ones, but nobody had done a rap mag that was inspired by *Viz*, *HHC*, *Private Eye* and *The Source*. Of course, with such high aims, you'd have expected the first issue to be a slam dunk classic, but the fact that it wasn't is largely my fault. We had ideas, but we didn't have a plan. We also didn't have a designer, and we'd given ourselves an unrealistic deadline – the forthcoming Fresh 97 concert in Folkestone.

Fresh 97 was the brainchild of Mick 'Blue Eyes' Mottesford, a rapper turned concert promoter who ploughed a fair amount of his own money into an extravaganza that combined shows from legendary rappers, graf demonstrations, breakdancing, UK artists and more. I'd interviewed Mick all about it for *HHC* at his home in my old stomping ground, Nottingham, and was impressed by his passion and commitment. In a pre-Internet era he was getting on the phone to rappers around the world and getting them to come over to an unloved piece of the English coast. It chimed with what we wanted to do with Fat Lace – all aspects of hip-hop culture, new and old, the forgotten and the as-yet unknown. A few months out, we thought it would be the ideal time and place to launch issue one. We'd sell it while covering the event itself.

At this point, the *Fat Lace* crew was three people. Myself, Dan Greenpeace and Mike Lewis. We got to know Mike through buying mail order records from him. While all the other record dealers distributed professional lists, Mike's had loads more personality. He also had bargains galore, and Dan and I had both ordered from him frequently. Dan being Dan, he'd also spoken on the phone to Mike, and built up a rapport. The three of us met up on a trip to London and hit it off famously.

We were all people who loved the minutiae of rap music, had strange passions for otherwise obscure records, and we also liked to make jokes about it. Mike had already dabbled in hip-hop with his own label, Mikey Mike Records. The artwork on the *DJ Mikey Mike and the Milestones of Funk* album from 1990 would be familiar to anyone who had ever received a letter from Mike, or bought from his mail-order list. Hand drawn, blocky and charming, it was underground personified, but in a very British way.

Mike was, and remains, one of the least hip-hop people you can ever meet, despite his involvement in it for nigh-on 40 years. B-Boy clothes and slang? Not for Mike. He's more likely to be making his own pesto and grinding coffee beans while watching a VHS of *Sweet Valley High* (of course, I'm basing some of this on my time living with Mike in the late 1990's. He may be watching something else by now). He and Andy Cowan were my first entries in what is now a long list of people who are absolutely fathoms deep in hip-hop, but you could share a coffee and pasta alla pesto with them and not have a clue.

Now, Mike runs Lewis Recordings, putting out fine records by Edan and DJ Yoda, among others, and is typically humble about the things he's done and places he's been, the rappers he's interviewed, photographed or even put into the studio. Such is Mike. He was one of the originals, the third of the trio, and he brought something entirely different to *Fat Lace*, something sillier and more slapstick. The magazine was all the better for it.

We didn't really have a major plan at that stage. It was haphazard. We had a couple of interviews we'd done that we either couldn't place in *HHC* or we just had more answers from the artists than *HHC* had space to run with. We started asking artists questions that they wouldn't normally encounter in a run-of-the-mill mag interview – Is Eric B the world's worst DJ? You're allowed one meat, two vegetables and a dessert, what do you choose? – and putting them aside for *Fat Lace*. I asked Andy Cowan if this was above board – could we use a couple of minutes of our interview time to gather material for a little magazine we had planned? Of course, being Andy, he said yes. We were worried that, as he was paying us to interview these artists, it would be out of order for us to use some of it for ourselves. As far as he was concerned, it was 'overmatter' that would be consigned to the bin otherwise. As long as our articles for *HHC* didn't suffer, he was game.

What's in a name? *Fat Lace* didn't take too much thought. We wanted something short, snappy, memorable and a little old school – the fat laces that B-Boys wore in their sneakers in the 1980s. Dan came up with it, Mike and I agreed with it instantly. However, piecing together the rest of the magazine wasn't all that simple.

We'd also had an idea about resurrecting a defunct *HHC* column called *Demoblaster*. The original saw unsigned artists submit their demo tapes to be judged by a panel, usually made up of other artists, along with a writer. It had served its time and we thought we could do something similar, with a feature called *It's a Demo* after the classic Kool G Rap & DJ Polo single. Thus, that first issue of *Fat Lace* comes complete with the subtitle 'Incorporating 'It's a Demo'. It's the first and last time it was ever mentioned. We didn't receive any tapes, we didn't even ask for any, and it got filed away in the bad ideas graveyard.

Which almost happened to the entire issue, especially with a man with the visual sense of Helen Keller at the helm. This was before the advent of home computers and laptops – the days of TIME Computers having a high-street presence were just around the corner. Instead, we had to make do with my access to whatever rudimentary design programs we had on the computers at the local library. We decided to put comments about the magazine at the bottom of every page, and it was entirely fitting that the one at the base of the content page said 'The magazine that won't win any design awards'.

I can't remember now whether it was PagePlus or PageMaker that I used to design issue one of *Fat Lace*, which says it all. If in any way at all I'd achieved mastery of either piece of software, I might be able to recall the name. But as anyone who has seen or read issue one of *Fat Lace* can tell you, that mastery was completely absent.

Black and white? That's fine. We didn't have the budget for even a single colour on the cover. The fonts? What was a font? I just picked the one I used to use for the college newsletter at Joseph Priestley College. How best to illustrate an interview with Stretch Armstrong? Why, how about me taking a picture of an arm and stretching it the full length of a page? Who needs Neville Brody?

The content was as ramshackle as the design. Interviews and reviews, a bit of humour. The response to that Zulu Nation fax. In effect, it looked and read just like a fanzine, rather than an actual magazine. I'm not sure we even had a flat plan to work from. Don't get me wrong – we still loved it.

Key to it all was the cover, and our very first cover hero – T La Rock. A truly legendary New York rapper who'd made significant records in the 1980s with the likes of Kurtis Mantronik, Hollywood, Greg Nice and more, his main claim to fame was the certified hip-hop hall of fame record *It's Yours*. This 1984 gem was the very first release on Def Jam, and it showcased his brilliant vocabulary and wordy style. He went on to release one really good album and then a bit of a stinker, but he remained an icon of the 1980s for us.

Like many 80s rap stars, the 90s weren't all that kind to Terry Keaton. In 1994, while breaking up a fight in the Bronx, he suffered a severe brain injury. After surgery, he ended up living as a patient at the Haym Solomon Nursing and Rehab home in Bensonhurst, Brooklyn, a one-time rap legend surrounded by the elderly Jewish men who were the home's bread and butter patient. We'd meet him later in life, after this story became known – there have long been rumours of a film being made about Terry – but we wanted to dedicate our first issue to the man not just behind *It's Yours*, but also tracks like *Tudy Fruity Judy*, *Back to Burn* and *Breaking Bells*. A man who started his recorded rap career with the lines, "Commentating, illustrating / Description giving, adjective expert / Analysing, surmising, musical / Myth-seeking people of the universe, this is yours!", which are as far from the ordinary as you got in 1984.

The only problem? We didn't know where T La Rock was. We had no way of getting hold of him. That's when we made the editorial decision that it didn't matter. That we could put someone on the cover without an interview and just talk about how much we liked them. We were prepared to just drop him in there and sing his praises, when all of a sudden fellow rap legends Special K and Grandmaster Caz helped facilitate a chat with Terry.

In retrospect, it's not a great or incisive interview. We passed our questions to T La Rock through a third party, which is never an ideal situation. But at a time when old school interviews were a rarity, we had ours in the bag, and he duly graced the cover. Elsewhere in the mag, there was that badly designed interview with Stretch Armstrong – choice quote: "I like broccoli. I can't think of another vegetable" – Roc Raida, a column by Dave Paul of *Bomb Magazine* fame, some ramblings of a taxi driver I recorded one night, some bits by future beatbox hall-of-famer Kela and an early shot at fellow Leeds rap acolytes Braintax.

I'll take a quick minute to here to double down on that, largely because my good friend and absolutely wonderful writer Justin Quirk[4]

---

4 Justin is a brilliant writer about art, music and all manner of culture, and I thought this even before we became friends. He was the man who told me to write *Wiggaz*, and his book on glam metal, *Nothin' But a Good Time* (Unbound, 2020) is wonderful.

insisted that all he wanted from this book was me banging on about what a dick Braintax was. As regular readers will know, Braintax were a rap group from Leeds who came through at the same time that Dan and I were trying our own hand in the hip-hop game. They released the *Fat Head* EP on Low Life Records, and then, after Joe and Aaron split, Joe kept up the Low Life label himself, but down in London. Joe also kept recording as Braintax, albeit as a solo artist.

The renowned London DJ, MK, used to drop into my office when I moved to London (sorry, chronology fans, for yet another spoiler), because Barrie helped design covers for his mixtapes. He'd become friends with Joe, who'd turned Low Life into a notable label, with plenty of fine UK artists on it. I'd still roll my eyes whenever his name was mentioned, because I had first hand experience of what a petulant little prick he really was. I was repeatedly told that I was wrong, that I was just being bolshy or jealous, and that Joe was actually a fine MC, label boss and all round humanitarian of the year.

It gives me no joy – okay, a little frisson, perhaps – to reveal that Joe later ripped off nearly everyone who signed to his label, and did an overnight flit with all the money. His name became mud in UK hip-hop circles, and it was all I could do to nod in sympathy and not proclaim from the top of the nearest bell tower, "I fucking told you all!" Rumours swirled about where he'd gone for years, with old friends swearing retribution. Well, guys, I know where he is. If anyone needs that address, I've got you.

Anyway, Joe Braintax had moaned about a review in *Hip-Hop Connection*, even though it was actually a good one so, on a page titled 'The Inaugural Fat Lace Awards', he won the Dry Your Eyes Award for 'moaning about a good review and generally being a humourless tit'. Time has blunted many of my opinions, but damn, that guy was always a bell-end.

The best stuff in that first issue was all from Mike, and his stuff really set the tone for what was to come. He had a three-page feature called *Mike Hard's Drama Addicts Club*, where he let his imagination run riot.

A fake interview where Schoolly D talked about his dream of being a *Bullseye* contestant but was worried about DJ Code Money's dart throwing? Genius. Columbo's gossip page where he revealed that Tupac was actually still alive because his subscription to *TV Quick* has just been renewed? Gold. And then, exclusive of exclusives, an interview with The Notorious BIG.

> *Fat Lace: What is your favourite colour?*

> *Notorious BIG: A hamburger. I just love to stuff my chops with as many as I can possibly fit into my huge cakehole and I even stuff them up my arse.*

Mike set the childish, piss-taking tone for what *Fat Lace* was to become, but I take all the credit because I was the editor and designer and that is the end of it.

There's a piece on the Red Bull Music Academy website called 'A History of Hip Hop Zines'. It features *Fat Lace*. That would be a point of pride – it's the only entry of the 10 that originates from outside of North America – if the Torii MacAdams piece wasn't a load of largely incorrect bullshit. I can't speak to the accuracy of the stuff about the other zines featured, but he gets off to a calamitous start with the following: "London's *Fat Lace* was a quarterly founded by DJ Yoda (Duncan Beiny) and Dan Greenpeace in February 1997."

Good stuff, except that the lovely DJ Yoda wasn't involved until issue 3, as a writer and then part of the editorial squad, that the magazine hailed from Leeds and it wasn't even close to being a quarterly (5 issues in 4 years). It leaves me out, and it also leaves out Mike Lewis, a core member of the editorial team for the mag's entire run. I then get referred to as 'staffer Drew Huge'. No, that'll be editor and publisher, mate. Finally, we're told that, "when *Fat Lace* petered out in 2001, much of the staff moved on to *Hip-Hop Connection*." *Fat Lace* ended in 2000, became an online mag published first independently and then by Uproxx, and we were already all working for *Hip-Hop Connection*. Other than that, it's all spot on. Pulitzers all round.

We managed to hit our deadline for the first issue, albeit by crowbarring in some real space filler and giving away a couple of adverts to industry contacts in return for future favours. We duly took piles of them down to Folkestone for Fresh 97. We imagined a scenario where we sold every single copy and returned as conquering heroes with a pile of money and a future as publishers. The reality was somewhat different. Sales were sluggish – rap fans can be real tight arses – even with Dan's brother, Rob G, acting as salesman and hawking the mag to every group of B-Boys in the building.

It picked up on day three of the event when Special K – a legend who'd once been one third of the Treacherous Three – held up a copy on stage and shouted, "Cop this mag, my brother is on the cover." Until then, I hadn't even realised that Special K – Kenny Keaton – and T La Rock were siblings. A mini sales rush emerged, and *Fat Lace* broke even. That's all it needed to do.

8: I'M NOT A PLAYER

Working for minimum wage in a dismal video shop, when the minimum wage didn't exist. Penning stuff for *Hip-Hop Connection* at night. Trying to get the *NME* interested in my stuff again. That was 1997. I'm approaching my mid-20's, and thinking that the real writing career might just pass me by.

Fat Lace provided one highlight, the takeover of *HHC* by Future Publishing another, securing the magazine's immediate future. In January, I hosted a roundtable 'state of hip-hop' discussion in London, in the office of the man who signed Take That. It was a 'great and good of UK rap put the world to rights' kind of thing, with a few label heads, producer Trevor Jackson AKA The Underdog and Mat C, who would go on to edit hip-hop magazines, including a notable rival publication.

At the same time, Dan and I were collaborating on some big *HHC* pieces together, truly relishing the opportunity to talk to some of our heroes. And when we weren't working together, I was up late at mum's, attaching some clunky recording device to her old rotary phone to make sure I could capture every word from my interviewees.

Dan and myself put together a comprehensive piece about the New York hip-hop hotbed Queensbridge where we spoke to Mobb Deep, Poet of Screwball, Noreaga of CNN, Royal Flush, Rob Swift, Akinyele and Mic Geronimo. In the same issue I wrote a preview of Fresh 97, where we'd get to see legendary Coldcrush Brother Grandmaster Caz, who I also interviewed the same month. I was slowly but surely amassing a catalogue of interviews and encounters with long-time heroes. And Mic Geronimo. And I was adding to my string of 1* album reviews.

The interviews kept coming thick and fast throughout 1997. Delinquent Habits, Camp Lo whose *Uptown Saturday Night* album I fell in love with, Tony D, Dead Prez, absolute rap royalty EPMD. As my mum slept upstairs, I spoke to both Salt and Pepa, with them guiding me through the tricky minefield of shopping for underwear for your girlfriend.

The Fugees second album, *The Score*, had been absolutely huge in 1996, and I got to interview Lauryn Hill over the phone in 1997. I rang a few times and got no answer, but kept persisting as this was earmarked for the *HHC* cover. Eventually, she answered. She hadn't heard the phone over the running water. The scenario: Me, in my pyjamas in Sylvia Emery's lounge in Beeston, South Leeds. Her, in the shower at home in America, completely naked. It was a first and a last – interviewing a rapper who was soaping up her nethers while answering questions about touring, the other Fugees and her dreams of working with RZA and Stevie Wonder.

Hill would go on to build a reputation as being quite difficult and somewhat prickly. She'd miss a lot of live shows or arrive so late that most of the audience would have aged out of her music by the time she took to the stage. To be honest, it's not particularly easy being a woman in the rap industry, especially when you achieve superstar status so quickly. I found her to be a fantastic interviewee. She gave long and thoughtful answers about the group's sudden success, how the perception of them had changed from being an underground rap group to an R'n'B group all because of the success of the *Killing Me Softly* cover. She talked candidly about the swirl of going solo rumours, addressed a perceived beef with Jeru the Damaja and the art of live performance. All of this while she was rinsing the Vosene out of her hair. She also told me, "I don't really like to write rhymes. My best raps come out of me when I feel it, like in the shower, for example. My best rhymes come out when I'm washing." Maybe it's also the case for her best interviews too.

By now, I was realising that many of the finest moments in interviews were hidden between the lines. You might get some gold from one of your scripted questions, but sometimes you just had to go with the flow to unlock something interesting. Equally, you might pick up on something when you were waiting to start your interview, some interaction between the artist and their PR that hinted at some tension or a different story to the one you hoped to tell. In the same month that I chatted to Lauryn Hill, I also got to speak to Scarface, long-time Geto Boy and arguably one of the greatest rappers of all time. He's definitely in my top 10.

He was another rapper who was a delight to chat to, largely because he was so surprising. "I'm not interested in hip-hop at all," he told me, "I don't even listen to rap." He then went on to sing the praises of Enya, Mazzy Star, AC/DC and Judas Priest. He talked about working with Tupac, his fatalism and future projects with the Geto Boys. But the real highlight wasn't prompted by a question. I'm in Leeds, he's in the offices of Virgin Records, Houston. I mention that the review copy of his new *Untouchable* album I'm holding has a track called 'Mary Jane' that, according to the liner notes, is supposed to feature Jay-Z. But Jigga is nowhere to be heard on it. Scarface, real name Brad Jordan, is not best pleased.

> *"Jay-Z? What the fuck are they talking about? Who wrote that muthafucking shit? I'm gonna dig in their pussy about this shit. These muthafuckers have got to respect me. I'm a man of respect. For anybody to fuck up my shit is disrespectful. I don't need no goddamn Jay-Z or whoever's names they putting on that tape."*

He then grabs another phone and I listen in as he makes several internal phone calls to deliver a number of bollockings. When he's done, his anger initially colours the interview – he's got a bit of a grump on. But eventually he thaws, warms to the task and gives some great answers. But it's the bit at the start that gives me my intro to the piece, and also something that reveals the mindset of Scarface at the time. Because, of course, he works with "goddamn Jay-Z" in the future.

There's a bit of travel within the UK sprinkled in. I head down to Bristol to meet Roni Size and Krust to explore their landmark *New Forms* album with them. I cross The Pennines to Manchester where Manc rap impresario Dave 'The Ruf' has put together a compilation called *Ruf Diamonds*. Gathered in Alaska Bar are rap groups Krispy, Hearts of Darkness, First in Command, Tribal Lordz and Numskullz. I interview every single one of them, and make a firm friend in the rapper Fluke, one half of another group on the compilation, Meta-phorce. Under his proper name of Tom Dartnell he starts writing for *HHC* and eventually becomes a colleague in a future day job. I haven't seen his partner-in-rhyme, Debut 75, for about 20 years, but he sent me a wedding present in 2022. Braintax aside, the UK rap scene is full of fine people.

At the same time, I begin the first of what would eventually be many, many regular columns for *HHC*. Take my advice – if your part-time video shop job isn't really cutting it in terms of funding your expensive record-buying habit, start a column called *Encyclopaedia Raptannica* where you deliver an A to Z of the rap world. With 26 letters to cover, at 2 a month, that's at least 13 months of cheques right there. And, more importantly, you get to deliver your highly subjective views of every rapper, DJ and group you can think of.

June of 1997 is a landmark for *HHC*. After nine years on shelves, it has reached 100 issues. It celebrates with a super-thick issue and a great De La Soul cover photo. I deliver a breathlessly quick overview of how hip-hop has changed in that period and, along with Dave The Ruf and Dan, a six-page guide to what went down at Fresh 97.

Remember when the Internet wasn't really a thing? Let's celebrate that with the very first edition of the dismally-named *Webheadz* column, which makes its debut in July, 1997. My column would be an attempt to chronicle the hip-hop content to be found online at the time, and the screen grabs on the page show that we're very clearly in Web 1.0 territory. Anyone who thinks the web was once all great and lovely and has only recently become a bin fire should take note of my opening paragraph: "As we take the first of our regular looks at what the Internet holds for hip-hop travellers, let us be mindful of the sheer amount of vitriol, prejudice and snooker-loopiness we can expect to encounter." Ain't a damn thing changed.

More important, especially in terms of my future writing career at *HHC* and beyond, was a piece I wrote called *The Playa Way*. The intro sets the doom-mongering tone:

> *In many ways, hip-hop is a sick puppy. Those of us who love it, and those of us who live it, must be prepared to admit that sometimes we're just a bit sick of it. De La's Trugoy is certainly sick and Stretch Armstrong revealed in HHC that he gets tired of it. That's no surprise. The most consistently innovative, positive, awe-inspiring, important and relevant music form ever can also be the most frustrating, disappointing, stagnant and negative. Since about 1993, that's the way we've been headed.*

What prompted this apocalyptic reading of the state of hip-hop music in 1997? Truth be told, some 26 years later, it's hard to accurately recapture the anger and disillusion that permeates this article. It's like trying to rediscover your youthful disgust at anything, especially when, over two decades later, hip-hop is still my daily soundtrack, and I now scoff at doomsayers who constantly try to tell me it's dead or dying. Some things stay constant in life. I'd say my hatred for Tories is as sharp today as it was when Thatcher was alive. But this particular article is like a time capsule of a period that has long since disappeared, taking those particular emotions with it.

In brief, the piece attacks the 'playa' phenomenon in hip-hop. In particular, the fake player – to segue back into some actual spelling – that was all over every record in the mid-to-late 1990s. Rap videos were populated with people in shiny suits, sipping from bottles of expensive but not very good fizz and talking about the player lifestyle. If you didn't like that, you were a player hater. And self-important and somewhat tetchy Andrew Emery was more than prepared to be a player hater.

I wasn't alone in this view, to be fair. The Fugees had given an interview to the UK's *Downlow* magazine, where they commented, "You can't drive through the ghetto in a Benz or Jag wearing Versace. That doesn't even make a bit of sense." Trugoy's stellar verse on the title track from De La Soul's *Stakes is High* was a masterpiece of tired anger at the player's pretensions.

I'd interviewed De La Soul for the same Mat Carter-edited magazine[1] in August 1996 as part of the promo they were doing for that album. Reading it back recently, I realise that I didn't write the introduction. It doesn't sound like me at all. But I echo most of its senti-

---

1 Mat and I used to call each other at home, and I loved how his dad would answer the phone in a true old-school style with 'Welwyn Garden two seven five nine oh three three' or whatever the number was. I invited him onto that *HHC* round table and he asked me to write for *Downlow*. It was for free, but I really wanted to meet De La Soul. Relations soured when he launched a zine called *Fatboss*, as we felt there was only room for one independent hip-hop magazine with 'Fat' in the title in the UK. And despite his protestations, it was clearly a sideswipe at us. We ended up organising a 'soundclash' at The Social in London that they put a lot more work into and ended up winning with ease. For the record, I always thought Mat was a great, enthusiastic guy and was sorry we'd fallen out. I also didn't really rate *Fatboss*. It looked the business, but the undoubted design mastery was often at the expense of being able to read the words. Mat has, I'm glad to say, gone on to other great hip-hop related things that I'm not at liberty to divulge.

ments. However, what matters is what the trio of Posdnuos, Maseo and Dave have to say.

Downlow: Are you directing your lyrics at a particular audience?

Dave: Some of them are aimed at rappers who feel it's a party at all times. We're just letting them know that when the party's over, it's time to take care of business. We've gotta wake up 'cos there's a war going on around us.

Posdnuos: We're not concerning ourselves with the rappers. It's the issue we're attacking. It's not a question of attacking Biggie or Nas, it's attacking the people who try to emulate what they're talking about."

The letters pages of magazines, the more eloquent rappers, the ranks of record buyers in hip-hop retailers – there was a divide happening, with many disgruntled consumers feeling that hip-hop had lost its soul. But had it, really?

After *Wiggaz With Attitude* came out, I was invited to be a guest on Romesh Ranganathan's *Hip-Hop Saved My Life* podcast. It was lots of fun, but one of the main stories Romesh wanted me to talk about was the time I called Jay-Z a 'cunt'. And no, it wasn't in print. It was this encounter with Jay-Z that prompted the whole article, and made me disappear down a rabbit hole of being a true school hip-hop purist for a decent period to come.

Jay-Z and Foxy Brown were promoting their Ain't No Nigga[2] single and I'd decided to take some of the questions that rap fans were asking on the *HHC* letters page to my interview. I cleared this approach with

2 Quite possibly my least favourite hip-hop record ever.

the PR, who said the artists would both be willing to address the whole 'player' thing and that it would make a change of pace from the usual glad-handing interviews. Only, once we were in a room together, it was clear that nothing had been cleared with Jay-Z. I had to explain that some of the questions were quite combative. He was okay with that. Foxy? She didn't turn up. Maybe someone told her I gave her a one-star review once.

HHC: Isn't your subject matter, with its cars and Moet, just an orgy of materialism? How do you justify what you rap about?

Jay Z: I don't have to justify anything I do. That's entertainment, that's what I do. I'm making records. I don't think people who say that have listened to my whole album. I tell a story. I tell a complete picture. I don't glorify cars. I tell you I was in that car. I don't talk about four or five cars. If you hear me talking about a Lexus then that is what I had. I'm not glorifying anything, no type of clothes or nothing. That's what I wear, that's what I drive.

HHC: However, even if you do like it, aren't you holding up an image of a lifestyle that's impossible for most people to attain? In effect, it's just showing off.

Jay Z: I'm not telling people to go out and get this. I'm telling people what I have. I'm telling a story about me. Have you got my album? On my album do you hear me say Versace more than two or three times? I can't change my life, I do what I do. I give people something they can feel, not all this 'I rhyme like this, I rhyme like that' – that's garbage to me. I'm not really with that. I'd rather touch on emotions people can feel and say, 'Oh, I was in that position'.

HHC: Do you represent hip-hop culture on your records?

Jay Z: I represent myself and my people before I represent hip-hop. No-one asks a doctor how does he represent medicine. I'm doing a job. If I'm contributing to hip-hop then fine, but if not, fine.

HHC: Do you ever feel guilty about giving out a negative image?

Jay Z: I just represent what I see every day. I don't feel guilty about anything, no regrets.

HHC: Do you think that Biggie's death was partly as a result of all these negative forces in hip-hop?

Jay Z: Biggie was my friend and I'm very dad, but I don't wanna talk about it for a magazine purpose. This music didn't have nothing to do with it. Forget that."

Despite me warning Jay Z in advance about the nature of the questions, it's a testy exchange. In fact, he winds the interview up there and then. Reading that back, he's got every right. I'm not sure I'd enjoy being questioned in a similar way. And in many ways, what he says is correct. Why did we ever expect young black men to represent a whole culture every time they made a record? It's a ridiculous expectation to hang on someone.

Like I say, I can't really understand what made me go down this path as a writer – and it's a path I stayed on for some time. I was bolstered by a really positive response from the *HHC* readership, who wrote lots of letters supporting my viewpoint. They enjoyed reading about one of the vanguards of the new era of hip-hop being properly questioned.

Jay Z didn't just bring the interview to an end, he was rude and dismissive. I made my case – you said you were okay with these questions, we'll get to some safer ground in a minute and talk about new projects etc. He wasn't having it. I can't recall exactly what he said next, but it was unpleasant. I can recall exactly what I said next: "You don't need to be a cunt about it, mate." And that was that.

I've got a few regrets. Not at how that day ended up, but about the piece. Being perfectly honest, it's nice to have a story like that on your CV. 'The day I called the future biggest rapper in the world a cunt to his face.' But I'm less proud of the article, of my stance. It felt right at the time, but reading it now it's hideously po-faced, and it holds Jay-Z up to a standard that's wholly unrealistic. Hip-hop has always done bragging, from its very inception, and here I am telling someone it's suddenly out of order.

It's a strange moment in time. The Roots were mocking the player style with their song *What They Do*, and even more explicitly with the video for it. Jeru told *HHC*, "Because it's our music, we need to police our own community. It's our music." Independent rappers and label owners were constantly telling us that they set up their imprints precisely because the major record labels only wanted to sign a certain kind of commercial rapper.

And I was swept up in that moment. It's not a take on the music that I think has aged well, although it played very well at the time. Is it that I've softened, or grown more fond of the records that typified the player type? A bit of both. I listen to mindless gangster rap allllll the time now, because it's just so funky. The stuff they're saying just rolls past me. But in my 20's, I was still the same self-important bloke who'd tried to set the world right in his lyrics as a failed rapper.

One more point on this. Jay-Z went on to be the world's biggest rapper, is regularly hailed as the greatest of all time and of course he's now Mr Beyonce. So my attempt at a takedown was entirely ineffective, as it was always destined to be. Journalists might be able to annoy a rapper one-on-one in a hotel room, but ultimately we are mere mortals next to them. All of which doesn't mean I like Jay-Z. I never liked his voice and still don't. And *Reasonable Doubt*, the album in question, widely hailed as a masterpiece, is absolutely flooded with the gaudy flaunting of wealth. Not Versace – he's right about that – but the effect of so much rapping about fine wines, Cristal, Moet and Lexus cars is still deadening to me over 20 years later.

9: STRAIGHT JACKET

In the rich circus of minor Leeds characters, Barry of Briggate[1] is a particularly weaselly one. He ran a newsagent, 'Barry on Briggate', whose familiar, cheery, 'heart and soul of the neighbourhood' name was pure façade. In reality, he was Dickens' Smallweed, a man hunched by his own meanness. With a prime position on one of Leeds' main shopping streets, his pricing was a miracle of rapacious optimism. With remarkable foresight, he'd predicted 2024 cigarette pricing in 1998. Items with a set RRP – a 10p bag of Space Raiders, for example – would be overlaid with a price sticker of 28p. Often there wasn't a price sticker at all, but Barry would take a look at your item when you went to pay and pull a price out of the ether. But this story isn't about Barry. It's about the bin outside his shop.

There's a peculiar hindsight unique to music fans. It combines legendary gigs you could have gone to but didn't, with rare records you had the chance to buy but failed to do so. I have both of those, but with the added touch of 'incredible hip-hop memorabilia I stupidly parted with'.

On the first, I've got plenty of cause for regret. From the coach I missed to the filming of the BBC series *Dance Energy* – when it was on TV I got to see Dan and Martin down the front as A Tribe Called Quest performed in the studio – to the time I got ran out of the Big L tribute

---

1 For the uninitiated, Briggate is one of the main thoroughfares in Leeds. Lined with classic boozers, fast-food restaurants, shops, a couple of theatres and full of buskers, street rappers and people who bump into you because they're looking at their phones while walking. In other words, like any other high street.

concert in New York (more of which later). Add in countless live shows missed during my London days, either because I was too busy drinking in pubs with colleagues or going out with a series of women with acute social anxiety. Or because I was too lazy. Then again, I was the only one of my friends to get the mini-bus from Leeds to Birmingham to see NWA, Eazy-E and Above The Law perform. We all have those moments.

When it comes to rare records, it's hard to even quantify how many I missed out on. In the early days of record collecting, you were using what little pocket money you had to buy the records you knew or wanted. Most of us didn't have the financial wherewithal or crystal ball necessary to plan shrewd investments based on scarcity. When I was 11 or 12, the purchase was often a toss-up, often decided by the strength of the cover. In later years, with a touch more money and a bit of rap on the radio, you might head into Crash Records and ask to reserve the Kool G Rap & Polo *Poison* single ahead of it coming onto the racks.

By the time I was shopping for records in London and New York, I knew the artists I liked, the posse or crew they were aligned with, the producers and engineers to look out for. I had favourite labels, whether contemporary ones like Rawkus or Fondle 'Em, or vintage ones like First Priority Music and Tuff City. My purchases would be guided by that. And while I was flicking through rack after rack and crate after crate, I was flicking past potential gems.

My view is that unless you're a record dealer, you shouldn't really be browsing or purchasing music just for the sake of scarcity. What you buy should always be an aesthetic decision, based on what you like, what you want to listen to or what you want to play out if you're a DJ. An unplayed record is a sin (there are caveats here, of course, we're going deep[2]).

---

2 It's absolutely fine to have unplayed spare copies of a record you love. At one point I had De La Soul's *3 Feet High and Rising* on cassette, UK and US CD's, UK and US vinyl. I also had a couple of spare, sealed US originals, just in case. You never know when you'll need them.

That doesn't mean life isn't full of record-buying mistakes. I know I've turned my nose up at things that in future years became worth thousands of pounds, in favour of something I wanted then and there[3]. I've also missed out on having backup copies of classic albums – and any serious rap fan will tell you that a backup copy isn't a luxury but often a necessity – due to my shallow pockets or short-sightedness. There was a great little spot in Manchester called Powercuts, which sold all kinds of genres and had a treasure trove of hip-hop albums. Dan discovered it on a shopping trip and took me along the next time we crossed the Pennines. Here you could find all of the Run DMC albums, US imports, sealed, for 99 pence. Why didn't I buy five copies of every single one?

Crash Records, the focal point of so much of my early hip-hop life, had a bargain bin where the unloved and unwanted ginger-headed stepchildren of the vinyl world were herded together and offered for the telling price of 25p. This is where you'd see offcuts of unlikeable novelty rap, truly dire albums by Three Wize Men and untold bootleg house records. It's also where, for one long summer, a thick stack of the *Culture Shock International* EP from 1998 was priced up at exactly one quarter of a pound. Perhaps it was the naff hand-drawn cover with the legend 'Rap Rap Rap Rappers' that put people off, but I never saw any-one take it to the counter to ask for it to be played. Depending on the staff member, you'd have probably been refused anyway – bargain bin records don't often get played. And so all of us missed out on a gem, a genuinely excellent eight track EP that now fetches an average of £125

---

3 It's hard to say which are the rarest and most valuable rap records of all time, as prices fluctuate and many are traded or sold in private transactions. An original Beat Bop can fetch a pretty penny, but records like Mr Magic's *Be Bop Convention* and Mistafide's *Equidity Funk* routinely fetch more. Some of the most sought-after pieces are original 'show vinyl' pressings, which are instrumentals of albums in very limited quantities. I personally sold my collection of A Tribe Called Quest show vinyl for quite a lot of money, but have also heard of a set going for £15,000.

on eBay and Discogs. I've owned two copies, both of which cost me north of three figures. And a batch for 25p each was staring me in the face for months.

That's not a serious regret, however, it's just a 'one that got away' story to share with like-minded collectors or on a Twitter thread. The one serious regret I have is around my most-wanted record.

I first heard Rammellzee Vs. K-Rob's *Beat Bop* on the *Electro 2* compilation. That collection of tracks is the most important in my entire musical life as it's the very first hip-hop album I heard, and the one I credit with having changed my destiny. Among the great tracks on there – including personal perennial favourites like *Two, Three, Break* by The B-Boys and Hashim's hypnotic *Al-Naayfish (The Soul)* was one of the most original and most important rap records ever. *Beat Bop* is over ten minutes of two MCs going back and forth with invented personas to tell a meandering narrative over a funk backing. K-Rob, a Profile records artist and very much a bread-and-butter MC, holds his own, but the futurist and graffiti artist Rammellzee is the real deal here.

There are lots of stories to be told about this record. One is about Rammellzee, his life and career. I got to write a brief piece for *The Guardian* following his early death, but there's so much more to unearth. Another is about how the record got made in the first place, on how the artist Jean-Michel Basquiat was supposed to rhyme on the track but got shunted back to just providing the now iconic sleeve artwork[4].

Much is the stuff of myth and legend. Other stuff is more mundane: Reportedly only 500 copies were pressed, it plays at 45pm (not unheard of, but still relatively unusual for a hip-hop 12"), it's the only ever release on the Tartown label. It's a track that has been endlessly reissued, but with so many pressings and variations it's often hard to discern one of the original copies from an ersatz version released four decades later.

---

4 You know something has transcended its genre when Uniqlo are selling a T-shirt of it.

And if you want to own a vinyl copy and listen to it, that's probably the best way to go. Get a nice reissue with reproduction artwork, or even pick up the Profile Records release from 1983 – either way you'll have change from £50.

I don't want to listen to those. I want to listen to an original. I want to frame the sleeve. I want to be able to say I have an original copy of *Beat Bop*. I want one of the 500. Can I say why? Probably not. I've never been one for reissues except for where the original is impossible to source, never came out properly or was released on such a terrible pressing in the first instance that the new version is essential. But do I want a reissue 12" of *Beat Bop* instead of an equally fine-sounding but somewhat vintage original? No, I do not.

The main problem? The price. Original copies now routinely fetch anywhere from £1,000 to £3,000. They'd probably fetch even more except for the difficulty of discerning an original from a repress on a global marketplace such as Discogs or eBay. I know many collectors who've been assured that the one they're buying is the real thing, only for a repress that plays at 33rpm to turn up in the post.

That price reflects not just scarcity, but also the subsequent importance of Jean-Michel Basquiat as a graphic artist (to give an example, his piece *Untitled* from 1982 fetched over $110m at auction in 2017) and the wonders of the record itself. It's both one-of-a-kind and hugely influential. You could argue that Cypress Hill's B-Real owes his distinct nasal rapping style to that adopted by Rammellzee on *Beat Bop*. And if they doubted you, you could also point to the use of the words 'Cypress Hill' on the track, subsequently sampled by the group. And if they still weren't convinced, you could just play them the 'Shoot 'em up' bit of the record which Muggs, B-Real and Sen Dog borrowed in its entirety.

Sorry for the digression, but such a record must get its due. Once upon a time, the eminent independent record shop Mr Bongo, situated on Poland Street in Soho, revealed that they were auctioning a copy of the original. This, in the mid-to-late 90's, before the market-place was flooded with facsimiles. It was authenticated, and they were inviting bids.

At the time, I was living in Mike Lewis' spare room in Belsize Park. I was earning £15,000 per year from my day job, topped up with a bit of *Hip-Hop Connection* writing money. My debts were mounting, I was running out of money before month's end without fail. I couldn't afford to bid.

Picture this as a time when the second-hard market in hip-hop was still in its infancy. While we were almost 20 years into hip-hop in the UK, this mostly existed in terms of swaps and trades rather than records fetching ridiculous sums on eBay. Values hadn't been estab-lished beyond those most fundamental ones: what you wanted and what you liked. We didn't know the value of a *Beat Bop* then but were still shocked when it fetched the princely sum of £125.

What seemed like a fortune then seems like a pittance now. I kick myself regularly over not just extending my overdraft a touch more to get this record. A near mint condition original, sourced by a reputa-ble record shop. I've subsequently owned rarer and even more valuable records, but this will always be the one that got away. A caveat: I did land one in 2012. I paid $570 for it from a German eBay seller. He described the cover condition as 'Excellent' – in fact it had a giant crease and all four corners were bent. He described the labels as 'clean' – they had 'toxie' written on them in marker. Most importantly, he described the condition of the record as VG+[5] – yet both sides skipped, crackled and sounded worse than the 5th generation dub of *Electro 2* I'd first fallen for. I got my money back; the search goes on.

---

5 Not everyone is going to be familiar with record grading, but a VG+ record should play through fine without crackles, skips or jumps, and should have only superficial visual flaws.

Speaking of price gouging, back to Barry on Briggate. This is the scene of my most foolish memorabilia faux pas. As well as records, many pieces of hip-hop memorabilia have also grown in value. There are countless Instagram threads devoted to the very best T-shirts, jackets, posters and promotional items sent out with review copies of albums.

I've acquired a decent collection myself. Dozens of desirable T-shirts, hundreds of original promo posters, many framed. Even that all-important DJ Jazzy Jeff and the Fresh Prince *Summertime* sunbed cover. But the kicker is I probably threw out more than I have now, both worthless and priceless.

The Bradford gig flyer signed by both members of 3rd Bass? Lost in a house move. The sweat-soaked Holiday Inn towel that I caught after Eazy-E threw it into the crowd during an NWA concert? I kept hold of that for around 10 years, but then threw it out when it became little more than a hard-to-authenticate unwashed petri-dish of potential contagion[6].

T-shirts came and went. Ones I purchased from shops (that hard as hell Demon Boyz one from the 1980s!), others the result of queueing after concerts (NWA again, Public Enemy, so many more). In my early journalism days, promo tees were a given if you visited a label. You'd come out with a bunch of promotional cassettes and perhaps a Slick Rick T-shirt in size XL. These were worn, washed and, eventually, discarded. But that's fine – you can't keep everything. Especially if you're moving home constantly or living with someone who, understandably,

---

6 This wouldn't be the strangest piece of rap memorabilia. Some of the official merchandise was quite unusual or witty. One Wu-Tang offshoot project saw journalists being sent a small container which had inside a solitary, dead bee. Black Sheep's label sent out condoms to accompany the release of their *Strobelite Honey* single, with 'Put your wolf in sheep's clothing' printed on the back. Jeru the Damaja's label went one better, offering up not just a condom but also some soap to accompany his classic *Come Clean* single.

doesn't want to sacrifice cat-swinging room for an ever-expanding repository of hip-hop bullshit.

A visit to Rawkus Records in New York saw one of their staff members, Blak Shawn, invite us into the warehouse to stuff our bags with their entire T-shirt range. We copped maybe eight or 10 tees each. One by one, they bit the dust from overwearing, gifting or just developing that weird white armpit crust from deodorant and sweat. Je ne regrette rien, even if a legion of people who came of age during the 2000's would now bite your arm off for them.

But the worst way to lose a piece of memorabilia is through a fit of pique.

When Loud Records was in its absolute prime – let's say from 1992 to 1997, when they were releasing game-changing records by the likes of Wu-Tang Clan and Mobb Deep – they were one of the finest labels in the world. Solid branding, a fascinating roster – Sadat X, Alkaholiks, Funkmaster Flex, Big Pun – they had it all. Their merch game was strong too. I was a relatively frequent visitor to their London offices even when I was still in Leeds, along with Mike Lewis and Dan. We'd go in with empty record bags and leave with them bulging.

They were also a label early in pushing the concept of the street team. At a basic level, this was a simple exchange where you'd give some fans some promo material, early access to music and such, in return for them doing some basic marketing work in their town. It's a grassroots approach to marketing that sees value in someone outside a concert giving away flyers or posting stickers up on lampposts. Anecdotally, it was pretty effective. Back when I was still in Leeds, and part of a relatively small hip-hop scene and also Leeds' only hip-hop journalist, I was invited to be on the street teams for both Tommy Boy and Loud Records.

It's an unpaid gig, but I was still enormously proud of the Tommy Boy opportunity. I was already on their mailing list, but even to be in some unofficial position for one of hip-hop's greatest labels was an honour. Tommy Boy were one of the pre-eminent rap labels in the early 80's and were still going strong in the 90's with legends such as De La Soul and Digital Underground. I'd happily stick their stickers up in Leeds city centre. Big up the late DJ Swing for the opportunity.

The Loud thing was a somewhat slicker operation – we were invited to a London briefing and sent on our respective ways with goodie bags full of flyers, stickers, press kits, promo photos and more. Best of all, Loud Records had commissioned a label jacket from Helly Hansen and their chosen street team were all given one for free.

At the time, Helly Hansen was a hip-hop approved clothing label. They'd gone from being an obscure Scandinavian manufacturer of waterproof outerwear to riding the backs of many major rappers. Few mid-90's hip-hop videos were complete without a glimpse or two of a HH jacket on the back of an artist, whether Mobb Deep or LL Cool J. Their name was being dropped in lyrics, and Loud had organised some sponsorship deals with them[7].

Yet while the name Helly Hansen was synonymous with technical innovation and advanced fabrics, the street team jacket was not blessed with the same care and attention. Instead of waterproof technology, it was seemingly manufactured with water-attracting and retaining technology. It was made of some form of rubber that wasn't just heavy (and unlined), but also had unique properties that ensured that even a slight rain shower would leave you feeling like you'd been to a water park.

---

7 Helly Hansen was founded in the 19th century, aimed directly at fishermen, as Hansen himself was one. It ended up being a pioneer of new fabrics and, a hundred years later, was being adopted in the north of England as part of the technical outerwear fashion scene that unexpectedly bubbled up football terraces and beyond. It became a popular label among rappers and rap fans in the 90s, but that trend was gone almost as soon as it arrived. By chasing the hip-hop market, Helly Hansen ended up taking some wrong turns. Rap fashions change fast, and Hansen had put too many eggs in that basket and had to refocus on its core market.

Another drawback was the look. On the peg, the bright yellow sailing jacket with blue trim looked wonderful. The front logoing – both 'HH' and 'Loud Records' was subtle. The sizable Loud Records logo on the back had real visual impact. It would have looked amazing in a mid-90's rap video where a bunch of Queensbridge kids were stomping around their patch close to some flaming braziers (what were they burning?) and aiming finger guns at the camera[8]. It looked less amazing on a still scrawny, lanky boy pacing the hard streets of Leeds City centre on his way from the Virgin Megastore to the market to buy a quarter of pick-and-mix sweets. There was a time and a place to rock certain items, and that wasn't it.

I found the jacket frustrating, the practicalities of it starting to outweigh its cachet of cool, and it reached a peak one rainy day as I walked up Briggate. The patented water-magnetic innovations of the jacket meant that as soon as the skies opened, I looked like I'd been drowned. I was soaked head to toe in moments and lost my rag with the Loud Records jacket completely. A 99p cagoule would have been more effective. As I passed by Barry on Briggate, I took the sodden coat off, balled it into an angry bundle and smashed it into a bin. I stomped off to get the bus home, realising that bizarrely I was keeping drier by just having a T-shirt on.

Recently, I saw one of the jackets sell for £750 on the internet. I wouldn't be surprised if it was that tight fucker Barry who sold it, having prised it from the bin on that stupid day. All of which is a long, roundabout way of saying, don't come to me for advice on stocks and shares.

---

8 The video for The Roots *What They Do* is a perfect dissection of 1990s rap video tropes. The brazier budget for labels back then must have been incredible. Women in bikinis dancing next to swimming pools, rappers stepping out of flash cars with bottles of Champagne, posses crowding the camera, fish-eye lens shots, yet more braziers. It's why the truly great videos from that era stand out – the vast majority were rotten with cliches.

10: THE FINE PRINT

When I look back, and consider the wide panoply of hip-hop magazines the world offered before the demise of print, I feel proud to have written for the best, and to have edited the most original. Many would disagree with that summary, however. Hey, write your own book.

The Source is widely regarded as the finest magazine covering hip-hop music and culture. I can't emphasise enough how much I loved it when I discovered its early issues. It had access to the latest records, the newest artists and was weeks if not months ahead of the news we got second hand in the UK. It bloomed into a well-edited, iconic mag that unearthed some soon-to-be-legendary artists and did particularly well at looking at the intersection of race, music and politics in the US. So why isn't it the best? Firstly, it shat all over its own legacy under the later editorship of Benzino. Secondly, it never had a consistently great writing staff, although it did have some fine editors.

That latter point might be seen as 'shots fired', but any scan of *The Source*'s back issues is always a triumph of hope over reality. A great cover shot[1], followed by some soft-soap interviews and some badly-argued album reviews followed by a dated and not very well drawn cartoon (to be fair, few cartoons age well and topical hip-hop cartoons

---

1 Some of *The Source*'s covers are absolutely brilliant, and reflect the benefits of big budgets and access. Rarely did the piece inside live up to the cover.

from the 1990's are nowhere near as bad as, say, racially charged *Punch* cartoons from a century earlier, but still).

They shone a light on racial divides in America with insight and verve, but were hamstrung in their ambitions to be the bible of hip-hop by some truly amateur-level writing from many of their contributors when it came to their bread and butter – the music. While they might have had the impact of being the first on the block (in the US, at least – *Hip-Hop Connection* magazine predates *The Source*), *XXL* and *Rap Pages* were often both better written hip-hop magazines.

It's no coincidence that the same people who made them so – Elliott Wilson, Jefferson 'Chairman' Mao and a select crew of others – were the people behind my favourite music magazine, *ego trip* – the 'arrogant voice of musical truth'. While we conceived of *Fat Lace* independently of *ego trip*, it was a magazine we all loved, and some of its later issues undoubtedly influenced our visual approach. I wrote a hip-hop magazine world cup article for *HHC* and crowned them winners, but was it really a hip-hop magazine? With its coverage of the punk and skate scene, it was laudably diverse (and hugely zeitgeisty), well-written and original, but its 13 issues vary widely in content and quality.

Hip-Hop Connection did too, of course, but over a much, much longer period. From 1988 to 2009, over some 232 issues, *HHC* was editorially very solid. It only had three editors for the entirety of that run, but it did have several publishers. One of those, Ministry of Sound, who owned the magazine from 2000-2001, had arguably the most deleterious effect on it. They chopped and changed, sometimes with reason, sometimes seemingly randomly.

It remained, whoever owned it, utterly independent in its opinions. While editors of *The Source* were resigning for being told to regrade album reviews, or in some cases toeing the line – or, even more egregious, being edited by an artist who spent large parts of each issue promoting his own music – *HHC* was critically diverse. I wrote hundreds of thousands of words for the magazine, and the only ones ever changed were my typos.

All writers make mistakes – some of us, many of them – but a good editor allows them the latitude to be right or wrong in their judgement, as long as it's well argued and persuasively written. I gave bad reviews to albums I subsequently came to love – or at least appreciate – but still stand by the reviews as honest reflections of where I was at the time. A UGK classic given two stars? Yes, I was way off – it wasn't the only time, as we'll see in a later chapter – but that summation was indicative of my listening tastes at the time, and I was being paid to express my opinion, not those of a collective or the wider world.

HHC was, increasingly, a broad church, and it found space for writers who embraced the new as passionately as those who cherished the old. It also realised that the same person could do both. In the time I wrote for *HHC*, people came and went. Some moved on to bigger and better things, others were just dipping their toes in the writing world and disappeared. All of them got to have their say, unfiltered.

This is why *HHC* is the greatest hip-hop magazine ever for me – I didn't enter it into the world cup feature that I wrote, as that would have been unbearably biased. But now, more than a decade after its death, it's something I feel strongly about. It did it in the face of low budgets – *HHC* staff were paid a fraction of what feature writers at *The Source*, *XXL* and *Vibe* received – and in the face of countless difficulties.

Chief among them was access. US hip-hop mags had a geographic advantage that put rappers in their backyard, while we had to wait for them to fly to us (with the attendant jet-lag) or fly to them (rare). Many US writers of a certain vintage have an inflated reputation purely because they lived in a city – New York or Los Angeles, largely – where they could walk around the block to see a rapper perform, or to interview them. They'd run into each other digging for breaks in a Greenwich Village record shop. I know this a) because it's obviously true and

b) because when we paid out of our own pockets to go to New York for a few days, we ran into rappers ALL the time.

When you're paid 5p a word and you're having to wait up until 3am UK time to interview a rapper down a phone line, you'd damn well be passionate about it. And it's that fervour of a pure fan that shines through in the very best years of *HHC*, tempered with a critic's wary eye. We were allowed to big up our favourites, but we had to do it with panache – or else what was the point?

Any beef in *HHC* was purely inter-writer rivalry, with several scribes taking a potshot at each other. I had run-ins with Will Ashon[2] (a writer I respect highly) and Spencer Kansa (a writer), because *HHC* was also a forum where we were allowed to debate our differences of opinion. We were never asked to have a pop at an artist to settle some beef, but nor were we told not to because they were advertising, or their label was sponsoring a cover CD. Without fuss or show – something anathema to the soft-spoken Andy Cowan – he protected our rights as writers to vent on music we all loved, then sent us a cheque at the end of every month. It's an editorial approach that should have been more widely adopted, back when magazines still existed.

Is there a part of me that maybe fell in love with annoying readers? Perhaps a little bit. Sifting through my cuttings, I have several regrets, but one is that I reacted to some negative letters by becoming more unpleasant about certain sacred cows. Tupac being one. I referred to him once as being a 'better corpse than a rapper', which was obviously silly. I'm not sure I believed it, which means I shouldn't have written it. But I knew it would annoy his fans who, to this day, happily ignore the less pleasant parts of his personality. And I also knew it would

---

2 I was going to write about this, but I recently contacted Will to apologise for being a dickhead at the time of our spat. He was very gracious about it, and apologised in return. He also said he couldn't even remember what it was about and didn't want to be reminded as he'd probably be mortified. So I'm leaving it out.

provide succour for those readers who didn't like Tupac. Sure enough, the next letters page had people hating me and loving me. So I definitely wrote that to provoke rather than just to tell some personal, perceived truth about rap music. I also wrote it to provoke Spencer Kansa, my fellow *HHC* scribe, whose one-note column was almost always about how Tupac was an angel sent to save us, when it wasn't about C. Dolores Tucker.

If you're going to write about music effectively and engagingly, I think it's essential that you ultimately do away with writing with an audience in mind. That's not the same as ignoring what readers will like, it just means you start somewhere else entirely and if you're a good writer, they'll enjoy it anyway. If your starting point is trying to please, you second guess yourself every step of the way. Many of my favourite writers across the entire spectrum of journalistic topics from news to politics, cinema to satire, have a voice that is uniquely theirs. It's their job to interest the readers, but not necessarily to please or placate them. It's the editor's job to publish or not, with all the necessary edits. The never-ending fountain of support and vitriol that is now underneath every online article is proof that you can't please all of the people all of the time, so don't even try.

While writing this book, I skim-read every issue of *Hip-Hop Connection*, and what I can say with some certainty is that the magazine is at its best when, towards the end, it just got rid of the letters page altogether. I know a lot of *HHC*'s readers – lovely people. But most of those who felt the need to put pen to paper or fingers to keyboard were horrible. Not just to me and my fellow writers – most of whom observed it with an amused eye – but to each other. There were long-running squabbles, racism, homophobia and sexism, threats of violence and an ongoing inability to understand the purpose of a music magazine.

These are angry people – the vast majority of them male, you won't be surprised to learn – who are apoplectic that a writer they've never met has a different opinion about the second Count Bass D album than they do. They're foaming at the mouth – enough to commit it to posterity by sending their complaint to a magazine's letter page – that a subgenre of hip-hop they don't love is being given column inches for the benefit of those that do. Their bitterness drowns the scattering of cogent letters that are advancing an interesting point, engaging with a piece, or disagreeing in an agreeable fashion.

Worst of all? The people who just get it wrong, but in an absurdly angry fashion. I was indifferent to the crunk genre when it dropped. It was embraced wholeheartedly by some of my colleagues like David Sadeghi and Rob Pursey. More power to them – they were right about a lot, especially in terms of which way the wind was blowing in hip-hop. They wrote about crunk consistently and well, along with several other *HHC* writers. I didn't write about it at all. And yet let's fast forward to May 2004, with a letter slagging me off for writing about crunk all the time. What could have provoked such anger? It's hard to tell – in the issues running up to it I wrote about The Visionaries, politics, Biz Markie, Jaylib and New York. But I was barely writing anything at the time, to be honest, and definitely not a single word about crunk. This was not an isolated incident.

The conclusion? Reader opinions suck. Most readers are far too sensible to want to write in to a letters page in the first place because they understand the purpose of the thing they're reading is to inform and entertain. But the ones who did put pen to paper or fingers to keyboard are the spiritual forebears of the trolls who pollute twitter with their anger, who create anonymous accounts so they can call people names underneath *Guardian* articles about trans rights.

Not that the publications are free from blame, however. Many have embraced comments sections as a way of driving reader engagement, or at least that's how they position it. Of course, the driving factor in the online era is that engagement boosts ad revenue, and with many publications and outlets struggling to survive, you can see why they might need to go down that route. If the cold, hard reality is they need clicks to survive, however, they just need to be honest. Because if they truly believe that all opinions matter, they're lying or deluding themselves.

Everyone is entitled to an opinion about music, but not necessarily to a forum for that opinion. Because many people, when given one, simply shit the bed. A good writer can write about something you care about in a way that can be amusing, transformative, reassuring, provoking, sad and many more things. They can say something about a piece of music that makes you understand it in a completely different way. It's also really good when a writer captures something you yourself knew inside you, but hadn't found the words to express.

Which is all why people do – and should continue to – look for new voices in writing. The people who write for the best magazines – and I realise I'm generalising a little bit here because we can all name writers we hate and perhaps other writers are more guilty of this than readers – are paid to do so precisely because the way they frame their opinions has value. Their opinions might not ultimately matter more than Steve0132888UK who is itching to comment, but the way they express it definitely matters more. It deserves remuneration.

Another bugbear – and yes, this chapter is really turning into 'ageing writer shakes fist at sky' – is commenters and letter writers who think the thing they've just read that you've written is the only thing in your life or the only thing you care about, rather than just a small reflection of the things you do and write about. I wrote a piece for *The Guardian* about motion sickness, a minor affliction I have that means I can't play certain video games, especially first person ones. I haven't even tried VR as I imagine I'd redecorate the entirety of the north of England in vomit. As someone who has played games since I was a kid, this wasn't a massive deal, but I did miss out on some of the communal first-person shooters my colleagues played at lunch. The crux of the piece wasn't really about me – it was also about other people who couldn't do it, with a wider theme of how democratic technology isn't always all inclusive. Perhaps the photos that accompanied the piece didn't help, with the photographer catching me looking like I've just been given some kind of terminal diagnosis rather than just pondering on not being able to play *Call of Duty* with my mate Nat.

The comments? Ugh. Every writer tells every other writer never to read them, but they all secretly do. I'd talked about playing *Doom*, a groundbreaking game which came out on PC before being ported to some consoles. I never played it on PC, I played it on Playstation, which somehow delights the readers. "That sounds awful. You thinking *Doom* was a playstation classic," says Imperfect Rex. "Lol at Playstation classic *Doom*" says Barbaretti. Okay, incels, not really the point.

Yet that's just comment dummies being comment dummies. My real ire is reserved for the likes of KelvinBristol: "This is your body's way of telling you to dump the console, get out of the house & play tennis, run, cycle, swim or anything." Yes Kelvin, because writing an article about games means that's all I do. I'm sure Jay Rayner, the estimable restaurant critic at *The Observer*, sometimes has to excrete all the meals he eats, but I don't want to read that column, just his ones about food, thanks. You've seriously logged in to your account to tell someone writing about one thing that they should be doing another? Thanks! JFarquhar has equally useful tips. "As a nice alternative you could also try some kind of tabletop game with a few friends (more creative and more social anyway) or simply reading a book." Never thought of that mate. I mean, I've been a book reviewer, but cheers. What happens is these comments take away from those readers who have experienced similar things and want to engage with the piece – as many did – or who haven't but want to know more and to understand what it feels like. Instead, they're entering a forum where their hobby is being mocked by people logging on to do exactly that.

This engagement, this endless content, is wearisome. It's TV vox pops with people backing Boris despite him being an obvious wretched liar. It's men finding any opportunity on twitter to belittle female sports players and commentators. When even a hip-hop magazine's letters page is full of mindless shit – and that has been filtered by the diligent editor – you wonder what the point of all this comment is? For me, there isn't one. It's pointless. I don't care what some other bloke thinks about Marina Hyde's latest column, in the same way I wouldn't expect them to care about the fact that I think it's obviously brilliant.

One more thought: Ironically, despite the lack of everyday access, the best overviews, retrospectives and histories of hip-hop in magazine and online terms have been from outside of the US. Book-wise, there have been superb entries from hip-hop's home, but if I want the true story of Tony D, Son of Bazerk or Chill Rob G, I have to look to European or Australian magazines and blogs such as Robbie Ettelson's great *Unkut* or Werner Von Wallenrod's blog.

The ephemera and marginalia of rap has always been most passionately sought after and chronicled by those beyond the US, at the same time as we haven't been able to truly tune in to the lived experience of it. Maybe that's why we do it. If you weren't at Bronx River Center in the 1970s or at The Tunnel in the late 90s, you can still excavate the story, but it's not the same thing. Many of my most calamitous moments as a hip-hop journalist have been through confusing the experiences of a man writing about rap in his bedroom with what it actually is in the wider world. Some people are still making the same mistake, but they do it on Twitter now. Maybe we should all go to clubs more.

11: HOW'S LIFE IN LONDON?

As 1997 rolls on, I'm starting to get frustrated with life in Leeds. It's lovely to be with my family, but so many old friends have moved on. The only people keeping me sane are two new mates – Rob and Lucy. They're passionate music fans, teachers and very proactive friends. Lucy will drive over to Beeston, pick me up, and the three of us will head off to Bradford for a curry, to the pub to talk music, and sometimes I'll cook for them in my mum's kitchen, which is about the size of a large bee.

This friendship acts like a pressure release, because my frequent visits to London to interview rappers are telling me more and more that I need to live down there, but the hoped-for full-time writing job on a weekly or monthly is still a dream. The day job could be worse, but there's a huge difference between having a desk on a music magazine and renting out *Jerry Maguire* and *Liar Liar* on VHS to the people of Beeston.

I've still got a lot of interviews lined up. I'm in Nottingham meeting Mr 45 and Lee Ramsey, then putting together a feature about Will Ashon's label, Big Dada. The hip-hop magazine world cup mentioned in the previous chapter has one tie being fought between '*The Source* Then' and '*The Source* Now', a sign of how that magazine had changed for the worse.

The November 1997 issue of *HHC* felt like a personal triumph. I was all over it. I've got two regular columns in there, a review of a De La Soul live gig and four features, including a lengthy cover story about

The Gravediggaz, a chat with The Alkaholiks, a piece about hip-hop and drinking, and a game of pool against The Beatnuts. I am living my best hip-hop life.

The Liks trio of Tash, J-Ro and E-Swift are a lot of fun, and we talk about west coast rap, our mutual admiration for their friend King Tee, and who in hip-hop can really handle their booze. It turns out they loved Ol' Dirty Bastard, but he couldn't get down like that: "That's another fool that can't drink as much as The Alkaholiks. He tried. Him and Keith Murray and the Beatnuts will get slayed."

Talking of the Beatnuts, the Fat Lace squad of myself, Dan Greenpeace and Mike Lewis met the Corona, Queens stars in Camden for a pool tournament. I set the tone for the games to come when I fouled the first break. Dan took his life into his own hands by wearing an Al Tariq[1] promo shirt, which the duo of Juju and Psycho Les mock gasp at. We get our arses kicked on the baize, but enjoy racking up the expenses by getting the best producers on the mic to review various types of alcohol, from Guinness to Budvar. Stella Artois wins the day.

This is all high jinks compared to my Gravediggaz story, where I waxed more than a little pretentious. I decided to meet their horror film stylings head on, and opened with a quote from Peter Hutchinson's *Hammer and Beyond* before I started to assess the psychological and metaphorical impact of horror films, throwing in quotes from Kafka's *Metamorphosis* along the way. Yep, this is what the readers of *Hip-Hop Connection* were fiending for! However, I will say that the quote I used from Robin Wood's seminal *American Nightmare* – "One might say that the true subject of the horror genre is the struggle for recognition of all that our civilisation represses and oppresses" – still feels totally on the money for an article about this particular rap supergroup. I'm a lucky

---

1 Al Tariq was formerly known as Fashion, and was formerly a member of the Beatnuts, before leaving under a cloud and going solo.

man – I got all four of them. Prince Paul, Fruitkwan, Poetic and RZA, who is, without a doubt, one of the best interviewees you can ever meet.

EPMD were also great value, the duo of Erick Sermon and Parrish Smith having reunited after a somewhat acrimonious split. Considering that they'd both slagged each other off on record and in interviews since calling it a day after four great LP's, they were surprisingly on message. The deaths of Tupac and Biggie had inspired them to get back together, and they were happy to laugh at their own missteps. I asked them what their least favourite tracks of their own were, and they matched exactly the ones their fans hated – *It's Time to Party* and *You Had Too Much to Drink*. Although, apparently, the former was Mike Tyson's favourite EPMD record – he must have been punch drunk.

In the background of all this, we were thinking about *Fat Lace 2*. While we loved bits and pieces of the first issue it was, overall, a bit of a tatty disappointment. It looked awful. We wanted the next issue to feel and look more like a real magazine. To do this properly, we'd need a bigger team and a bigger budget. Rob Pursey wanted to be involved, so did Barrie Smith, who was now a professional designer[2].

We got together at the Leeds cafe Indie Joze and hashed it out, ending with an agreement to all contribute some money and to expand the editorial pool. We were already sitting on a few reader's cheques, lovely people who'd liked issue one enough to send us some of their hard-earned for the next issue, not realising they'd have to wait about 18 months for it. With five equal share-holders in place, Dan and I put together a flat plan for issue two. We wanted more pages, glossy paper, perhaps even a smattering of colour on the cover. And we wanted it to look good too, after my dismal efforts on the launch issue. With Barrie in place, we could rest easy on that count.

---

2 Barrie was the artist formerly known as SADE – Skilfully Applying Distinguished English – who appeared on some of our demo tracks and featured in *Wiggaz*.

The next challenge was to gather the material. There'd need to be a mixture of interviews – some leftovers from *HHC* work, some original – and some features. We were determined to push the humour even further. We were going to do all this while holding down day jobs (part-time in my case), working for *HHC* (Mike had joined the fold in July 1997 with a piece about *Star Wars* and music) and trying to have a social life. All this is by way of apology to those readers waiting for their cheques for £2 to turn into something tangible.

I also had another big plan for 1998: get that dream journalism job in London. Thanks to Barrie, I didn't have to wait too long, as he knew of an opening for a sub-editor at the company he'd just joined in London. If I came down, he'd introduce me to the editor to see if we hit it off. At last, the day I could lock up the video shop after a day of rewinding the likes of *The First Wives Club* and *A Time to Kill* for the very last time was drawing nearer.

I headed down on the train, crashing at Dan's house for a couple of nights. The interview was in Soho, a part of the West End I didn't know at all, and which would later come to feel like home. The interview was mostly conducted in the pub, The Lyric on Great Windmill Street. Actually, scrub what I said earlier, that would become my second home. The editor asked to see some of my writing, so I unveiled the much-thumbed cuttings, and then he tasked me with writing a couple more bits in the office. There was no job offer just yet, but it seemed to be going well. His final question to me that day took me by surprise: do you play cricket?

I did. And so a few minutes later, the editor ushered me into the back of the publishing company owner's Rolls Royce. We drove out to the suburbs where a bunch of writers, designers and publishers from the same company were dressed up in cricket whites, about to play their annual friendly game against their solicitors. I'd been drafted in to make up the numbers and, as there was no spare kit floating around, I was going to play in the jeans and shirt I'd turned up to the interview in.

The editor, Rob Swift, introduced me as a bit of a ringer as I'd played league cricket in Leeds, and while I didn't blow the opposition away (not helped by Swift himself shelling about three catches off my bowling), I bowled out their openers, then hit a rapid 25 not out before retiring to the pavilion (the side of a field). After beers and canapes we were driven back into London, and I was offered the job of sub editor, starting at £15,000. I'd like to think I was hired for my editorial skills, but perhaps it was merely my probing left-arm swing and hint of genuine pace that convinced them I was a good bet.

I returned to Leeds with a job offer and a month to sort out my life before moving to London. I was thrilled – and just as excited to hand in my notice at the video shop. My mum was sad I was leaving – and I was sad I was leaving her – but she was also excited for me to go to London to make my way in the world of music journalism.

Yeah, about that.

My job offer wasn't from one of the illustrious music magazines I'd long dreamed of transforming the hip-hop coverage of. It wasn't at a newspaper where I'd learn the ins and outs of investigative journalism, on the phone late at night to anonymous sources, breaking a big story. It wasn't on one of the growing numbers of middle-shelf lad's mags, packed full of attempts at gonzo journalism and reviews of the best headphones, interspersed with *Brookside* stars in their underwear. Nor would it be for an esteemed literary magazine, where I'd arrive all bright eyed and soon discover that I was nowhere near as well read as I thought I was.

No, I'd be going to work for PRO. The Paul Raymond Organisation. Legendary purveyors of top shelf magazines such as *Men Only*, *Razzle* and *Club International*. I'd got myself a job in porn.

Still, it's all a means to an end, eh? Get myself ensconced in London, keep ticking over at *HHC*, make some contacts and get myself poached by one the legitimate mags I really admired. Right? Not quite. My family were very understanding and supportive of my move into the world of tits and arse, but there must have been some disappointment that they couldn't really go into a shop and buy, with pride, a magazine I was writing for. My mum wouldn't have been able to take an issue of *Club International*, where I was sub-editor, along to her club and crack open the centrefold. "Ignore the fanny, Jean, look at the quality of that headline. That's our Andrew." No, that wasn't going to happen.

Dan, Barrie and I had planned to get a house to rent together, but they were locked into contracts at their current places for the time being. My *Fat Lace* brother Mike Lewis very kindly stepped up, and offered me his spare room. Mike had a lovely basement flat in Belsize Park where he lived with his girlfriend Clare, who was also beyond charming at suddenly sharing what was quite a small space with a 6'2" hip-hop nerd. Mike was the most welcoming of hosts, and I'd wake daily to the sound of him grinding coffee beans, the aroma drifting into the bedroom. Belsize Park is a lovely area, a place where I'd never be able to afford to live, and only a few stops from my Soho office on the Northern Line. And did I mention Mike didn't want any rent either? What a mensch.

In the background of all this, there was a revolution in hip-hop. There had always been independent labels – in fact, in the earliest days of hip-hop, that was pretty much all there was – but from 1997 into 1998, there was a huge growth in the numbers of non-major label rap imprints. As already mentioned, much of this was a backlash to the direction the majors were taking, with many artists and producers sick of the money-obsessed, commercial side of hip-hop. But that wasn't the sole factor. When considering hip-hop labels, you always have to look at other potential motivations. Vanity, money laundering – they all play a part.

For fans like myself, this was a much-needed breath of fresh air. As my Jay-Z piece showed, I wasn't loving the landscape of hip-hop as offered by the major labels in the mid-90s. As a writer, it was an opportunity to chronicle a new movement, to be in on the ground floor of something exciting that might just change the face of rap forever. Years later, myself and Dan are indelibly associated, in some minds at least, with pioneering this independent movement in the UK music press. Dan already had his vital *Independents Day* column, and I was all set to interview many of the major players in this scene. But, credit where credit's due, another *HHC* scribe was the first person to interview two of the most important artists of the indie era – Company Flow and Reflection Eternal. I tip my hat to Chris Elwell-Sutton[3].

Both of those artists were signed to Rawkus Records, which in many ways was the most significant label of the independent era. How independent it really was is up for question – it was backed financially by James Murdoch, son of Rupert, and I'll leave it up to you to decide which character in *Succession* was based on him. He was friends with Jarret Myer and Brian Brater, who'd launched Rawkus as a dance label, rapidly pivoting to become an influential hip-hop imprint instead.

The early Rawkus rap releases started making their way over to the UK in 1997. Sir Menelik, Company Flow, Mos Def, Shabaam Sahdeeq, Indelible MC's, B-1, L-Fudge, Reflection Eternal, RA the Rugged Man – all fresh artists, all sounding different to each other, all a world away from the glamour and glitz of major label artists. The output was far from perfect, not everything has aged brilliantly, but at the time it was definitely the standout of an exciting bunch of new labels promoting a notably different underground sound.

Head to a hip-hop record shop in 1997 and you'd flick past records from Rawkus, Fondle 'Em, Duck Down, Rhymesayers, Raw Shack, Stones Throw, Dolo, Eastern Conference, Solesides, Correct, Knee Deep, 25 to Life, ABB, Blunt, Fortress Entertainment, Ekapa, Funky Ass, Hydra,

---

3 Chris went on to edit *Muzik* magazine and now, like many other casualties of the disappearance of specialist music magazines from the shelves, he has a completely different career as a lawyer specialising in data protection.

DITC, Guesswhyld and countless more. Many shined brightly but briefly, some only mustered a single, unforgettable record before disappearing, a couple are still with us today. It had the feeling of hip-hop rediscovering its past as a cottage industry, and the assembled press corps of the UK's magazines duly shuffled into position to cover it.

The move to London definitely made life easier for me in that regard. There were still phone calls to New York and Los Angeles at all times of day and night, but being in the capital meant better access to visiting rappers, record labels and rap shows. And 1998, as I settled into my new job, my new city, felt like a sea change. The interviews and features I pitched became markedly less mainstream, and suddenly I was talking to the likes of Sir Menelik, Killarmy and Shabazz the Disciple, all in the same month. All three voiced the dissatisfaction they felt with the way the rap scene had been in recent years. Killarmy saw it as a war to win, Shabazz thought that interesting artists had been pushed on to independents by the major labels. And Menelik? Well, Menelik thought our chat was being bugged by Puff Daddy who will steal any new musical ideas he discusses. That's Sir Menelik for you.

I took up arms in the same edition of *HHC*, writing a hit-piece on the new album from The Firm, highlighting how far Nas has shifted from vivid teller of street parables to 'seeing the streets through the crystal of his glass of Cristal'. If battle lines are being drawn up, I've chosen my side. Or maybe I've just written myself into a corner[4].

---

4 In cheerier news, I also got to write a piece on the worst albums in hip-hop history. In a rare moment of democracy, I opened this up to the readers as well. Many awful albums were discussed, from Bobcat's *Cat Got Ya Tongue* abomination to the Party Posse LP that was always invoked during such chats. The actual top 3 seems really unfair, in retrospect. PMD's *Shade Business* solo was in third. Fair enough. It's shit. Number 2 was Coolio's *It Takes a Thief*. The landslide winner was Snoop's *Tha Doggfather*, which wasn't well received at the time but surely doesn't deserve such opprobrium. Or maybe it does – it does contain *Snoops Upside Ya Head* after all. The people spoke.

12: WRITE MY WRONGS

etting stuff wrong, sometimes calamitously, is all a part of journalism. This is why newspapers publish apologies for things they've misreported or facts they've cocked up, usually hidden away on page 17 in the bottom right corner and never given anywhere near the prominence of the original piece with all the mistakes in.

Due to music's ephemeral nature, multiplied by the subjective nature of our response to it, getting stuff wrong about artists, albums and songs is incredibly common. When I was growing up, poring over every page of the *NME*, their unfailingly boosterish writers were constantly telling everyone about the next big thing. Piss Flaps were a math-rock four-piece from Surrey and their self-titled EP was going to tear the dour indie scene a new one. And then we never heard from the bunch of private school Crispins ever again.

When you're claiming everything is the future of something, you're going to have a low hit rate. It's probably easier to slag things off – at least you'll be right a lot more often. But then, what happens when you've written a group off entirely and they go on to reshape the genre, blow up worldwide and then marry the most desirable people in the universe. You look pretty stupid, that's what. Is it then, a good idea to stay in the middle, to offer only bland observations on the sound you're hearing? Hell no. No one remembers those writers.

This tells us something very important about music journalism – and about lots of other types of writers too. It's not just about the music.

It's also about the writer. You the consumer might just want to know the guest feature line-up and who does the production on the 16th Conway the Machine album of the year. But, more often than not, the writer who is going to tell you some of that is also trying to carve out a career. They want their words to read well, to be noticed. They want their review or feature to be appreciated by not only the reader, but also by their various bosses at the publication or website they're working for. This, inevitably, leads to some writers trying too hard, some getting the balance just right and others not trying hard enough.

Many *NME* readers hated Steven 'Swells' Wells' approach to reviewing. Others adored him for it. But no one ever forgot him. I read his stuff even when I couldn't care less about the artist involved, because I knew it would be entertainingly over-the-top regardless. It's why Christopher Hitchens was box office – even if you didn't find yourself aligned with his position, he'd argue it with such force of character mingled with a suavity of phrasing that it would still be a pleasure to read.

This is all a roundabout way of saying: writers get stuff wrong. A lot. And usually that's fine, we all move on. It doesn't, usually, end up in a fatality. Sometimes a musician takes offence, but the power of reviews to sway a buying audience one way or the other is overrated. That's why they need to be entertaining – you can get the dull facts elsewhere, and the review doesn't really matter in terms of success or failure. Each music review written is actually, when you come down to it, more important to the writer than to the artist.

I got lots wrong. Some of it I put down to changing tastes or the follies of youth. Other reviews I just didn't have enough time to really get into the music, or the recording was dreadful or it was at a listening party where you don't get to appreciate the nuances. That can impact what you write. But I have to admit I also got stuff wrong out of stubbornness or inflexibility at times. You have to be big enough to look yourself in the mirror and say, 'I gave that a bad review because

I wasn't expected to like that kind of thing'. That's what I meant about writing myself into a corner, earlier. You can easily come to stand for or against something, and you write to bolster that view, to support that movement, or to tear it down. And that can affect how you think about music, how you write about it.

I was only three months into my career as a *HHC* writer when I gave my first 1* review. It was for the UK rap act Without Warning and their album *Land of the Lunatics*. That I didn't get wrong – I stand by that entirely. It was a special kind of rubbish. I'm also pretty happy with the 1* for Too Short's *Gettin' It* the same year, even though I do like a lot of his music. No, the first one I'm a bit concerned with is my 2* review of UGK's *Ridin Dirty* in the November 1996 issue. This was UGK's best-selling album, a hugely influential one, and regarded now as a Houston landmark. And here's what I had to say:

Once you get past two of the least prepossessing names in rap history – Bun B and Pimp C being the terrifying monikers of this Texas duo on their third LP – it's clear that this is would-be Too Short by numbers: drawling, slanging and not saying a great deal. Not that it's all bad. There's a streak of southern soul throughout that lifts up the set before it finally crashes and burns. One Day summons up a plaintive melancholy while Murder is dramatic and pretty pacey. Curtis Mayfield's classic Future Shock break is used to some effect on Pinky Ring, but after these lonely high points it's all downhill in a lowrider. There's no lyrical hook to draw you in, the lazy twang is pleasant on the ears but both rappers might be speaking in tongues for all the interest they engender. On Murder, one of the emcees chimes in with, "Well I'm Bun B bitch and I'm the king of moving chickens." It's reassuring to know that if his rap career ever stalls there'll be a bright future for him in poultry transportation. Now that's living fowl.

Ok, I'm still happy with the last line. I'm right about their names. But otherwise this is just nonsense. This is an album I can play end to end with no skips. Reading it back I can tell I'm just getting on my high horse about a lack of vocal content, as if everything I was listening to back then was either wholesome or some 'spiritual lyrical miracle' stuff.

1997 is peppered with 1* reviews, some of which I wouldn't change at all[1] and some of which are unduly harsh. One out of five for Westside Connection's *Bow Down*? The same for The Dayton Family's *FBI*? Crazy. By April I'm really leaning into giving albums a spanking, culminating in me going to town on the *Young Southern Playaz Vol.* ' compilation.

> *It's all playing and no work for Memphis, Tennessee's motley collection of rappers judging by this compilation. The names of some of the artists involved – Lil' Milt, Lil' Blunt, Lil' Keke – only serve to convince the listener that Tennessee is populated entirely by midgets, hip-hop's version of Time Bandits.*

I go on to pour further scorn on a compilation that features the hugely acclaimed likes of Gangsta Pat, Three Six Mafia and DJ Screw. It would appear from all of this that 'playa' is a real trigger word for me, but I'm also not alone. That same page has scathing reviews of albums by Kingpin Skinny Pimp, Gangsta Blac and C-Loc, penned by Tom Dartnell and Dan, that carry on in a similar vein. One star all round, lots of disdain for regional rap. Anyone who ever complained that southern rap didn't get a fair shake at *HHC* until the axis of Robin and David Sadeghi arrived has plenty of evidence to cite from this one page alone.

---

1 Of Mo Thugs' *Family Scriptures* album all I can say is "A compilation put together by Bone Thugs N Harmony showcasing some of their proteges? Pass the razor blades and run the bath mum."

At this stage, I think I was too tuned into the New York sound, and the burgeoning independent scene, to give southern rap my full attention, although that seems like a feeble excuse. Why ghettoise music? But there are glimmers of hope. I give Tela's *Piece of Mind* album four stars, the same as Camp Lo's NY classic *Uptown Saturday Night*. Crime Boss gets the same rating as a none-more New York album like Boot Camp Clik's epically disappointing *For the People*. So it's not all unbalanced regional hate, but I've clearly got it in the neck for the pimps and players. Ultimately that's not the worst standpoint to have, is it? To not like pimps? To think that making music about exploiting women is somehow a bit crass? But then again, I love Big Daddy Kane's song *Pimpin' Ain't Easy* so I'm not sure how to reconcile that.

At least there's honesty to my reviews. I had a lovely time speaking to Salt N Pepa, but the following month I could only bring myself to give their *Brand New* album two stars, which is exactly what it's worth. I thought Tony D was brilliant, but his *Pound for Pound* project on the UK's Grand Central Records was only 40% as good as it should have been – in other words, two out of five. Other notable one stars from that period that will either enrage you or have you nodding in agreement are for Mic Geronimo's *Vendetta*, Mase's *Harlem World*, DMX's *It's Dark and Hell is Hot* and Foxy Brown's *Ill Na Na*. I don't think I'll be budging on any of those, even if there's pretty much a whole generation of rap fans who regard them as classics. They're just wrong[2].

But I could be too. In fact, I'm very wrong with my review of Cam'ron's *Sports, Drugs and Entertainment* album in November, 2000. I don't think it's as good an album as *Come Home With Me* or *Purple Haze*, but it certainly didn't deserve the absolute pasting it gets from me:

---

2 Or maybe I am. I plan on relistening to all the one and two star albums for a feature on my new blog, adventuresinrap.com

It could be argued that the likes of Cam'ron and his long-time pal
Ma$e add a dash of colour to an otherwise dull hip-hop scene.
Equally, it could be argued they should be lined up and shot so
that we can all get on with listening to Yakballz.

Yakballz, of course, had a career that was as precisely as long as you'd expect a man called 'Yakballz' to have. Cam'ron is still releasing records now, and is one of the more interesting rappers of the last two decades. As he was then, if I'd cared to listen properly. And as for lining them up to be shot? That was just stupid.

One review I feel was very far off – despite giving it three stars – is for Bubba Sparxxx's *Deliverance*. In a long feature review I call it 'pretty decent space filler' and 'likeable enough'. I also take exception to what I perceive as a wheedling, paranoid tone that permeates the album:

How does Bubba spend his second album? Well, he spends quite
a lot of it taking a pop at haters who thought he'd disappear after
his initial success, those who thought he was a one-hit wonder.
Can anyone actually say they spent any time casting aspersions
on Bubba or dismissing his chances of recording another album?
Isn't everyone too busy to worry about average rappers? Get over
yourself mate.

I'm happy to report that it didn't take me 20 years to regret this review. A few months later, in an encounter you can read about in the *Guess Who's Comin' to Dinner* chapter, I share ribs with Bubba, and the piece includes a mea culpa:

Those who have lived with the album Deliverance can report
that it does what an LP should do – hold together as an artistic
concept while remaining interesting and varied. A confession:

When I reviewed the album for HHC, I was a bit sniffy about it, thinking it was all a bit whiney. Let me point out that I changed this view before I met Bubba, because I started to see what it was about. So what is it about? It's about an emcee getting to say what didn't get said before.

It was a classic case of not listening to the album enough before reviewing it. Two decades later, *Deliverance* is in steady rotation. I think it's a genuine classic, a 5* album. And the tone of whining and whinging I detected on that first listen? Nowhere to be heard.

It's also very possible to be wrong in the opposite direction. To overpraise, to hail the next coming of Rakim when listening to an artist who's, you know, Yakballz or similar. There aren't too many concrete examples of this, but I was certainly guilty of getting caught up in the indie rap whirlwind, riding hard for artists who, in retrospect, weren't all that amazing. There was lots of 'more of this stuff, less of that stuff please' from me, but I think my tastes truly matured as I got into my mid 30's. By then I was listening to anything and everything, something that has stayed with me. Geography doesn't matter, as it clearly shouldn't. Equally, I'm not going to fall out with the many Kanye West albums I love just because he's a bit of a knob. Okay, a lot of a knob.

I'm not now one of those writers who only has time for 'positive' hip-hop – although, as we'll see, I certainly flirted with that limitation a time or five. Academics and intellectuals have submitted dense analyses of the genre over decades and the takeaway seems to be, generally, that they love that politically committed, non-violent corner of the music that, in reality, represents only a tiny portion of it. They don't have a lot of love for the drug tales, the shootings, the misogyny. Even Michelle Alexander, in her brilliant and important *The New Jim Crow*, couldn't resist a swipe at gangster rap.

To me, that's a failure of imagination that we can reduce to 'Good rap? Thumbs up. Bad rap? Thumbs down.' Trust me, there's a world of nuance they're missing out on. If you're going to engage with hip-hop in any real or meaningful sense, you're going to have to realise early on that while Sir Mix-A-Lot's *Baby Got Back* might not seem to have as much 'enriching' content as, say, Ras Kass' *Nature of the Threat*, they both have their stories to share with us. They both have depths worthy of study that reveal something about history, culture, gender, race and more. The only real difference I can see is that only one of them is a banger, and it's not the one that bangs on about Yacub, a made-up evil scientist.

I think the best music writing treats party rap and drug rap with the same attention to detail as a political or positive track. I personally feel that there's more depth and witty wordplay in a Clipse track like *Virginia* than in a record from the complete opposite side of the tracks such as Young MC's *Just Say No*.

Equally, journalists often fall into the trap of only writing in detail about music they think reflects their own politics, and ignoring stuff that doesn't. I did this for a while, and boy was it limiting. It's vital to get out of your comfort zone when it comes to rap music. The day I wrote this section, someone wrote a piece for *The Guardian* about how she was saying goodbye to the misogynist rap that was the soundtrack to her youth, because her daughter didn't like it. Well, that's up to her, and it's certainly a good idea to be mindful of what you're playing around your kids, but all the artists mentioned in the piece[3] aren't merely misogynistic, they all offer a lot more besides. Eminem, Lil' Wayne, Fat Joe – yes, they can drop some crass and sexist lyrics, but each of them has a body of work that contains a whole lot more.

---

3 How seriously you take such a piece will depend on your view on rap lyrics, how easily offended you are and whether or not you have a tolerance for writers who make obvious blunders such as calling R. Kelly a rapper.

So, it's in the job description to get things wrong. Even my favourite *HHC* writers were often way off on some things. It's something that can wind people up, and *The Source* 5 mics rating system used to be a constant source of irritation to artists and readers alike. To this day, people are still scanning in reviews they disagree with and posting them to Instagram. Often, the whole debate is baffling. Some writer gave an album you love four mics twenty-eight years ago and you're posting in high dudgeon because you think it's worth 4.5? You surely have better things to do. My response is always the same: why do you think *The Source* would get it right? That magazine was only good for a few years. Jonathan Shecter left it in 1995, and no other editor came close to his reign.

In the end, you have to attribute the review to the writer, not the magazine. It's not *The Source* that gave Lil Kim's *The Naked Truth* album five mics. It was Michael 'Ice Blue' Harris[4]. It's not *Hip-Hop Connection* that awarded The Jungle Brothers' *VIP* LP one star. It was me. But history tells it another way. "*The Source* gave it this...", "*Vibe* gave it that..." – it's an easy shorthand we all fall back on, but ultimately it does both the writer and the magazine a disservice. I recall one livid UK rapper writing in to *HHC*'s letter page calling the magazine all kinds of names for a less-than-positive review of their album. I wrote back – 'it wasn't HHC, mate, it was me'. Whether you're wrong or right, if your name is at the end of the piece, you can't hide behind the magazine.

---

4 To be fair, it's a bit more nuanced than this, as all the mic ratings in *The Source* were decided by committee. For me, that's highly weird, but I also understand it as *The Source* was inseparable from their mic ratings. It was their calling card. But Michael Harris wrote the damn review, which is as bad a piece of writing as that magazine ever published. The 'committee' didn't do a great job on that rating, with plenty of rumours abounding that one of the bosses at *The Source* was dating someone from Lil Kim's camp at the time, hence the incredible generosity of the review.

13: AND THE WINNER IS

Despite my passion for hip-hop, despite my love of travel, by 1998 I'd still only been to New York once, when Dan and I headed there in 1991. It was time to remedy that, and the boom in indie rap was the perfect excuse.

Small genre magazines don't have the budget to fly their writers around the world. If you were lucky, you'd get a plum assignment on a big cover story where the record label would pay to fly you across, but even then you were down the pecking order behind the lad's mags and the mainstream music press.

So we started to do it for ourselves. Dan, Mike and I started planning our first writing trip to New York in early 1998. We'd get cheap flights, we'd share a room and we'd do our best to pay our way by cramming in loads of interviews and features for *HHC*. As a bonus, we'd try and get some content for *Fat Lace 2*, which was rapidly taking shape.

We'd already got the cover story in place. I'd gone to interview Philly rap legend Schoolly D at a London hotel, accompanied by Mike who just wanted to meet him. Stalwart *HHC* photographer Paul Hampartsoumian is also in the building. The places you interview rappers can be quite jarring. I've done it in recording studios to a soundtrack of hip-hop beats. I've done it in record label offices, in rapper's houses, at the back of nightclubs. But the hotel interview is always the strangest. Sometimes it's because the rapper is in bed, and has no intention of getting out of it (Method Man). At other times it's because you can hear the artist's mate flushing the loo and then trying to hide their shame with more than one spray of Glade.

On this occasion, it's because we're with one of rap's hardest to ever do it, and we're in a room with a fake aviary complete with piped bird-song, a grand piano idling in the corner and elderly couples taking afternoon tea. The reverie of the fake birds and cucumber sandwiches is somewhat disturbed by Schoolly D saying 'motherfucker' every few words and me laughing uproariously at his vivid stories.

HHC: Is is true you were going to sue The Beastie Boys for sampling Gucci Time?

Schoolly D: I was going to but that was just talk. My manager wanted to. What the fuck for? I was morally, 'How the fuck can I go and sue The Beastie Boys when James Brown, George Clinton, Bootsy, Aretha Franklin, should be knocking on my motherfucking door?' So how could I go do some shit like that? Lawsuits are no fun because I was sued by Led Zeppelin and that wasn't a pretty sight."

To be honest, the interview was so good that I wanted to use absolutely everything for the *HHC* piece. The only *Fat Lace* stuff was a quick sidebar about what Schoolly D likes to cook and how he relaxes. To be honest, you didn't need a massively insightful interview to get a *Fat Lace* cover. You just needed to be an artist we liked. 1/2 page of questions like 'What would you cook for a romantic dinner for two?' Yep, that's enough to put you on the front.

The trip to New York would have to be a balancing act. Get enough material to write stuff up for *HHC* and get the trip to pay for itself. Cram in some extra stuff to fit into *Fat Lace 2*. And enjoy ourselves in what was then still the most vibrant hip-hop city in the US, even if the lustre had come off it somewhat. We had a very long hit list of clothes shops, record shops, bars and diners to visit.

The major downside of sharing a hotel room with other men is sharing a hotel room with other men. There's not much space, there's no privacy. Sleep is fleeting. Cheap New York hotel rooms – our choice for this one, as it would be for several subsequent trips, was the Washington Square Hotel – don't come with much storage space or clothes hanging room. We'd live out of our suitcases, damp towels hanging everywhere, and try to fall asleep to a cacophony of the noises men make when they're settling down for the night. On the plus side, it definitely encourages you to get out of your room and make the most of New York.

The city had changed a lot since my last visit. By 1991, some of the rough edges of the city were being smoothed off, although it was still in your face. Times Square remained full of sleaze and fleapits. For better or worse, the city had cleaned up its act. Whatever your views on gentrification and Giuliani, a place that had peaked at 2,245 murders in 1990 had brought it down to around 660 in 1998. It certainly felt like a safer place to visit.

Before we'd arrived, we'd tried to piece together an agenda. We made some calls, put interviews in place and, once our feet touched the ground, pretty much all of that fell apart. People stopped returning calls. Others cancelled. But we discovered it was actually easier to arrange things in the flesh. Blak Shawn, one of the people running things at Rawkus Records, invited us to their office on Broadway. The lift was full of Keith Haring graffiti, as his studio used to be on the 5th floor – it was now the home of the Keith Haring Foundation. Rawkus occupied the 4th floor.

Blak Shawn had been the man orchestrating the label's press relations, and had done a great job of ensuring the UK market had access to the whole Rawkus talent family. On this trip, he went above and beyond. First up, he opened up the doors to the merchandise room, and let us fill our bags with Rawkus tees. Then he asked us who we wanted to interview, and he made sure we got every single one lined up. We even got some bonus artists who just happened to drop into the office when we were there.

As a sign of the way Rawkus was stirring things up, their artist Mos Def was on the *HHC* cover in May 1998. The month after, the issue was a Rawkus special, complete with the headline 'Exclusive! The Inside Story of Hip-Hop's Hottest Label'. Inside, there were a couple of other bits before we got to the main event. An interview we did in New York with rap legend Doug E. Fresh. A chat with producer EZ Elpee for another of my new columns, *The Producers*, which had kicked off the previous month. And then there's the Rawkus story, with Dan and myself putting together a heap of interviews and Mike Lewis taking photos – there was more than one string to his bow.

I chatted with label owners Brian and Jarret, who are upfront about having taken a loan from News International, the Murdoch family company. "Yes, we got a loan, but they are completely disconnected from the company and are definitely not in this office." I can see why he gave this answer, but it's not entirely true. We literally saw James Murdoch in that office, and he may or may not have been smoking weed with Brian and Jarret. That's one for the lawyers.

Let's not let that distract from the music, however, and the passion that Brian and Jarret had for their label. It may not always have been smooth sailing, but ultimately they delivered some genuine classics to the hip-hop market and, for that short but sweet period, they could lay claim to being music's coolest label.

It helps, as a writer, when your ego is cuddled a little. Most of us walk into interviews and are introduced by the press assistant or we tell the artists who we're representing. Inevitably, halfway through, they'll ask us who we write for again. That's fine – they might be doing a dozen half-hour interviews throughout the day, and why the fuck should they care?

But when I walked in to chat to Mos Def and Talib Kweli, they greeted me by name and mentioned how they'd liked a couple of articles I'd written, quoting me a few choice bits. The cynic in me says this was fed to them by Blak Shawn to make the journalist feel well disposed towards them, but I'm inclined to accept it at face value. They were two artists at the start of their careers. They cared what the press had to say about them and, right then, the UK press were way ahead of their US counterparts in paying attention to what the artists of Rawkus had to say.

After that, I spoke to Shabaam Sahdeeq, one of the Rawkus' earliest rap signings, who as well as a smattering of really good singles also ran the street promotions team for the label. His career didn't quite pan out there in the end, but he more than held his own on the likes of *5 Star Generals*, where Eminem delivered a guest verse ahead of his fame that had rap fans in NY and beyond sitting up and taking notice.

We saw Sir Menelik again who, last time he spoke to *HHC*, spent a part of the interview dissing Q-Tip for making the same music over and over again. This time, I asked him "Any more emcees you want to snap on since the last interview?" and he graciously acknowledged that Tip was stepping up. We spoke to El-P about Company Flow. We left laden with interviews, T-shirts and Rawkus promos. We also left laden with a rapper.

RA the Rugged Man only released one record on Rawkus, the really very good *Till My Heart Stops* in 1997. He was, however, in the office at the same time as us, and we got chatting. Today, RA is a well-known rapper with a strong catalogue and a big following in Europe. At the time, he was fresh off a busted deal with Jive Records, who didn't take kindly to some of his behaviour in their office, and tracks with titles like *Cunt Renaissance*[1].

---

1 A collaboration with The Notorious BIG, no less. The lyrics from either don't bear repeating.

Nevertheless, we hit it off very well with RA, and he came out for a few drinks with us. It had been a long day, and it turned out he'd missed his train back out to Long Island. Hey, why not invite one more person back to our already overstuffed hotel room? And thus it was that RA the Rugged Man accompanied us back to our digs.

It was Oscars night, and RA was and is a genuine film buff, with a wide-ranging knowledge that takes in Rainer Werner Fassbinder's more difficult films (RA is of German stock, and later moved there) as well as horror and standard Hollywood fare. We decided to write a feature based on his Oscar predictions, as we sat down to watch it with him, sharing a few cans of shit American lager and a Chinese takeaway.

It was the year of *Titanic*, a hugely popular and not really all that exceptional film that swept all before it. It turns out that RA doesn't love the film either, but he had seen it, and he proved very adept at picking the winners.

Best Actress in a Supporting Role:
RA's Pick: "Kim Basinger for LA Confidential. Just 'cos I predict her doesn't mean I give a fuck about her. It doesn't mean I like her. I'd rather fuck the old bitch on the Titanic just to say I fucked her before she died." HHC photographer 'Mad' Mike Lewis spits out his sweet and sour pork in mock outrage.
And the winner is… Kim Basinger.

He doesn't get many wrong. In fact, he gets the first six picks correct, correctly surmising that the 'The Academy is on Titanic's dick'. He gets to 8 out of 10 after a choppy run on the short animation and short film categories which, lets be honest, no one watches or gives a fuck about. He kicks HHC's arse, that's for sure. Until the 'Original Musical or Comedy Score' round, that is.

RA's Pick: As Good As It Gets.

And the winner is… The Full Monty. Cries of 'The Brits are coming' and several rounds of Rule Britannia from the HHC contingent. The war of independence[2] is reenacted with chopsticks. "You can't get these ones though," RA protests. "These are the hard ones, fucking music."

I'm not going to lie, we were having a great time, but I was still slightly outside of the experience. There was a part of me that was watching from above, telling me that I was on my first writing trip to New York and we'd got an actual rapper in our hotel room, eating takeaway, cracking open beers and watching The Oscars. Let me never become jaded about this stuff, I'm saying, because this is what you wanted. Okay, you wanted to be in the studio with them, kicking lyrics, but that was never going to happen, so soak up every moment of this.

After a serious slump in his predictions – "I'm falling to pieces here," he said, and that's before he gets nowhere near the Actor in a Leading Role pick – he rallied. In the end, he scored a truly excellent 17 out of 24. It was 1am and yet, for all of us, the night was only beginning.

The beds were all full. Where was RA going to sleep? He didn't care, to be fair, and we managed to rustle up some spare bedding and pillows so that he'd be relatively comfortable in our bath. Our actual bath. But it's not like he ended up spending much time in it. Sleep was fitful that night – it had been a long day, we were all suffering from jetlag, and the gassy beer and takeaway food, as well as the presence of a rapper in our bathroom, meant that none of us were slumbering securely that

---

2 I actually wrote 'The Civil War' at the time in *HHC*, which I suppose is why I'm writing this book and not a six-part history of America. Then again, Ken Burns knows bugger all about the Bay Area rap scene.

night. Actually, that's not true – Dan could sleep through the bombing of Dresden, so he got his seven hours.

After a day on the booze, the middle of the night wee is inevitable. But where to go when you've got a guest sleeping in that room? To hell with it, when you've got to go, you've got to go, so I shuffled to the loo in the dark, trying not to wake the MC who, I assumed, was curled up foetally in the hotel bath. Nope. He wasn't there. I finished my wee and pondered where the hell our guest rapper had gone. He wasn't in my bed. He wasn't in Mike's bed, as Mike's bed was also my bed. I couldn't see him getting into Dan's, as Dan was snoring the whole place up. Had he decided to walk to Long Island on foot? Had he decided to head to LA to take umbrage with the Academy because *Vices and Virtue* took the Oscar for Short Film Live Action instead of his prediction *It's Good to Talk*?

No, neither of those. Because as I headed back to my bed, RA came in through the hotel room door. He'd been for a 'walk'. What kind of walk, I asked. Couldn't sleep? At this point, most men would mumble something and head off to bed. RA isn't built that way. No, he fessed up straight away.

It turned out he'd been for a stroll to a few peep show booths – back when they were still a thing in New York. He's got kids now, so I'll spare you the rest but, suffice to say, that wasn't a one-off visit 'for obvious reasons concerning entertainment' as JVC Force[3] might have put it. He was up and out of that bath at least one more time in the wee hours to check in on the welfare of women putting in a nocturnal shift. By the morning, the bath was the perfect place for him to wash off the grime of a memorable New York night.

---

3 JVC Force have one of the finest forced rap acronyms of all. Justified by Virtue of Creativity For Obvious Reasons Concerning Entertainment. I did all this acronym stuff in *Wiggaz*, so I won't be revisiting any more.

That Rawkus issue felt like the start of something special, at the time, but maybe in retrospect it's already the beginning of the end. I called the label 'without doubt the preeminent label in the current climate of hip-hop,' with a 'special aura that goes beyond beats and rhymes and cuts and reaches into the core of why we follow the music in the first place'. And that's something I certainly felt at the time – and I wasn't alone. But within months, the first stories of unhappy artists started to do the rounds. The ones whose releases kept getting pushed back. The ones who weren't happy with the amount of studio time or support they were getting. Rawkus might have been at the vanguard of a new musical movement in hip-hop but that doesn't mean it was any better at artist relations than other labels. There has hardly been a rap label in existence that hasn't had artists who've left it complain about being jerked around. Sometimes rap artists can be very hard to deal with, but often they are simply jerked around.

The Rawkus dream withered on the vine, eventually, but that's not an unusual story. It burned briefly but oh so brightly. Many regard Mos Def's *Black on Both Sides* as a bona fide classic. Others will go to bat for Company Flow's *Funcrusher Plus*. Albums by Black Star and Pharoahe Monch still get plenty of play. But for me, it was the 12"s they got right. They gave shine to interesting artists like Mr Complex, Thirstin Howl III and The High & Mighty, with attention-grabbing artwork and B-sides worth flipping the records over for.

I never really got to write much about Mos Def during his Rawkus career, but I did get to sit in on a couple of the studio sessions for *Black on Both Sides*. Dan, Mike and I shuffled into the legendary Chung King Studios and sat quietly as the rapper worked with producer 88 Keys on the track *Love* and possibly on *Speed Law* too. Despite the incredible access to the recording of what is considered a classic, I can't say it has given me an abiding love of that album or of Mos Def. In fact, I think both it and he are incredibly overrated. He's best in small doses, and

Black on Both Sides – later dubbed *Wack on Both Sides* by my *Fat Lace* colleague Rob Pursey – outstays its welcome. You'd think I'd be able to get a whole chapter out of being at the recording of part of this alleged landmark album, but the experience elicits a shrug compared to the memory of watching the Oscars with the Rugged Man.

Another studio session, another late night. We headed to Battery Studios on West 44th Street to join rapper Mike Zoot and producer EZ Elpee as they recorded the track *Urban Harvest*, invited by Guesswhyld Records founder Matt Fingaz. It was the first time I'd seen a rapper go into the booth to do ad-libs. Those 'uhs' and 'ahs' that lurk behind the vocals of many a hip-hop record are usually added afterwards, by a rapper or his mate as they listen to the original vocal. It really does sound like they've gone in there to pleasure themselves.

Even more studio sessions awaited, but these are for radio shows. We'd decided to explore the world of New York hip-hop radio and, over one long day and night, we did exactly that. We went to a space just off Broadway to meet the people at 88 Hip-Hop, probably the world's first Internet-only rap radio station. Clearly a lot of money was being pumped into it. We sat in on a show by Evil Dee, of The Beatminerz and Black Moon, then went to a party where Wu-Tang affiliate Cappadonna and his crew rapped to a room of music industry movers and shakers. Like many things .com of that era, it was all gone within two years.

Our next two radio visits were to two stalwarts of the late-night New York scene. Tucked away somewhere in a New York University building, we observed DJs Riz and Eclipse as they juggled the latest records for their *Half Time Show*, while MC duo Cocoa Brovaz jumped on the mic. Photographer and honorary Beastie Boy Ricky Powell arrived to be interviewed about a new book (he seemed like a proper knob, to be honest), and then it was time for us to head off again.

The final stop was at an institute of rap radio, the Stretch Armstrong & Bobbito show on WKCR. It's a show that has aired many a rap legend, and Bobbito shares tales of the famous night that Nas arrived with Akinyele and Lord Finesse and served notice of his precocious talent. We don't enjoy quite that star wattage – we get Sporty Thievz and Lord Digga – but it's still a privilege to sit in on a show that combines dope music with outright silliness. The trio – Stretch and Bobbito are joined by co-host Lord Sear – often go over the line between humour and self indulgence, with endless in-jokes, but they always manage to pull it back.

During a break, I asked Sear if I could make him the subject of a piece I was writing for *ego trip*. It ended up being about him showing me some weird and very complicated handshakes. I just wanted to be in *ego trip* and, sure enough, they printed the piece. I was thrilled at the time, but for reasons that will become obvious later in the book, I don't even have the issue or even the cutting now.

All of which would be quite enough for one trip, but yet another highlight is still to come. After using a second-hand interview for the cover of *Fat Lace 1*, we actually get to meet the man, the myth, T La Rock, in the flesh.

Mike, Dan and myself were invited to his apartment on a day that was cripplingly cold. It was an abode that spoke volumes about the life of a rapper whose heyday was in the 80's, and who didn't enjoy the riches and fame granted to later rappers. The producers of *Cribs* would not be troubling Terry Keaton to explore his small one-bed place, and that's a shame, because to me he's a giant of the genre. Every rapper who tries to bust vocabulary-charged, complex rhymes will forever walk in the shadow of T La Rock. His life story is one of incredible potential short-changed by shonky label deals, a traumatic head injury and the battle to rediscover himself afterwards.

Mike snapped away as Dan and I sat on T La Rock's bed with him. He rifled through boxes to play us tapes both new and old. Tracks for a mooted comeback. Recordings from his early days. There was that inevitable disconnect between T's plans – "I'm hoping to work with DJ Premier, Mantronix, Marley Marl, Pete Rock and Q-Tip" – and what we know would be the reality. Rappers from T La Rock's era rarely get that kind of producer attention or label interest. All of those people will be fans of T La Rock, in particular his masterpiece *It's Yours*, but we knew, even as he was telling us about his hopes, that none of it would come to pass.

He told us a story about MC Serch, of the group 3rd Bass. Serch, famously, was a constant presence at many hip-hop shows[4] before he found fame as a rapper, releasing records on Def Jam. "I can't even get Serch to return a phone call," T told us.

> "I don't want to sound mean, but I want to talk about rappers who I helped get where they are today and Serch is one of them. There was a time when Serch couldn't get in a party. This was when The Roxy was open and I used to get him in. I'm the one he used to hang around, and when he wanted to quit rap I talked him into hanging in there. Now I can't even get the time of day from him."

This trip didn't just take over a fair chunk of *HHC* for two issues, it also fueled much of *Fat Lace 2*. As part of our time at T La Rock's house, he pulled out some of his film collection and we do a page all about his movie recommendations. It's the only time the film *Anaconda* would be mentioned in the pages of *Fat Lace*. We had Sir Menelik talking about

---

4 A couple of years ago, I listed a bunch of old photos I'd collected over the years on eBay. Pete Nice, formerly of 3rd Bass and now a hip-hop historian and collector, bought one of them from me. It was of The Fat Boys performing live at a long-gone New York venue called Red Parrot. I wondered why he wanted it, but then closer examination of the picture revealed a familiar face in the crowd – a very youthful MC Serch, Pete's former partner in 3rd Bass. The two are not on good terms these days, and soon enough Pete was using the picture to make fun of Serch on social media.

the Rawkus Records roster. We had a quick interview with storied graf writer Phase 2 who we'd bumped into at the Rawkus offices designing a cover for a Company Flow record.

There were several things that marked the new edition of Fat Lace out from its predecessor. Firstly, there was the design. Barrie Bee was on board and no longer am I allowed anywhere near the layout. This was for the best. We had a new writer in the form of 'Rob Bringur the Cornershop Terrorist', a key member of the team going forward. We had freelance contributions from Mr Ree.

Mostly, though, the difference was in just how we maintained the silliness and irreverence while actually looking 300% more like an actual magazine. The mission statement, if I can use so lofty a phrase – was in full effect, with the promised mixture of old schoolers – T La Rock, Schoolly D, Jungle Brothers – with new talent like Mr Thing, Siah and YESHUA DapoED, Loot Pack, Frankenstein and Dilated Peoples.

The features started to become ever more esoteric, while retaining a connection to hip-hop. What other rap magazine had a feature written by an actual teacher about a fictional teacher schooling his pupils in 'Alfonics'? Where else would a writer adopt the persona of rapper Blackjack to talk about *Coronation Street*, pointing out that 'Ken Barlow, father of Gary, was in the original pilot episode and in the Bayeux Tapestry'?

My growing disinterest in the graffiti that I was supposed to like as a hip-hop fan had led to a growing interest in collecting pictures of obscene and hilarious graffiti, mostly on the streets of Leeds. This formed the basis of *Crap Graf*, where we published gems like 'Bastard' and 'Neil Shaw is fucking fit' and wrote about them like they were masterpieces of graffiti.

Best of all, and already mentioned, was the Notorious BIG autopsy. An idea of Mike and mine's, but written by him and then given a big assist by Barrie with the design. I nipped to the shops and bought the board game Operation[5] and then Mike worked his magic: Too young to die, too fat to live.

Is it hugely disrespectful to mock a dead rapper? Yes, I suppose it is. But that's no reason not to do it. We wanted Fat Lace to occupy a space somewhere between a standard hip-hop magazine and a satirical publication. We wanted to speak reverentially about hip-hop we adored, but caustically about things we didn't. We wanted to do something different, and sometimes you have to commit to pushing the limits of what most hip-hop fans find acceptable.

For me, it ultimately comes down to this. If Biggie can appear on records like *Cunt Renaissance* and, on others, utter lyrics like 'shoot your daughter in the calf muscle', is it too much for some writers to speculate that the contents of his corpse included Shergar, a wine lake and not just an Adam's apple but 'everyone else's apple too'? I don't think so. Our piece about Biggie is the same as what he does on the mic – it's largely just fantastical words. He isn't shooting your daughter in the calf muscle. We're not finding Lord Lucan near his shinbone.

> *Examination of the stomach contents were amazing. We found 3,000 undigested pies, 2,000 cream teas, a number plate from a Volkswagen Beetle, a small wooden boy named Pinocchio and an elderly gent answering to the name of Jonah. Samples of his blood were found to contain five times the legal limit of Kit Kats.*

I love a lot of Biggie's music. It doesn't mean I or my colleagues had to worship his every breath. Listen to dream hampton – another writer conflicted about much of what she hears in hip-hop – tell stories about him dressing down Lil' Kim for not wearing enough make-up, and you might think he perhaps wasn't the loveliest man to ever live. Same goes

---

5 Later regifted to my niece Hayley and nephew Richard.

for Tupac. Same goes for countless rap heroes. Feel free to put them on a pedestal, but we don't all have to. Fair enough, hampton's[6] critique was a bit more erudite than our collection of fat jokes, but as *HHC* writers we often put our hearts into long and considered takedowns of rap's murkier corners. *Fat Lace*? That was just for jokes.

---

6 hampton is probably the best of all the writers *The Source* produced and exempt from any criticism of that magazine's scribes. She was prickly, honest and heartfelt, and never anything less than stimulating to read. Her name, with its lower case 'd' and 'h' is no friend of autocorrect, but is in tribute to the feminist thinker bell hooks, who I basically rinsed the hell out of for my undergraduate dissertation about representations of women in the films of Spike Lee which, with every passing year, seems like an increasingly ridiculous thing for me to have ever taken on.

14: LIVE ON STAGE

Even the very best writers and journalists have their Achilles heel. It might be something they're not necessarily good at, or it just might be something they don't like doing. For me, reviewing rap shows was a bit of both.

You'd think getting paid to go and see artists perform was all gravy. No paying for a ticket. No missing out on the hottest shows in towns. You get to jump the line and head straight for the guest list queue. If the PR person has done their job properly – not always a given[1] – your name is on it, and you head inside. If you're incredibly lucky, and you're combining a review of the gig with some reporting, perhaps an interview, you might get a backstage pass.

---

1 I'd say I turned up and found my name was NOT on the guest list about 15% of the time. This is a guess, not a mathematical fact, but it feels right. In some ways, the worst thing about this isn't that you don't get to see the show or do your work – although on the rare occasion you're desperate to watch the gig, it's just annoying that you can't when you could have gone and bought a bloody ticket. It's not the disappointment in your contact at the label or the group's manager not doing their job properly. No, it's having to exit the guest list queue. Even when you've done it a thousand times, there's still a frisson about going straight to the front. It's like a fast pass at a theme park. But that tiny joy is as nothing compared to the walk of shame when you're not allowed in and you have to backtrack. I have literally been jeered by people in the normal ticket queue when the security couldn't find my name on the list and I had to trudge off into the night. Once I had a mobile phone I could try to style it out by holding a fake conversation, like I'm waiting for a friend or making some important shit happen in the business of show, but that's hard to carry off.

Actually, it's not that lucky. Let's be honest, being backstage is not very exciting. The only time I've enjoyed it was at the Rock Werchter festival in Belgium, and when I accompanied Dan to a Ghostface Killer show in London. Mainly because Ghostface is hilarious. Most of the time, however, you're just ignored, having to remind people why you're there, sitting outside changing rooms until you get a snatched 10 minutes with someone whose mind is on their performance, not an interview.

I could write endlessly about hip-hop music. About the charisma of the artists, the history of the genre, the meaning of the lyrics, the derivation of the slang. About the producers and the samples and the inspiration and a thousand different things. What is there to write about at a live show? What songs they did and whether they were good or not. A paragraph about the support act if they're worth mentioning. I'm simplifying, but not by much. Another part of this, for me, is that if a show is good, I want to enjoy it in the moment. I don't want to be standing there formulating sentences in my head for how I'll write about it. It's a distraction.

One particularly tough assignment is being asked to review a DJ set. I'm not talking about skilled acts of turntablism, or genuinely original AV experiences like those put together by DJ Yoda. No, just someone playing some records. What's to say? I got to go to a Mary J. Blige concert in Manchester because DJ Shadow was supporting and the editor wanted a review of that. I wasn't even a big Shadow fan, but watching him press some buttons and move some records around on a couple of turntables turned me off him even more. It wasn't in any way bad, but what do you write about that? On the plus side, I got to see the queen of hip-hop soul perform, and that was an all-timer.

At other times, it has simply been someone playing a selection of records but, because they're a legend – let's say Grandmaster Flash or Afrika Bambaataa – it warrants attention and gets to be treated like an actual performance. It's not. DJing well is a fine skill, but it doesn't need chronicling over 400 words. Again, you just want to be in the moment, experiencing the vibe, not struggling to work out how you'll write anything remotely interesting about the DJ's choice of records and how he segues between them,

There are some excellent live reviewers out there, people who can take a performance that's good, bad or indifferent and turn it into a nice piece of writing. I'll be honest, though, they're generally something I skip. They're never going to be that interesting to read, are they? Especially if you weren't there and don't plan on seeing them on the rest of the tour. The only times I find a live review of interest is if it's someone I'm seeing later on that year, or a show I was at. For the former, I want to get a sense of if it's any good, what they're playing, whether I'd be better off passing the tickets on. For the latter, I like to see if the critic has had the same experience as me. Very occasionally, you can tell they weren't actually there and they're bullshitting, because they've left out a major event, a special guest, or they've mentioned a song that wasn't performed. They probably got kicked out of the guest list queue too, but didn't want to lose the fee.

The main problem with reviewing rap gigs, however, is that they're largely rubbish. You wait around for someone to come on late, they haven't soundchecked properly, and then they spend the first 10 minutes cursing out the sound engineers, who is probably getting paid fuck all to take this abuse. Then you'll spend a few minutes scanning the stage to see if all the people who were billed to be there have actually turned up. The Wu-Tang Clan were notorious for no-shows. You'd be hyped up to see Ghostface and ODB, but you'd get U-God and one of the extended crew like Street Life or Cappadonna. Seeing some weed carrier[2] fill in for a Method Man or Genius verse is a woeful experience.

---

2 Big up Robbie Ettelson for coining this handy catch-all term for a rapper's mates.

Even worse is when expectation is met by crushing reality. When Stetsasonic played London's Jazz Cafe in 2019, it was their first London show in 28 years. The first ever hip-hop band only released three albums in their career, but they were much loved, and alumni from the group such as Prince Paul had become rap greats. I headed down from Leeds to London and hooked up with some friends for the show. There were people I knew who'd travelled from Nottingham, Newcastle and further beyond to see some genuine legends in action. It could have been a truly memorable night. It was a complete and utter shitshow.

I just looked up some footage of the night on YouTube and read the comments below. Somebody has written "Salute to the OGS for still being able to rock. Daddy O could not make the show.. deal with it.. Shit happens. IF YOU TRULY LOVE HIP HOP CULTURE.. THEN YOU CAN UNDERSTAND THAT. They clearly apologized and did the best that they could without their leader. They could have just said fuck it and not come to the stage."

Whoever wrote that was clearly not at the show. Everyone would have been happier if they hadn't come to the stage. It wasn't just that Daddy O wasn't there, although his loss was keenly felt. For many, he was the main voice of Stet and, once again, seeing someone else perform his lyrics was jarring. It was that four members of the group were absent. It was a shoddy, amateurish performance that spit in the face of fans who'd come from far and wide.

It started badly, and got worse. Are there just these people on stage? Ah, surely Daddy-O is going to arrive for a big reveal halfway through the track! No, maybe next track? Still no sign. Okay, now the rappers are telling us why some of them couldn't make it. It happens. But have you guys even practised these songs, because this is abject? The crowd went from amped to hushed to angry within about 10 minutes. We'd filtered through to halfway towards the stage. 10 minutes in, we filtered back out to the bar, to watch from afar as the show went nowhere fast.

20 minutes in, people started to leave. They'd completely lost the crowd. After 30 minutes, we left, to head out, go for a drink and try to rescue the night. It's still not the worst rap gig I've ever seen, but it's up there[3].

The consistently great rap performers are few and far between. Public Enemy is a banker. They never miss. Same goes for De La Soul. They do the classics, they work the crowd, they give energy back. I've only seen Kanye West once – he was fantastic. The Beatnuts were brilliant. Ice-T was amazing. The Roots can sometimes get a bit lost in jam sessions, but generally do a great show. Mostly, however, you're at the whim of whether the artist can be arsed or not.

I saw EPMD, 30 years past their prime, twice in 18 months. The first time was awful. They were out of sync, out of puff, phoning in a greatest hits set that felt like an excuse for collecting money. They obviously had done no preparation whatsoever. The second time round, they were brilliant. Taut, trading lines, finishing off each other's rhymes, their ease with the material translating into a rapport with the crowd. It was a direct result of them actually putting some effort in.

Every rap fan has sat through a lazy gig. Fortunately, UK crowds don't usually put up with that shit, and so artists have had to step up. It used to be that a big name rapper could have a global hit and book some shows in the UK. They'd arrive, make you wait for 90 minutes too long, then perform said hit over the vocal track so all you can hear is reverb and echo. They'll have 95 people on stage with them who are also given mics and do their best to ruin every other line. The rapper then performs two other songs, does the hit again, and leaves. The end result? People boo, bottles fly, fights start, the artist gets a terrible write up and people swear never to see them again. Rinse and repeat. London crowds have got so feisty so often that the Lil Wayne's and Snoop Doggs

3 Other YouTube reviews are way more accurate. "Absolute crock of shit." "Worst gig I have ever been to." "It was absolutely dire."

who once tried this approach now arrive and do proper shows that treat the crowd like they deserve to be treated.

It's hard to define what makes a great rap show. Crowd interaction, a bit of call and response, can help create a fun evening, but I've seen rappers barely look at the crowd, never mind speak to them, and they still carried the night. Too many hangers-on is usually a bad thing, but it's okay for a solo rapper to have one person with them to help hype the crowd up. Playing the classics is a must, but don't perform them more than once. I saw Lord Finesse support Ice T in Sheffield before Finesse had become an actual legend. He'd only had the excellent *Funky Technician* album out, and was about to release his second. He decided just to perform stuff from the new record, that absolutely nobody knew. Not a great idea. He stank. I saw him a couple of decades later, his status in the rap pantheon secured, and he played hits from across his career and had the crowd in the palm of his hand. Play a new song or three, sure, but earn the right to do so by giving the crowd what they paid to see.

A good DJ can make or break a live show as well. De La Soul's Maseo always added an extra element to their shows, jumping on the mic and fizzing with energy. A DJ with turntable skills should always get his or her chance to shine and show what they can do – although it's a relatively rare sight today as we have moved a long way from the 'he's the DJ, I'm the rapper' approach of the 1980s. Even a warm-up DJ can be a factor. I can't bear the ones who play all the hits by the group you're about to see – what's the point of that? – or who jump on the mic constantly to try and get you hyped up but fail because you can't hear a word they're saying. A good warm-up DJ knows how to set the mood, the tracks to play for that audience, but without stepping on the main event.

Recent years have seen the arrival and growth of the nostalgia tour, with groups performing classic albums in their entirety or banding together with other crews to perform the highlights of their careers.

The former can be a really great way to celebrate landmark albums, but then you do have to sit through the inevitable weaker tracks that wouldn't normally get a live airing. The latter is bigger in the US, as it's more expensive to take this kind of stuff on the road, and was a huge part of the celebrations of hip-hop's alleged[4] 50th birthday in 2023.

What's good about these shows is that they usually put so many artists on the flyer that even if a couple don't turn up – which invariably happens – you're still getting to see plenty of performances. It also means the artists come out and do two or three of their best-known tracks, and don't outstay their welcome by being given too much stage time. This contrasts with the big tours of the past where everyone got 50 minutes whether they had 50 good minutes of material or not.

One of the most important rap shows in the UK was held at London Docklands Arena on Saturday 3rd November 1990. Public Enemy were headlining – and they delivered an incredibly good set – but they'd also brought with them a really strong and interesting support line-up. Tragedy the Intelligent Hoodlum. EPMD. Master Ace, DJ Mark the 45 King. Some of the UK's finest were on the bill too, with She Rockers, MC Mell O, London Posse and Demon Boyz[5] all performing. The show is usually remembered for two things – how good Public Enemy were, and the horrible welcome that Young Black Teenagers got.

---

4 I say alleged because not everyone is convinced that hip-hop was fully born at the storied Kool Herc party on Sedgwick Avenue in 1973. It depends on how you look at music genres and what actually constitutes one. I don't have a massively strong view either way but probably lean to them beginning when there's actually some recorded output. This might be my least committed footnote ever.

5 I always thought it was nice of US rap giants to have UK artists supporting them at their shows. However, in the 80s and 90s the UK acts were often on a hiding to nothing, with everyone waiting in the bar for the main event or just being completely indifferent to their homegrown heroes. This does seem to have changed, with genuine UK stars now selling out their own shows, but it was rough for some excellent UK rap acts for a very long time.

Famously, YBT were a white rap group, and many took offence at their name. I thought it was a good one. It spoke to how they had grown up with black culture and were now operating within it. The name was actually given to them by Public Enemy's Chuck D, and they were signed to Hank Shocklee's – of PE producers The Bomb Squad – S.O.U.L label. Apparently the group had wanted to be called Leaders of the New School, another name coined by Chuck D, but lost out in a battle for that moniker to Busta Rhymes, Dinco D and Charlie Brown. Instead, they got Young Black Teenagers, and a whole lot of resentment from certain rap fans from day one.

Did it help their cause that they had songs called *Proud to be Black* and *Daddy Kalled Me Niga 'Cause I Likeded to Rhyme*? Probably not. But when they took to the stage at London Docklands Arena, they hadn't even released their debut album, and the nuance of their lyrics and stance were lost in translation from second one. They had hardly been announced when boos began and coins began to rain down on them. They barely made it through a song before they retreated from the stage. That must have hurt – and not just from the hail of 2p coins lobbed their way.

Yet even that is a blur compared to the main thing that sticks with me from that show – the performance from The Afros. Now, on the nostalgia circuit, they'd possibly get to do one song, their 1990 single *Feel It*. Then, someone had the bright idea of giving this novelty group who would release one not very good album in their entire career 30 minutes of stage time. It felt like two hours. Led by DJ Hurricane, who'd worked with Davy D and The Beastie Boys, the group was just a bunch of blokes in Afro wigs, and that joke was stretched gossamer thin. Seven songs on their album – which only came out two weeks before the Docklands show, so nobody would have had time to get familiar with it even if it hadn't made zero splash – had the word 'afro' or 'fro' in. But they didn't have Afros, they had wigs. Wigs. They were playing dress up. Why Jam Master Jay signed them to his label remains a mystery, but even the combined skills of Sherlock, Columbo and Jessica Fletcher can't get to the bottom of who let them perform their zero hits for 30 minutes to a London audience waiting for Public Enemy to come on. Baffling.

Strangely, after starting this chapter writing about how tough and unrewarding I find writing about live rap shows to be, I ended up enjoying writing about the Docklands Arena concert. However, as writing about rap is already a niche career, I don't think there's much future in only reviewing rap shows from 33 years ago.

15: DESTINATION EARTH (1999)

What a strange, tumultuous year 1999 was. Everyone was worrying about something called the 'Millennium Bug', with IT companies making a fortune out of anxiety about the world's computers failing and planes falling out of the sky. Nothing happened. The UK government thought we'd be interested in the contents of a building called the Millennium Dome, with attractions sponsored by Tesco and arms company BAE. We weren't[1]. We were told the River Thames would turn into a 'river of fire' as 1999 turned to 2000. I was there – it was like a particularly bad municipal fireworks show. All that fuss about one year turning into another.

On a personal level, I didn't want 1999 to end. It was a strange and tumultuous one for me as well, and also for *Hip-Hop Connection* and *Fat Lace*. I started the year with a cover story about Method Man, after a particularly disappointing meeting, and ended it by writing an in-depth investigative piece into the unsolved murder of Notorious BIG. The *Fat Lace* autopsy was not admitted as evidence.

Inbetween I wrote endlessly, relentlessly. My *Webheadz* column is still somehow going, joined by a regular column where I interviewed producers, another column called *Go See the Doctor* where I prescribed medication for rappers having career woes, and my favourite of all, my cookery column.

---

1 6.5 million people went, which isn't bad, but they were aiming for 13 million so it was still a white elephant.

I started *Def Chef* in January, 1999. 'What's cookin' in the *HHC* kitchen' was the tagline, but in reality it was my kitchen in North London. I'd always been fascinated by food, and I thought it would be fun to ask rappers for their favourite recipes and then try to recreate them. Andy Cowan liked the idea, and also didn't mind me claiming the shopping on expenses. It kicked off with Monie Love's chicken curry.

To be honest, it wasn't always easy to get rappers to talk about food. Some just didn't cook. At other times I couldn't cram the question in at the end of a busy interview. I put out feelers to the other *HHC* writers, and sometimes they came up trumps with a good dish for me, but sometimes I had to rely on a book of rap recipes. At the time, there was precisely one of these. These days, there are hundreds. We pioneered that stuff.

In the coming years, through several redesigns, sometimes solo, sometimes accompanied by Mike to take better photos than I could manage, sometimes with guests, I cooked dozens of meals. Each one came with a suggested playlist – all of them puns on food[2] – an ingredient list, a drink recommendation, and me or my guest summing up how good the food was.

Recipes came in from the great and the obscure, but I gave each one their due. Mike G of the Jungle Brother's salmon fishcakes. Styles from Mountain Brothers' 'tasty ass' garlic and onion fries. Yo Yo's burritos. Sometimes the dish would be simple beyond belief – Method Man gave me a 'recipe' for a grilled cheese sandwich. At other times I had to step up my chef game – Yeshua DAPO Ed's fish soup, for example.

The column would go on hiatus when *HHC* changed ownership at the end of 1999, but then came roaring back in 2004 and ran for a few more years. Pretty Toney's macaroni, Andy Cooper of Ugly Duckling's 'Tacos del Cooper', Devin the Dude's gumbo. We even delved into veg-

---

2 A few random selections: OC *Thyme's Up*, Beatnuts *Broth The Books*, Various *I Saw Mummy Dissing Santa Claus*.

etarian and vegan dishes such as Giant Panda's steamed vegetables in almond-ginger sauce and Tajai's vegetarian sloppy joes. The column and the cooking became a fun fixture in my life and, much later, I even tried to turn it into a TV show[3].

New York beckoned again, and we were determined to take a suit-case full of *Fat Lace 3* with us. We had an incredible response to issue two, getting write-ups in *The Face*, *The Guardian*, *Echoes*, *Select*, *Urb*, *Spin*, *Blues & Soul* and *ego trip*. We'd sold a lot more copies, both through mail order and in record shops. My man Zane at Selectadisc in Soho was like a one-man *Fat Lace* sales machine, and I was taking in fresh copies every week for him. We had to step our game up further for issue 3.

We decided, for the first and only time, to have a new school star alone on the cover. In fact, we were so excited about this cover star that we didn't even wait for anyone to take a photograph of him – we used a video grab. Interscope had sent us an early video of Eminem's *My Name Is...* and we were determined to publish our cover story on him before anybody else got to what we considered the hottest new rap artist in a long time[4].

A few years later, I saw a piece in *Arena* magazine where a *Rolling Stone* journalist had claimed that they'd been first on Eminem, with his first cover story. We weren't going to let that lie. I wrote in to correct the record, and Arena published my letter, with an aside saying how great *Fat Lace* was. Take that, allegedly racist *Rolling Stone* founder Jann Wenner.

---

3 Dan and I met with a TV producer – one who had helped pitch and launch *Dragon's Den* – and we worked up an idea which would involve UK rap and soul stars cooking food for their fans. If it came off, I'd give up the day job and become a producer on it. It was a dream that died very quickly – even with a powerhouse producer on our side, we couldn't get a channel to bite.

4 A long time in hip-hop being about three months.

Dan hooked up the interview, putting part of it aside for *HHC*, and the rest for us. It was brief, but it was very punchy, with Em threatening fellow white rapper Cage.

"I'm gonna beat the shit outta him. You can print that. I hear he's still running around talking shit about me. This dude is gonna get his ass whipped. Fuck the rap shit, this dude is taking it personal."

Cage didn't get the shit beat out of him, but we got our cover. Elsewhere in the issue we spoke to Q Bert of the Invisibl Skratch Piklz, Prevail of Swollen Members, the Mountain Brothers delivered a guide to Philadelphia and Mighty Mi and Mr Eon of High & Mighty gave us the rundown on their favourite porn films. In response to the endless lavish car shots in US rap mags, we did 'Saab Story – UK rappers & their rides'. Blade showed us his travelcard, Krispy introduced us to 'Shaquana, Queen of the Road', their C-Reg 1985 Volvo 360 GL.

'Rapperz R N Day Jobz', a pun on KRS ONE's track *Rapperz R N Danja* (hip-hop spelling is basically fucked at this point), had indie darlings Unspoken Heard and Raw Produce telling us about their day jobs as VP of Technical Services, Account Manager, Product Manager and Teacher of Maths and Science to 7th graders.

The *Fat Lace* squad were overflowing with ideas for this one. We did the world's first ever Wu-Tang Name Generator[5], before the Internet copied it. We asked three women who worked in the media to review love and sex related songs by male rappers. Each song was marked out of 10 for 'crapness', 'misogyny', 'romance', 'sickliness' and, erm 'wetness'. Unsurprisingly, they hated Necro's *STD*, but were sliding off the sofa (their words, not mine) at Eric B & Rakim's *Mahogany*.

---

5 483? True Shit Child. 355? 36th Rugged Jesus. The accuracy is 100%.

Other hot scoops? Scaramanga told us his real name is Phil Colling-ton. Del tha Funkee Homosapien talked about his love of video games while not rising to our bait about the ZX Spectrum. Non Phixion's Sabac revealed that he likes, "Filipino ladies. I like women with nice hands and painted fingernails around 37 years old." Elsewhere, there was lots of made-up stuff, such as the continued adventures of Mike Hard's Drama Addicts Club and the debut of Bill Rhodes Rap Agent – "the 8th biggest rap agent in southeast Cardiff" – who looked weirdly like Dan in a Will Smith 'Big Willie Style' hat, but was actually written by debutant Ben Isaacs.

Having been called the 'rap version of *Viz*' by several people, we leaned into it and did our version of their incredible fake collectibles (already a parody of real-life shit collectibles), with an ad for a Roxanne Shante doll, 'individually hand-numbered by someone who knew MC Shan'. I am incredibly proud of this issue. It looked good, it read well and it was completely unique. However, how it looked was going to cause us some problems when we arrived in New York that year.

For a change, we didn't cram every single available moment with an interview or a visit to some far-flung rapper's house. We were letting the trip breathe a bit, but we had a few things lined up. I was with Dan, Mike and Pete Cashmore, who was a colleague from my day job but had also started contributing to *Fat Lace*. We were taking the tried and tested approach of sharing two beds in one room. Pete was really my friend – and could be a bit difficult[6] – so I shared with him.

The trip got off to a great start. We swung by record labels and sorted out some interviews and studio visits. We dropped *Fat Lace* off at vari-ous places, and we made sure we had guest list for one of the shows of the year. Lamont Coleman, better known as Big L, had been shot dead in February of 1999. We were all huge fans of his, and a tribute concert

---

6 To say the least. He has a chapter all his own coming up.

had been organised to celebrate his memory at Tramps in NYC. Some of his DITC crew would be performing, as were Gang Starr. The crew from Fat Beats records invited us along.

All four of us went, but soon we were down to two. Mike had headed off with his camera to capture the event. Dan had got a very badly-timed bout of diarrhoea and performed a rapid 180 almost as soon as we got into Tramps, heading back to our hotel to spend the night on the toilet. In retrospect, I envied him.

That left Pete and myself to rattle around until the show started. The Fat Beats guys got us into a VIP area, but then left to work the room. We ordered beers and waited for the fun to begin. There was to be no fun, as five men descended on Pete and I and formed a small circle around us. Your standard rap show taxing or beat down? Nope. This was the entire editorial team of *ego trip*.

I've said it before, and it bears repeating. *ego trip* was one of my favourite magazines of all time. I'd written that Lord Sear piece for them, and I was also trying to contact a long-lost British punk star for another feature they'd wanted from me. When we'd gone to their office, we'd hit it off well – another bunch of rap journos who wanted to do things differently. Who wanted to celebrate obscure artists, make jokes, be funny, shake things up. The guy I always met up with was Jeff Mao, and we'd leave the *ego trip* office – yes, the one where the Biz doll from Master Ace's *Me and the Biz* video lived – laden with promos he'd passed along to us.

We'd had a bit of a mutual appreciation society going on, and we'd run an advert for them in *Fat Lace 2*, free of charge. I gave them the title in the *Hip-Hop Connection* rap magazine world cup. But this was not a warm reunion.

Let's take a step back. We didn't just like *ego trip*. We loved it. Our designer Barrie loved it, and the distinctive visual style of their designer Brent Rollins. When we were putting *Fat Lace 3* together, Barrie wanted to pay tribute to that, and adopted some fonts and design styles in homage to them. In retrospect, perhaps it was a bit much, but we ran Fat Lace as a democracy and Barrie was an equal shareholder. He also felt, as we did, that they'd take it as a sign of our admiration for them. Did they? They did not.

As the *ego trip* team of five surrounded Pete and myself, I said hello to Jeff Mao. I did not get a warm response. One of them, Gabriel Alvarez, pushed me in the chest. I still didn't know what the problem was. I soon did. Jeff told me that *Fat Lace* had bitten their style. We'd stolen their font. He actually said that – we'd stolen their font. I tried to explain it was a homage, that our designer Barrie Bee loved their style. I can't remember which one of them it was, but an actual adult human male said the sentence "Barrie Bee? The B is for biter," to me. I would have laughed if the current situation hadn't held the real possibility of five men stomping the shit out of us. Pete was also getting pushed, and so I told Mao that Pete had nothing to do with the magazine, that it was on me. Dan, redecorating a hotel toilet, was getting off very lightly. Mike was having a fine night.

I managed to diffuse the situation. No-one threw a punch. I mean, let's be real, little Jeff Mao wasn't going to hit a 6 foot 2 man. But their main concern was probably getting tossed out by security for beating up two pasty British journalists. They told us it wasn't just that we'd copied their design – again, homage – but that we were rubbing their faces in it by being in their city. They'd seen the magazine on sale in NY record shops, and they were mad.

When I look at the issue now, I can understand their annoyance, if not their reaction. The Eminem piece, in particular, looks like it could have been plucked from *ego trip*. There's a letter in issue three from someone who worked at Tommy Boy Records in New York, who wrote, 'The magazine for ageing B-Boys is probably the most picked-up magazine in my office. Kinda reminds me of *ego trip*, but with the edge one usually associates with English humour." So yeah, there's some overlap, and I can see why they might have taken umbrage. They could have dealt with it in a more grown-up manner, however.

The situation came to an end, but the evening had soured for us. We knew it could easily flare up again, especially if the *ego trip* crew got a few more drinks inside them, or if the evening got rowdy. We conferred and decided to leave, before the evening had even got started. We hailed a cab back to the hotel, swapping a potentially amazing show to listen to Dan visiting the toilet repeatedly. It summed up the whole evening. We saw no point in stoking the situation, our only response being a short line in *Fat Lace 4*. Our approach of topping and tailing each page with boastful lyrics taken from records we loved continued, and this time we went for a line from the Ultramagnetic MC's 12" *Raise It Up*. Right at the top of the contents page, it reads, "Yo money grip, money grip, yo this ain't no ego trip."

We did manage to rescue the trip, however, and in some style. We wangled an invite into D&D Studios[7], courtesy of Evidence of Dilated Peoples, who we'd interviewed for *Fat Lace* and *HHC* before, and who was recording a new single with his group. We arrived in the evening to find Alchemist working on a loop, DJ Babu trying to perfect a scratch for the chorus and the two MCs, Ev and Iriscience, sat in separate corners writing their lyrics. In these situations you have to strike the balance between not getting in the way and making sure you actually get some material to work with for an article. Luckily, our guests were charming, making plenty of time for us.

---

7 D&D Studios, which was in New York's Garment District, was founded by two friends called David and Douglas. As well as providing a base for countless rappers and DJs – Gang Starr were pretty much at home there, starting from the recording of *Daily Operation* in 1991 and 1992, it's where Jay-Z recorded all of *Reasonable Doubt* – it also gave birth to a short-lived hip-hop label. In 2003, DJ Premier bought the studios from D&D and renamed them HeadQCourterz, dedicated to a late friend of his. It officially closed in 2015.

Between vocal takes, we'd sit and chop it up with the crew, taking photos, sipping beers. At one point, we took some photos in the booth with Ev and Iriscience either side of me, rapt at some killer lyrics I'd just kicked. As if. There was an open-door policy, and visitors included Bumpy Knuckles, Lil' Fame of MOP and both members of Gang Starr – DJ Premier and Guru.

Gang Starr, as you might imagine of such a prominent and celebrated group, had featured in *HHC* countless times, but relations had soured a little bit. In 1998, my colleague Burhan Wazir was given their *Moment of Truth* album to review, and decided on a novel approach. He felt that Guru was lagging behind his partner in terms of contribution to the group, and so rather than give the album an overall mark, he gave Guru and Premier separate ratings, the former low, the latter high.

It did not go down well with readers or, indeed, Guru himself, who had a letter published in the July issue taking exception to pretty much every aspect of the review. I'm a bit torn on this one. On the one hand, it was somewhat disrespectful to separate the contributions of a rap duo, especially such an exalted one, on an album that received positive reviews pretty much across the board. But then again, it also wasn't the worst idea ever conceived of. There definitely have been rap duos where one member has been more talented than the other. It might be that one MC is markedly doper or the DJ is carrying the rapper. Fans and critics have absolutely no problem, it seems, writing Eric B out of history for his leaden scratches while Rakim was busy redefining what it means to be an MC. We all have our favourites, but Burhan's mistake was probably to say the quiet part out loud.

I wasn't sure if Guru still harboured a grudge, but when he came into the studio where Dilated Peoples were recording *The Platform*, he was fine when we introduced ourselves as a team from *HHC*. I asked if he'd be up for an interview during the rest of the week, and he said he'd be in the studio most nights. We'd been invited in again for the following evening's Dilated session, so we set a date. I dropped Andy Cowan a message to say I'd sorted out an interview, and we could theme it around *Full Clip*, the same year's compilation of the group's first decade.

I was always going to ask about the Burhan Wazir review. My run up to it in the piece that followed has me more on Gang Starr's side – "Burhan Wazir's rather misguided review" – but time has softened that stance:

> *Burhan thought it would be a jolly wheeze to break the album review down into separate ratings for rapper and deejay. While no artist is sacred from criticism, his error was in failing to take into account the classical chemistry between Gifted Unlimited Rhymes Universal and DJ Premier. So what did Guru really think?*
>
> *"That was ridiculous and unjustified," he says, animated. "He probably just didn't like me. I'm professional. If I don't like you I won't deal with you. I wouldn't go and talk about you. The only reason I spoke on that whole thing was because other writers and people like Westwood had said they didn't agree with him either. I've also learned that any press is good press. That meant that Guru had some definite relevance in the hip-hop scene today or he wouldn't have mentioned me."*

The interview went swimmingly. We shared some Heinekens and reflected on the past and future of the chain and the star. I was not asked to pass on wedgies to Burhan Wazir. It's one of those nights you reflect on later. An interview with a certified legend. Crew and extended family popping in and out. And seeing a new hip-hop song being created from scratch through to the very end. Of the numerous studio sessions I've sat in on, that's my favourite – and the best track I heard being pieced together as well. Photos aside, I have one souvenir, given to me by Iriscience – a piece of paper with his lyrics for *The Platform*. Flip it over and it's written on the back of a D&D studio timesheet. History on paper.

Despite the contretemps with *ego trip*, *Fat Lace 3* was a big success. We'd managed to secure distribution, so we were now on the shelves of Tower Records in London and HMV across the country. We had momentum on our side and, after a meeting where the entire *Fat Lace* crew crammed into the lounge of my small Greenwich flat, we had ideas galore. Issue 4 was go.

16: INDEPENDENT LEADERS

at Lace 4 and 5 were the most fun you could possibly have putting rap magazines together. Issue 4 came out at the very end of 1999 and, because the millennium bug didn't affect us because it wasn't a real thing, we managed to get issue 5 out in early 2000. The word I'd use to sum up both issues is 'restless'.

That restlessness was in the design. Our decision to overhaul that aspect of the magazine wasn't because of the *ego trip* situation, but something we'd done with every issue already. We'd decided, once again, that the following two issues would have different design approaches and new mag logos to boot, which would feed into us launching a new T-shirt with every issue.

The restlessness was also in the mix of editorial. New issue? New album and single rating system again. New mini columns and space fillers. New contributors. Every one of the editorial team and the writers brought their absolute A-game, and where there'd inevitably been some press-day panic on previous issues – "We've got 1/2 a page left to fill. Ring RA the Rugged Man!" – this time we had more ideas for issues and articles than we had pages. We also had enough following out there to be able to approach artists without the *HHC* imprimatur.

The generous acclaim the magazine had got from newspapers and other magazines meant we were determined to ride the wave while we were still young(ish) and cool(ish) enough to get away with it. That window was closing fast – it always does in magazines – which is why we went full steam ahead with back to back issues. I say 'back to back', they were still six months apart. We weren't Stakhanovites. We had day jobs. We were also realistic enough to realise that there wasn't going to be a publishing house ready to snap us up. EMAP or IPC were not going to come knocking. We served our market well, but we were still niche to an almost exaggerated level.

Case in point issue 4. Inside you'll find fake prison letters 'written' by Slick Rick, an article about members of rap groups who don't actually do anything (apologies to Danny Boy of House Of Pain, Sen Dog of Cypress Hill and 'all of the Lost Boyz except Mr Cheekz') and new regular contributor DJ Yoda's *Ugly People Be Quiet*, about rap's ugliest people.

The Mexican One From Black Eyed Peas
Don't pretend you know his name. He looked in the mirror and
his reflection ducked. His birth certificate was an apology letter
from the condom factory.

We were being kind. J-Zone, before he blew up and started writing for, er, other underperforming UK rap magazines, was a key new writer for us. He wrote a connoisseur's guide to ignorant rap songs[1], while 7L & Esoteric – a full 65 years before they finally got paid off their Czarface project – wrote a guide to their favourite bits of Boston. Ugly Duckling kindly supplied a column too, writing about their working summer vacation touring with the Jungle Brothers. It contained details about Mike G's bowel movements, which was something of a 'scoop'.

Interviews included Vance Wright, Blak Twang, Phife from A Tribe Called Quest – with sporting questions set by our man DJ Mighty Mi – and Thirstin Howl III. We just wish we'd hit upon the wheeze of get-

---

1 We thought we knew a lot of rap, but Bustdown's *Nasty Bitch* was a new one for us. Warning: Contains the lyric "I farted in her mouth and made her cheeks inflate."

ting rap groups to write their own articles for free themselves earlier, rather than us having to transcribe them. The cover was reserved for two legends from two different generations of rap – Pharoahe Monch and Spoonie Gee.

We'd met Monch outside of the Rawkus Records office in New York, for whom he'd recorded a genuinely marvellous solo album. As hip-hop fans will know, before that he was a member of Organized Konfusion, with fellow rapper Prince Po, who together recorded a good debut album (with excellent singles), a brilliant second album[2] (with brilliant singles) and a crap third album (with okay singles). We were hoping to schedule a proper interview with him, but had to make do with chatting to him while he hung out of the side of his car on Broadway. Yep, that's how all the great interviews happen. You might have expected that, as traffic and NY pedestrians roared on either side of us, Monch would hurry his answers and inject a bit of urgency into the situation. As Dan wrote in his introduction to the cover story, that didn't happen:

We just about made it through the interview, although it was a learning process. Ask a question, wait patiently for the considered answer, on average 20-30 seconds and voila. 10, 15, 20, 25…

We didn't even talk to our other cover star, Spoonie Gee, who is crammed into the bottom corner with the caption "wow! Look at how big Phaorahe is!" But we did get an appreciation of him from Aaron Fuchs, Tuff City Records head honcho. It was a last minute addition to the magazine, but one we were keen to hold off on printing for, due to our love for Spoonie.

---

2 Right now you're thinking, 'Kudos to Andrew Emery for not falling back on the tired 'sophomore album' cliche that every other writer has always used to describe a second album.'

Aaron Fuchs is the dictionary definition of divisive, when it comes to hip-hop label heads. He founded Tuff City in 1981, a label that released many seminal rap tracks. Classics by the Cold Crush Brothers, The Fearless Four, Grandmaster Caz and Freddy B & The Mighty Mic Masters were all sought after by UK rap fans when they arrived on import. Many others discovered the label when the important *Electro* album series in the UK licensed tracks by Davy DMX and Spoonie Gee. The label would go on to host other key artists such as YZ, DJ Mark the 45 King, Hot Day and Lakim Shabazz.

It can be hard to judge how record labels do their business sometimes, when your only contact is a rapper who has been fucked around by said label. Tuff City managed to keep many of its artists happy for quite a long time, especially in rap terms but, equally, others had stories to tell of being ripped off by Aaron Fuchs[3]. You never know if they've been a difficult artist to deal with, or whether they were actually screwed. Both are equally likely. I can attest to Aaron Fuchs being very welcoming when we visited him at Tuff City HQ, inviting us to raid his record room, but then again we weren't contracted to his label.

That's probably not his most controversial area of business, however. When we went to his office, he showed us many original studio reels of soul and funk classics, key among them *Impeach the President* by The Honeydrippers. This 1973 single, recorded by Roy C, of *Shotgun Wedding* fame, with a bunch of high-school students, contains a drum break which would go on to become one of the most sampled in the history of hip-hop. It has underpinned classics such as Audio Two's *Top Billin*, Eric B & Rakim's *Eric B Is President* and MC Shan's *The Bridge*. More contemporary readers will recognise it from songs by Dr. Dre, 2Pac, Notorious BIG and Janet Jackson. It has been rinsed to death. The man who owns the rights to it? Aaron Fuchs.

---

3 You can read what YZ had to say about him later in the book. No skipping ahead!

Once sampling stopped being a free-for-all and became a cash cow for lawyers and licensing companies, there was a stampede to buy the rights to some of the most-sampled songs. Whether you feel this is legitimate or not is largely a matter of how much you can actually discern about each deal struck. Did people like Aaron Fuchs pay a fair price to the original artists or their rights owners for the songs they knew to be valuable? Or did they snaffle them up for a bargain price and spend the following years hunting down everyone who sampled their newly owned track? I honestly don't know.

There's a temptation to see every white label owner in US hip-hop as being the rap equivalent of Hesh Rabkin from *The Sopranos*, investing in racehorses and hiring high-class escorts while stiffing the families of the artists he exploited. And, in some cases, there's probably some truth to this. As for Aaron? Opinions differ. Was this a bit of savvy business or an age-old tale of Jewish business moguls capitalising on black talent? Was this a man who put out countless records by rap pioneers who may otherwise have gone unheard? It's a minefield I don't know enough about to tread in. Apologies for sitting on the fence.

What Aaron definitely did do, however, was pen an article about Spoonie Gee. Spoonie, real name Gabriel Jackson, was the nephew of Bobby Robinson, owner of Enjoy Records, one of the earliest and most important rap labels. Robinson came from the world of soul and had produced records by Gladys Knight & The Pips and The Shirelles. Enjoy has existed since the 1960s, but enjoyed – sorry – more success as the home of early rap and electro artists such as The Treacherous Three, Grandmaster Flash & The Furious Five, Doug E. Fresh, The Fearless Four and, yes, Spoonie Gee.

Spoonie was no nepo-baby, however. His *Spoonin' Rap* is a funky slice of 1979 rap simplicity, but as he matured his style kept pace with him, leading to gems such as *Love Rap* and *The Big Beat*. His Tuff City records included *Street Girl* and the international hit *The Godfather*. The latter came out in 1987, which meant that Spoonie had already managed an eight-year long career, at a time when many of his pioneer peers had disappeared for good. Fuchs did one of his favourite artists justice.

> *Was Spoonie the old school's greatest storyteller? Yes. While most rappers of his generation invited you to either rock a party or step up to the mic and compete, Spoonie told you the stories of the street – from the corner to inside the car to inside the bedroom – that the rappers left behind in the clubs. Was he one of the architects of the new rap language? Yes.*

It was a perceptive tribute to one of rap's forgotten, a man whose name lives on only among those who were there to see him or who bought those records in the late 70's through to the late 80's. Spoonie's influence on hip-hop was undeniable, his place in the pantheon a little shakier because most chroniclers of rap can only rely on the same old trio of legends. We didn't want the usual suspects on the cover of *Fat Lace*.

What Spoonie himself would have made of the rest of this issue, who knows? Rob spoke to his man Cesare, a scientist, so we could do some deeply mathematical illustrations about hip-hop's trademarked motion, the head nod. Each of the writers wrote deeply personal battle raps about each other. We invited the don dada himself, Andy Cowan, to be interviewed about his cats, just because we liked the title *Cowan on Cats*. Our comedy writer friends Nat and Chris did a three-part script that purported to be a lost hip-hop soap opera called *Frozen Soaps Songs*[4]. A personal highlight, however, was the centrefold, *Steady Mobbin'*.

You may have heard of Madlib. Rap producer extraordinaire. Col-

---

4 Possibly the most niche joke in the history of *Fat Lace*. Frozen Soap Songs was a publishing house associated with hip-hop label Wild Pitch Records. I don't think Nat and Chris know to this day why we called it that, as they weren't really rap fans.

laborator with MF Doom, J Dilla, The Alkaholiks and many more. Jazz artist, Quasimoto's alter ego, one third of Stones Throw group Lootpack. It's in the latter guise that we met him, albeit in different environs to those we usually meet rap royalty in[5]. We were in Mike Lewis' Belsize Park basement flat, and Madlib, DJ Romes and Wildchild were sitting around the tiny table that sat at the bottom of the stairs. It's a spot where Mike and I had shared many of his freshly ground coffees or recently pounded pesto pasta dishes. Madlib was wearing a mask, as was Wildchild. They'd just happened to arrive on the day we were doing the one and only *Fat Lace* fashion photo shoot.

It wasn't, to be fair, your average photo shoot. We'd been kicking around the idea of showcasing all the rap T-shirts we'd been picking up on our travels, but rather than just put them on models, we decided to theme it. And if you're planning a rap tee fashion showcase, is there any idea more obvious than recreating a botched Philadelphia bank robbery conducted by two formerly feted rappers? No, there isn't.

Steady B and Cool C were Philly MCs from the Hilltop Hustlers Crew. In the mid to late 80's, they had genuine success, with plenty of UK fans – Steady B came to London with his wonderfully named DJ Grand Dragon KD to perform at Wembley Arena at UK Fresh '86, alongside giants of the time like Mantronix and Grandmaster Flash. KRS One collaborated on Steady B's absolutely filler-free 1988 album *Let the Hustlers Play*. Cool C did well with singles *Juice Crew Dis* and *Glamorous Life* and also released a brace of well-received albums. That was as good as it got for them.

Many of the biggest and most beloved rappers of the 1980s never made much real money. Or if they did, it didn't last. By the early 90s,

---

5 To be strictly accurate, Madlib wasn't really rap royalty then. He had a handful of production credits and the first Loot Pack records to his name. His major success was to follow.

Steady B and Cool C had fallen out of favour. They formed a trio with another rapper called C.E.B. which stood for Countin' Endless Bank, bank being slang for money. The title was ironic, because they only really counted one bank – the one they attempted to rob in 1996.

That botched robbery could not have gone more wrong – not for them, but for their victim, Lauretha Vaird. She was the police officer who responded to a silent alarm that went off after they tried to rob the PNC Bank in North Philadelphia suburb Feltonville. And she was the woman shot dead by Steady B as they tried to escape. Many rappers boast about who they've shot, most having never squeezed the trigger in their lives. Steady B has nothing to boast about – he and Cool C were headed straight to death row.

This is another of those things where you have mixed feelings about one of the best days of your lives. For our fashion shoot, I had the idea of us recreating that very same bank robbery, albeit outside of the Belsize Park of HSBC. Barrie had been tasked with creating masks of Cool C and Steady B, and had done a bang-up job. And it's these masks that two-thirds of Lootpack were wearing in Mike's flat as the photo shoot began.

The trio then walked with us to the bank – helpfully closed on a Saturday so we didn't get into actual trouble – where we enacted a highly unrealistic recreation of said heist, complete with my then girlfriend playing said police officer. Between each shot we were changing rap promo tee-shirts, although it's really hard to tell in the finished product as they're all black and XL, like most rap tees. Barrie played the getaway driver, while Rob and I mugged it up as the rappers. In an aside, Dan wore false teeth as a bank teller, and our bag of money was helpfully marked with 'swag' like in all good comics.

The street was quiet, but not all that quiet. In addition to future hip-hop legend Madlib, who seemed to be enjoying himself, passers-by were gawking at some men in masks pretending to shoot a police officer while wearing T-shirts saying 'Swollen Members' and 'Fondle Em Records'. This is not why they moved to Belsize Park.

I was buzzing afterwards. The shoot was fun to do. Mike's photos came out brilliantly. Lootpack appeared to have a good time, and subbed in for some of the photos. My ambivalence only came a couple of years later when I was commissioned by that most august of publications, *Nuts* magazine, to do a piece on the very same robbery.

I had a few friends who worked on *Nuts*, and when they weren't gurning at models and writing lists about Dave Courtney's top 10 most hilarious tortures, I'd get the occasional bit of work. It was usually along the lines of 'Funkmaster Flex's 48 favourite cars' or 'The sexiest murders committed by rappers', but this time they asked me to do a full, serious, investigative piece on the Cool C and Steady B robbery. They offered a decent amount of money and a decent amount of lead time, meaning I could actually do a proper job. And I did[6]. I tracked down the original court documents. I tracked down a member of the policewoman's family. I spoke to the governor of the US prison where Cool C had been held pending his execution for the best part of two decades. I tried to schedule interviews with Cool C, but that ultimately proved impossible. It was, however, enlightening. I learned about the victim's family. About Lauretha Vaird herself, a black woman and single parent. I learned about how tawdry and pointless it all was – some rappers who'd got used to the glamorous life dealing with the end of their rap careers by shooting a woman dead. Their reward was to lose the rest of

---

6 I hasten to add it was all in vain. The piece got spiked before I even turned it in as the commissioning editor realised it wasn't really very them because it wasn't about a) tits b) sports or c) tits in sports. But at least they paid me what is called a 'kill fee' in full, which is more than I can say for Mark Ellen, *Old Grey Whistle Test* and *Live Aid* presenter at tit-free *The Word* magazine who got cold feet about an idea he'd commissioned from me and totally fucked me over after I'd written it twice. *Nuts* in more ethical behaviour than *The Word* shocker.

their lives to an unforgiving prison regimen, forever fighting for stays of execution. And if that doesn't make you reflect on you recreating the day of a woman's death as a comedy fashion photo shoot, nothing will.

Jarring change of tone alert.

The main photo shoot in *Fat Lace 5*, by contrast, doesn't give me any nightmares, but I can't speak for the people who saw it, however. As with many of the best ideas in all journalism, it starts with a simple pun. Remember Color Me Badd, whose hit *I Wanna Sex You Up* had a pretty ingenious hook based on Shuggie Otis' *Strawberry Letter 23*? Yep. Do you remember how they curdled the vaginas of a generation of people – men and women – when we actually saw what they looked like? Well, we weren't going to do that. We were just going to turn 'Color Me Badd' into 'Cover Me Badd' and recreate some of our favourite rap covers. However, we did also do that, because said photo shoot involved me, a 6' 2" man, wearing a swimsuit owned by a woman eight inches shorter and 10 stone lighter than me.

The whole crew assembled – something that wasn't all that common by then – and myself, Dan, Barrie, Yoda, Rob and Mike put a day aside to do our takes on classic album covers. And I use the word 'classic' loosely, because one of the albums is *World Class* by The World Class Wreckin' Kru'. I love a lot of the music on this 1985 electro album, but it's best known now for its status as the first LP to feature the talents of two future members of NWA – Dr Dre and Yella. It's even better known for what the crew chose to wear on the cover, a set of outfits that make them look part Jonzun Crew, part Prince's backing band. Yella wore lace gloves. Dre was clad in something that you might dress a pinata in, but also had a stethoscope dangling around his neck because, you know, he was a doctor. Our budget just ran to shirts, make-up, some gloves for Yoda/Yella and I wore a keyring around my ear to stand in for Lonzo's earring.

The other covers were chosen with equal care. Alliance's *We Could Get Used to This* is a moderately obscure 1988 album, but one we all loved. Why choose this above a thousand other rap album covers with people living the good life? Maybe it's because Alliance weren't allowed to get used to this, what with it being their one and only album. Rob did a great job standing in as the token female on this[7].

Kool G Rap & DJ Polo's *Live and Let Die* from 1992 had always struck us as a silly cover. The duo are in the foreground, balaclavad up, feeding steak to two salivating dogs while two other blokes stand on chairs, nooses around their necks. Are they literally living and let(ting the two fellas at the back) die? Bloody hell, that's on the nose. I can't tell you why our recreation of this involved no meat – perhaps Mike's local butcher was shut on the Saturday in question. Instead we were all set to torch a toy dog in a cover that was otherwise IDENTICAL in all regards. Honestly, you can barely tell them apart.

Lastly, the main event. A cover that I'd personally put in my top 10 of all time. The triptych of Ice-T, his then partner Darlene and DJ Evil E, lined up for his 1998 album *Power*. This is a cover so iconic it has been spoofed by other artists, on mixtapes and on other magazines. But they all did it after we did it, and that's because we did it sexily. The cover's strength lies not just in the imagery, although that alone would carry many a rap album back then. A scantily clad woman holding a big gun, two men concealing something behind their backs – simple but not special. No, the power here lies in the back cover revealing the reverse of the image, with more guns on show, the deceptively simple design and spacing, but also in the word 'power' and how it relates to the image you're seeing. The power of sex. The power of violence. The power of surprise.

The *Fat Lace* remix? The power of retching. I don't think I'm giving too much away to people who've seen the issue to reveal that my girlfriend's

---

7 It has taken me a long time to realise that this book hasn't got any photos in, unlike my last one, so the context may be missing for some people. Tough. You should have bought *Fat Lace 5*, suckers!

swimming costume was splitting my difference. The reverse shows how hunched over I was as the size eight cozzie battled against the frame of a man more accustomed to two bin bags Sellotaped together. I'm not lying, as uncomfortable as this was, I'd joyfully recreate four different rap album covers every month for the rest of my life with these guys.

Our cover star for issue 5 was Milk D, formerly of Audio Two, but then a solo artist following a calamitous fall out with his brother which, as far as we're aware, still hasn't been sorted out. It's a shame, the duo of Milk & Giz were much loved for their two albums, and as part of the First Priority Posse helped bring us such artists as the aforementioned Alliance, Positive K and their sister, MC Lyte. Audio Two recorded one of the most important hip-hop songs ever, the iconic *Top Billin'*, a song so important it has been sampled by everyone from 50 Cent through to Mary J Blige., Dr. Dre and Snoop Dogg. As an example of how these things work, the original beat was based on a sample from *Impeach the President*, which, as we've mentioned, was owned by Aaron Fuchs. Interestingly, it was the way that Audio Two recreated that sample that a) made it so amazing and b) means people have to sample them, rather than the original.

Dan also interviewed De La Soul, but even though they're my favourite rap group of all time, we never really considered making them the cover stars. We just felt it wasn't very '*Fat Lace*' to do so, even though they gave us great answers. Also interviewed for this issue were Quannum, Big Scoob, Mr Complex, Quasimoto and Arthur Baker. A real scoop for us was getting two highly original MCs, Kool Keith and former cover star T La Rock, to chat to each other for a piece. T did the questions, Kool Keith did the answers, and they didn't disappoint.

TLR: So what are your rhymes saying now?
KK: My album answers a lot of questions. It was getting too weird. I had niggas coming to my show with pickle jars. These kids don't know I grew up in the projects. That I grew up in pissy elevators,

motherfuckers throwing couches out the window, motherfuckers
throwing spaghetti on your shoulders out the window.

Shoulder spaghetti. J-Zone was back with more brilliance, conjuring up a list of imaginary posse tracks, followed by a guide to crap TV that included a section on *Ally McBeal* that is basically just a love letter to Lucy Liu. DJ Design delivered a guide to scratching using a zip (or zipper, as our American 'cousins' have it) and DJ Yoda showed off that he'd got an English degree by doing a guide to grammar complete with copious hip-hop examples to make it relatable.

> *Personification*
> *The attribution of human qualities to an inanimate object.*
> *Examples include I Gave You Power by Nas, in which he pre-*
> *tends to be a gun, Stray Bullet by Organized Konfusion, in which*
> *they pretend to be a bullet, and Ouch by the Fat Lace Crew,*
> *where we pretend to be elastic bands.*

We chronicled the 13 separate times that Tupac was shot, with a total of 824 bullets entering his body at one time or another. Shooters included Tim Roth, Dr Dre, his mum, himself, Snoop Dogg, Damon Albarn, Lisa I'anson and Erika Eleniak from *Baywatch*. Speaking of crime, our latest predictor let you put the rapper together with his crime and sentence[8], while our social affairs correspondent Penny Ashfield told the horrifying story of Donny King, a normal man abducted by breakdancers, in a hard-hitting expose called *They Made Me Wear Tracksuits*, written very much in the style of *Take a Break* magazine.

---

8 14-13-04? Eric B gets 100 hours community service for public urination. 19-10-11? Jurassic 5 most definitely deserved the electric chair for chimp tampering.

And that's just scratching the surface of an issue I'm so proud of I could burst. It's crammed with ridiculousness, overflowing with love and reverence for some rappers, while full of porn-mag parodies, a running joke about the questionable lyrical prowess of Group Home's Melachi the Nutcracker[9], the return of Crap Graf and the Corner-shop Terrorist, repeated spoofs of the *Worst Case Scenario Handbook* reimagined for hip-hop, Nat's round-up of lost hip-hop movies (among them, *Crimes and Missy Misdemeanours* and *Breakdances With Wolves*) and a half page that is literally about rap stars with half the normal amount of eyes.

It's a magazine that is at the top of the game when it comes to servicing its relatively small market of loyal hip-hop nerds who have a sense of humour. Who knew it was to be the last issue ever?

---

9 Real-life lyrics: "Yo it's a wonderful world, a world of wonder."

17: CRITICAL BEATDOWN

"F a rip critic". The words of Method Man on *How High*, his 1995 collaboration with Redman. He went on, in the next line, to point out that critics talk about it while he lives it. It's a well-known line, and a well-known sentiment. Obviously, it's one I disagree with.

What's the purpose of a rap critic? Well, for starters, let's take issue with that nomenclature. I might bill myself as a rap writer or a hip-hop journalist, or a combination of the two, but the word critic – especially the way it drips with disdain from the lips of many a rapper – is loaded. Maybe if you just review albums and singles for a living, you're a critic, but most writers also conduct interviews, compose all-encompassing features and thinkpieces. We spend hours pursuing fruitless leads in search of a story and, for those of us who are fans, we do it for not very much money. Yet still we're maligned by rappers, labels and, indeed, many fans. They use the word 'critic' as an insult.

Why is this so? Part of it is that there is no other music culture in the history of the world that has a sense of self-preservation and injustice like hip-hop does. Everyone who writes about it isn't supposed to just be an objective writer or even merely a fan, but a full-time cheerleader. To criticise one artist or one song is to criticise the culture, as though it's still a homogeneous but timid beast that will flinch from every blow. In other words, as far as many artists are concerned, rap music should be exempt from critique.

Now, I see the point of part of this. Maybe back in 1983, when rap was still in its nascence and a pretty much clearly defined culture that encompassed rapping, graf, DJing and breakdancing. When it needed all the help it could get. But by the late 80's, and most certainly by 1995 when Method Man was taking aim at critics, that wasn't really the case. Hip-hop was global by then, selling millions worldwide, a cultural phenomenon that steered not just what people listened to but how they spoke, what they wore, how they shopped. Many rappers were millionaires, fixtures on the radio and on television. What makes them exempt from criticism?

Let's be realistic, all this is, is a fit of pique. It's not my fault that Method Man, a truly gifted MC – and latterly a really good actor too – went from being the darling of fans who loved him all over the Wu-Tang Clan debut album, where he was arguably the standout, to an artist who has never recorded a classic album. He's got some good ones, sure, but while his group mates such as GZA and Raekwon dropped instant classics off the back of the Wu's runaway success, he fell down the pecking order. His debut, *Tical*, had some stellar moments, but was at times a muddy, unfocussed and weirdly mastered mess. And that's still his best album. Feel free to criticise critics for criticising your album, but that doesn't make them wrong.

Rappers have a pop at each other all the time. They record tracks implying that their rivals are rubbish, snitches, homosexual and a combination of all of the above. They say personal things about their mothers. Sometimes they'll actually fight each other. And, occasionally, they'll shoot each other. But a 5p-a-word writer saying that your album tails off towards the end? That's beyond the pale.

I've been a hip-hop fan since 1984, and it has dominated my life pretty much ever since. I tried – and failed – to be a rapper, but I've always known a lot about the music. I've obsessed over artists, labels, liner notes. I've bought thousands of records, CDs, cassettes, been to hundreds of shows, travelled across the Atlantic to interview my heroes, stayed up late at night doing pieces for free because I wanted to shine a light on a rapper I liked. Am I disqualified from doing this because I didn't have a successful rap career? Am I fuck.

I'm not singling Method Man out for any other reason than that he delivered that famous line. He's far from alone in his hatred of people who write about music. The *Hip-Hop Connection* letters pages used to be full of people writing in complaining about an album review. I've disagreed with many myself. But there's a difference between disagreeing with how an album is received and dismissing the person's right to write about it the way he or she sees fit. I've given many a lauded album a terrible review because I didn't like it. An honest writer should be upfront about his personal reaction to music. It's not his or her job to act as a booster for the artist or label, but to put that aside and focus on a visceral reaction to what they're hearing. As long as they're interesting, funny, enlightening or all of the above, job done. Give the same album to another member of the same magazine's reviewing team and you might get a wholly different take. It has always been this way.

Yet artists, fans and readers alike have never been able to get past this. They argue that the magazine has it out for them – when the same magazine has probably given them 10 great reviews and several cover stories before. No, that was the writer. And good on the editor or editorial team for letting the writer do their own thing. I've said this elsewhere in this book, but the editor at *HHC*, the estimable Andy Cowan, never once steered a writer on how to review something. Did he occasionally select an album to send me to review because he knew I'd go to town on it? Perhaps, but you'd have to ask him. A bad review of a major artist whose record label advertised regularly? Never censored, never spiked.

Do music writers have a purpose? Of course they do. Hip-hop magazines were sold and websites were browsed for more reasons than people just wanting news and rehashed press releases. Many of us buy magazines purely for opinion or the quality of the writing. We want the best writers to shine a light on the music we listen to, to take an angle we haven't considered before and to help deepen our experience of the art. Ultimately, what rappers, DJ, producers and labels have to realise is that music criticism doesn't exist for them, it exists for the reader. I've written in-depth, hard-work pieces about albums that people have forgotten about. I've read articles that were much more interesting than the music or artists they were tackling.

Talk about what? Live what? If we take Method Man's point to its logical end, no-one can speak or write about anything they haven't done for a career. So that means we'd have to take him to task for every metaphor or simile he's ever employed that lies outside of his chosen career. Butchery? Woodwork? NASCAR driving? Take 'em all out Meth, you know not of what you speak. Many rap critics are more knowledgeable and passionate about rap than many of the people who do it for a living. It's not a well-paid job, so you'd have to be.

It's not just a throwaway line in Meth's case, as so many are. I've witnessed his disdain for journalists in real life not once, but twice. The first time was in Paris, a rare foreign press trip when he was publicising his second album, the equally underwhelming *Tical 2000*[1] in late 1998. I was ushered into his hotel suite for my allotted 30 minutes, and that rapidly became 15 minutes as he spent the first quarter of an hour giggling to a woman on the phone. He stayed in bed for both that and our desultory interview. The opening quote sets the tone:

"I never like doing interviews so don't even ask me," yawns Method Man. "I hate interviews, man. I hate pictures too."

---

1 Is there a lazier form of album naming than taking an older record of yours and appending a number to the end? Other than self-titling it, no, there isn't.

To be honest, that's a cherished memory compared to the next time we crossed paths.

In 1999, he and Redman released *Blackout!*, a collaboration album on Def Jam. This time the press junket was in a London hotel, and I had the standard 30 minutes lined up. I got zero. Despite being scheduled for the second interview of the day, when I got there, the first interview still hadn't taken place. And nor did it for the next two hours. Instead, the ever-growing press corps fidgeted restlessly while, behind a VIP rope, Method Man and Redman passed spliffs back and forth. Occasionally, an increasingly exasperated press rep would lean over to tell them that the journalists were waiting, and were summarily dismissed with a wave of the hand. After two-and-a-half hours, they still hadn't started the interviews.

At this point, my patience/temper snapped at the lack of basic human decency. I was going to get £125 for writing circa 2,000 words on this duo, having traipsed across London's tube system, sat on my arse for hours, travelling back, then transcribing the interview. Rappers who've just got off the red-eye from New York? They've got an excuse. Artists who are delayed because of studio time/traffic/whatever – fine. Keeping people waiting for hours because you're a bit of a twat? No.

It helps if you've got the support of an editor who knows you can write an interesting and compelling piece about the album and artists without a single quote to work with. Who gives you the latitude to do exactly that, without getting angry that you haven't stuck around for a further X hours to get some mumbled quotes from two stoned rappers. Because he's been there too – he's sat around, recording device in hand, re-reading their questions for the 38th time waiting for someone to perform their part of the unwritten contract.

Armed with that knowledge, sometimes it's easier to walk away rather than be at the whim of artists. Although if you're me, and a bit bolshy, you probably can't resist calling over the beleaguered press person first and saying, in what should be sotto voce but most definitely and deliberately isn't, that you're going and not "waiting around for this pair of twats."

If rappers don't feel the press is on their side – not that it's their job to be so – then you can understand why they treat us like shit. But it's hardly going to fix the problem, is it? I'm not really sure if Jay-Z had taken rap journalists to task in his lyrics, but as he was also rude, late and distinctly unpleasant when I was sent to interview him, I called him what I called him. I'm sure he'd have decked me if he could have understood my accent or cared about it, but all I know is that, as he kept me waiting, an idea for a wholly different piece than the one I'd been sent to write was forming in my mind. One that argued that as hip-hop got bigger, as rappers became superstars, some of them began to treat not only the press but also, by extension, the fans, with disdain. Not a new story in terms of music, but not one that rap journalists often told, even though I knew many of my colleagues were equally angry about the way they were sometimes treated by people they'd given up time to interview.

I didn't have this knowledge at the time – it came later – but the rapper turned TV presenter Xzibit provided the perfect case study for this phenomenon. I first met him at the Loud Records offices in London in late summer, 1996, having travelled down from Leeds. He'd made some waves with his debut single, *Paparazzi*, and his excellent first album, *At the Speed of Life* was soon to drop. He was affiliated with both King Tee and The Alkaholiks, West Coast artists I really liked. The interview was a cracker – he was honest and open, addressed everything with candour and was a completely engaging interviewee. The piece was a doddle to write. The album didn't pull up any trees, sales-wise, but was a good calling card.

When it came to the follow up, 1998's *40 Dayz & 40 Nightz*, I was again pressed into action. This time it was a phone interview, conducted while the lead single *What U See is What U Get* was giving the rapper – real name Alvin Joiner – one of his bigger hits. The interview went okay – it didn't have the chemistry of the first meeting, but phoners can be more difficult. He was, literally, phoning it in somewhat, but it was still fine.

By the time I came to interview Xzibit for the third and final time, some years later, his career was in a different place entirely. Dr. Dre has brought him into the fold for his *2001* album, opening up Xzibit to a much bigger audience, and he was on records with Eminem, Limp Bizkit and Snoop Dogg. He was in a number of films and a regular on TV, hosting MTV's *Pimp My Ride* for several years. Our third outing was a shitshow. It was in the flesh in London, and he was surly, rude and uncommunicative. We all have bad days, so maybe I'm reading too much into it, but he was cynical and monosyllabical in comparison to the hungry, bright-eyed rapper I'd met a decade earlier.

We can all get jaded. By the time of our third encounter, the frictionless journalism career I'd envisaged in London hadn't panned out for me either. I was freelancing every evening to bolster my wage. The Guardian column where I could deliver some weekly inconsequentialities for silly money like Tim Dowling didn't pan out. But that didn't put basic human communication beyond me. I would still fulfil my part of the bargain, because I truly believed then, as I do now, that hip-hop criticism has a place and a purpose.

The late – and very great – Prodigy of Mobb Deep was someone else I got to interview three times, along with his partner Havoc. Prodigy was a tricky man to truly understand, which made him even more intriguing. The early Mobb Deep records might lull you into thinking they were just a duo of ghetto kids with a gift for cold-hearted street narratives and not much else. But then Prodigy would go on to release solo albums with titles like *Hegelian Dialectic* and would happily record records about the UK's queen being a lizard, like a rap David Icke. In other words, there was more to him than met the eye. He wasn't always up for shining a light on this part of his personality in the studio, but peers of his told me he could get deep over a smoke or two in the studio.

He was, in two of my meetings with him, charming, if a bit aloof. He gave good answers to the rote questions. So why is he in the chapter about worst interviewees? Well, because in my third meeting with him, he was fast asleep.

He started off awake and, to his credit, he and Havoc both warned me that they'd just landed that morning on a red eye flight from New York and were running on fumes. He wasn't kidding. Havoc had to carry the interview, while Prodigy's eyes flickered and his head slowly lowered in stages, like someone trying to stay awake on the sofa during a TV show, until he was pushing out some serious Z's. I didn't take it personally or as a slight on my interviewing skills, personality or lack thereof (you'd have to ask him. Although that may prove difficult). He was just knackered. As interviewing experiences go, however, it's more than a bit disconcerting. After I'd done my 30 minutes, I left, Prodigy still counting sheep. I should have offered to tuck him in.

These encounters – occasionally spiky, sometimes disappointing, frequently vexing – do lend themselves to an article, however. Miserable meetings that go wrong can be turned into something fun to write and hopefully to read. And these events, rare as they were in the hundreds of interviews I carried out, were still better than the alternative – a genuinely boring interview.

Whether on the phone or in person, you can tell pretty much straight away if an interviewee is going to be good value or deadly dull. Mumbled, rote answers. Complete distraction. Your heart sinks as you try to inject some energy into the chat and it just disappears. In many cases, you're going to have to tell the editor that this is going to be a 400-word piece instead of the three-pager he's got in his flatplan. In others, you just plug away, forcing answers out of your subject until you've got enough to work with, to shape into something that isn't going to be too laborious to read.

The real shock to me is when it's a rapper that's incredibly fluent and verbose on record, but can't string two words together in real life. They've made a really good album packed with wordplay and engaging topics. You ask them what a song is about and they just say "That's just us keeping it real." Cheers.

One group you might not expect to find in this chapter is The Beastie Boys, but here we bloody well are. I interviewed them in 1998 when they were about to release *Hello Nasty*. Known for being sometimes controversial, sometimes thoughtful, but always interesting, I was expecting this to be an interview to treasure. This was a trio who didn't just make fine and varied records, but who had experienced a lot in a short time, had witnessed the ups and downs of a musical career, and who also did interesting things like publish their own magazine, practise Buddhism and dabble in side projects.

After a long preamble about the group's back catalogue and how important an album *Licensed to Ill* was, the piece takes a turn as I sum up what it was like to speak to them:

Perhaps we might have expected a slightly better interview, one where our more searching questions weren't met with silence or a desultory 'I don't know'. Maybe they've said it all already or maybe they were just being annoyingly disingenuous, but this story was almost replaced at the last minute by the wonderful tale of a man who removed blood from a stone. Monosyllabic grunts don't fairly represent a verbally inventive group and so, faced with the oh-so-decadent luxury of 30 minutes down a mobile phone to Finland, we struggled to come up with something worth reading. Perhaps the group feel they don't need the help of magazines to sell their records and perhaps they're right, but magazines are bought by music fans who want more than just the music – they want to know something about the life of

the group, what else they have to say for themselves. In this case
it wasn't very much…

I'd met Ad-Rock before, interviewing him in the flesh along with Amory Smith about their BS2000 project[2]. That had been an annoying afternoon. They gave stupid answers, did in-jokes and left me with the square root of fuck all to write about. Yet that was a deep and meaningful chat compared to this one. There really was a lot of silence from them. A bunch of questions they simply didn't have answers for. Yes, phoners can be tricky, yes they were on tour, but that shouldn't strike you dumb. It shouldn't make you actively rude.

The very same month I also had a great phone chat with Ultramagnetic MC's legend Ced Gee and met Malcolm McLaren in London, who literally wouldn't shut up and gave me enough stuff for a book. I spent a fun afternoon at the house of Blak Twang, talking football. A fine chat with the Beasties would make it a truly remarkable month for me, personally.

I don't think I've ever been so disappointed. I was a huge Beastie Boys fan. I'd bought every record, every 12", every remix. I thought they were cool. This chat spoiled them for me forever. I know that might sound dramatic, and it probably is an overreaction, but I haven't bought a thing they've put out since. A couple of years ago, my sister-in-law Claire bought me *The Beastie Boys Book* for Christmas. Apparently it's incredibly good. I wouldn't know, I haven't touched it[3]. 26 years later, I'm still too annoyed. I really do need to move past it – one of them has died, for god's sake. Maybe I need to reconnect with what they did so well – make records, not give interviews. A long overdue replay of *Paul's Boutique* might be the place to start.

---

2 It came out on Grand Royal. Like most stuff on that label that wasn't Luscious Jackson, it was pretty rubbish.

3 Claire, I will.

18: BREAKDOWN NEW YORK STYLE

The City That Never Sleeps is slumbering. Hibernating might be more accurate, to be honest. Rebuilding its energy, licking its wounds. Before it comes roaring back.

September 11, 2001. It's about 10.30am, Barrie is in my office and we're booking flights to New York. We're planning to be out there with Mike, Robin and Lucy. We're planning on nothing else but relaxing with friends in the world's greatest city.

Two hours later, we're having a liquid lunch with colleagues in The Lyric pub on Great Windmill Street, when the landlord puts the TV on. We watch repeated replays of a plane disappear into the side of the World Trade Centre. We watch real time footage of another one doing the same. The news ticker at the bottom of the screen tells the tale of more planes, of deaths, of confusion. We watch the twin towers come down.

Late October, 2001. New York isn't just slumbering, it's smoking. We can see the plumes curling up from where the towers once stood even as we walk across the Brooklyn Bridge into the Financial District. It speaks to the scale of it. The ruins still belching out an echo of what happened some six weeks before.

The thrown-up walls surrounding the site are full of Polaroids and posters. Missing relatives. Cries for help. It's awful. The worst thing for me is the bike. Tied up to a lamppost, less than half a mile from the epicentre, covered in two inches of dust. A bicycle someone rode to work, and which will never be ridden home.

I've never seen New York like it. The normally teeming bars where you have to jostle to the front with liberal use of your elbows are hushed. It takes seconds to get served. You can get a table to dine anywhere. What amplifies the sombre mood is that there is a World Series on. The New York Yankees are playing the Arizona Diamondbacks. We head to sports bars to soak up the atmosphere. We are the atmosphere. The city is in mourning.

In the East Village, at a place Mike loves and says is always buzzing, there are about seven patrons, and Mike, Barrie and myself are three of them. A girl comes up to us and gets chatting. She tells us how the city has changed and may never recover. We tell her of course it will. It's New York. She then tells us how it's more important than ever that people connect, and she invites Barrie back to her place for a drink. He declines, he has a girlfriend. She asks Mike next. Same. I get the final invite, I too am spoken for. Normally, this pecking order would be a source of jokes, but we're all too depressed at what she has to say, how she's saying it, the pall that hangs over the city.

I don't believe in much in life. I don't believe in god. Ghosts? Nope. But New York? I believe in New York. I believe in it like I believe in London. That it has a hidden power, an innate energy that drives it. It's a magnet of a place. When people tell me they don't like 'that London', I always think it tells me more about them than it does about London. The same goes for New York. It's a smelly, sprawling mess that's either red hot or clap cold. It's hideously expensive[1]. It can be unfriendly. It can be daunting. It's fucking magic.

There's a whole world out there, but I'm a creature of habit. When you're not rich, I think it's natural to keep going back to places you know you like. I have no problem with couples and families who've

---

1 RIP the days of $2 to £1, says everyone who used to go to New York to buy records in the 1990s.

been going to the same caravan park in Wales or beach in Benidorm for 25 straight summers. When you work all year, you deserve to have a nice time, and sometimes you don't want to take a risk.

I've been to New York, as of writing this, 11 times. Barcelona? 8 times. San Sebastian? 5. There are myriad places I haven't been, and could have gone to – Rome, Prague, Budapest, Venice, Tokyo, San Francisco, all of Australia. I want to go to those places, but equally I also want to go back time and again to places I know I love.

New York in 2001 isn't the city that I know, but it is still the city I love. Wounded, but still upright.

Normally, I'd have scheduled a bunch of interviews to pay for my trip, but not this time. It's nothing to do with the events, it's that I'm not really writing much for *HHC*. From May through to December that year, I contributed a handful of reviews, two interviews and two features. We had the monthly *Fat Lace* page in the back that started in April that year, but most of the time I just organised that, and rarely wrote it.

It's strange, because that is the year when Andy Cowan bought *HHC* from Ministry. Long unhappy with the way they wanted to push elements of the editorial mix, there had been talk of Andy leaving the magazine altogether. I was invited in to chat with the publisher about possibly taking over, but I made it abundantly clear that a) I thought Andy was the best man for the job and b) I agreed with him that some of the editorial changes Andy disliked weren't for me either. I'd have happily taken over if Andy had left of his own volition, but I wasn't looking to swoop in and replace him. And if Andy was to leave, I wouldn't have just wanted to go in and be a yes man.

While I was certainly looking for a mainstream magazine role, I was loyal to the man who had given me my real break. As long as he remained editor, I would remain a contributor. Andy's experience was essential at this point in the magazine's history. He had dealt with the reader backlash to the cover featuring Mariah Carey with his customary grace. In fact, the new owners had been determined to have a woman on every single cover, a policy that crashed and burned after just three issues – there simply weren't enough female rap artists of stature to grace a cover. And especially not ones with new releases timed for the publication date. It was a silly idea, and a battle that Andy won.

New readers arrived, others left – twas ever thus in publishing. Beyond the 50 Cent's and Jay-Z's on the cover, *HHC*'s editorial mix under Cowan was as diverse and sprawling and fair-minded as ever. His editorial policy – a hand gently guiding the tiller – never fluctuated to my knowledge. When he stayed on, I didn't see it as an opportunity lost for me, but as the rightful situation. Andy bought the magazine and became publisher/editor at a time of record industry upheaval and crashing ad revenues that killed hundreds of mainstream magazines. Those last few years of the magazine were, in what was a ridiculously challenging arena, among its finest, with perhaps its best and most unsung writing line-up.

I've never really thought about what I'd do if I'd edited *HHC*, until exactly now as I write this. I've never thought about what writers I'd have hired, which I'd have culled, whether or not I'd have tried to capture some of the tone of Fat Lace, or whether I'd have looked to emulate the US rap magazines of the time. It was never my ambition, because I got to scratch my editorial itch with *Fat Lace*, and for me *HHC* was a place where I could talk to rap's great and not so great, theorise and postulate about the state of hip-hop, and receive a somewhat too small monthly cheque.

I was delighted when Andy bought Ministry out. The final issue under James Palumbo's ownership was January 2001. The February issue didn't exist, with Andy relocating the mag away from the Brutalist Ministry building back to his home in Ely. And for a while it looked like I was going to be all over it. For the March relaunch, I wrote a piece about hip-hop and sex, and ran through the greatest sex rhymes of all time. I spoke to Xzibit for the umpteenth time in the next issue, and the *Fat Lace* column made its debut. And then that was pretty much that. Some single reviews. A piece on bad British rap. A cosy chat with DJ Yoda. I was treading water.

What this interregnum did give me is breathing space. Doing a 9 to 5 then heading home to write up more articles had taken its toll on my personal life, on relationships, on friendships. Writing less let me go out more. No more making excuses when colleagues headed out for after-work drinks because I had to do a phone interview with somebody who had recorded a B-side with the cousin of a guy who once drove RZA's sister to the doctors.

It made for a wholly different trip to New York, despite the gravity of the times. We didn't have the stress of hopping from cab to subway to venture out to a record label office or a rapper's house. No more trekking endlessly in search of a radio station that is tucked away in the back of a garment building behind an unmarked door. Instead, I could row a boat with friends around the lake in Central Park. I could sit on the swings with them and watch the city go by, albeit at a much gentler pace than normal. I could eat a slice of peanut butter cheesecake at Virgil's in Times Square that is so vast and calorific that I visibly grew as I ate it in front of an impressed/worried Robin and Lucy.

There were the usual expensive trips to record and clothes shops across the city to fill our cases, but instead of snatching moments in between work assignments, we could take our sweet time. There were meals in diners, late night drinks in bars. We played pool, we talked shit. I took Barrie to the oyster bar in Grand Central Station and fell off my stool laughing at his very first attempt at eating a bivalve. It actually felt like a holiday.

I think the nature of that trip also let us understand 9/11 in a way that we wouldn't have if we'd just watched the famous footage on television. We got to feel the slowed pulse of the city, the way that the dust was still settling, in every possible sense of the word. You don't want to be a tourist at the site of somebody's else's grief, but we were all people with a passion for New York, and being there let us pay our respects. And while the city was bloodied, it remained unbowed. We also got to meet some of the people in the bars and restaurants who wouldn't let the attack on their city make them cower. If there's any city you back to rise up again and again, it's New York.

19: FOR PETE'S SAKE

'm at a party on the penthouse floor of a generally anonymous office block in Manhattan. DJ Premier is DJing and his partner in Gang Starr, Guru, is also there. We've been invited by some friends from Fat Beats Records, and myself, Mike, Dan and Pete Cashmore have jumped at the chance.

The four of us have spotted a few rappers we know – Scaramanga says hello, Guru has remembered us from interviewing him at D&D studios. What we don't know is that this isn't just an ordinary party. Whoever has organised it has also arranged for a number of girls to attend, girls whose job it is to lapdance for the guests and then offer to take them out the back. One girl jumps onto my lap and whispers, "What can I do for your cock?" I rather ungraciously reply, "Nothing at all, thanks." She slides over into Mike's lap and gets similarly short shrift. As a professional courtesy, I won't mention the name of the rapper who takes her up on a similar offer and disappears 'backstage' with her.

Instead, my somewhat appalled attention is focussed on Pete. I'm talking to Mike when Dan taps me on the shoulder and says something along the lines of, "What the actual fuck?", pointing to the middle of what is passing for a dance floor. I follow his finger to see Pete, in the company of one of what we have to ultimately call 'prostitutes'. She is sitting in a chair, one leg extended into the air, like something out of an amateur dramatics version of *Flashdance*. At the end of that leg is Pete, standing, cradling her calf in his hand and slowly sucking her toes one by one. I catch Scaramanga's eye – he rolls both of his. The rest of the partygoers look either amused or aghast. I'm not sure what I am, although I'm not in the least bit surprised.

On that New York trip, I was with Pete almost constantly. Dan and Mike occasionally went off to do their own thing – like interview Peter Gunz in the Bronx, as you do – but Pete was an ever-present by my side. He was excellent company for that kind of trip because he not only loved doing all the hip-hop stuff – the record shops, the interviews, the pilgrimages to places mentioned on hip-hop tracks – but he was more than happy to do a bit of daytime drinking like myself.

I'd read the words of Pete Cashmore long before I ever met him, something I've only just realised. Reading back through all the back issues of *Hip-Hop Connection* in preparation for writing this book, I found that they'd printed one of his letters on the Biteback page, and then the following month featured a deluge of replies that were all about his letter. This was always the Pete way. He could start a fight in an empty room, but he much preferred starting a fight in a real room with actual people he could fight in it.

I can't write about my life in hip-hop journalism without writing about Pete, however, and I have to write about him in the same way he would do it – unflinching, unfiltered, unrelenting. I never knew Pete to compromise, to take a backward step, to temper his words. And this was all amplified once he'd been on the Merlot. There was no appeal to his better nature because there wasn't much of a better nature once his claret of choice hit his bloodstream.

Here's the best of Pete. Incredibly clever and quick. *Countdown* champion[1]. *Countdown* champion of champions. The most incredible,

---

[1] Most UK readers will know this, but for the handful of readers in other parts of the world, *Countdown* here doesn't refer to my former DJ, Countdown, but to the long-running Channel 4 quiz beloved of mathletes, word nerds and those who chuckle with delight at receiving a Werther's Original advent calendar.

restless source of journalistic ideas I've ever known. Frequently hilarious. Passionate to the point of absurdity. A generous laugher. A really good writer, and a very funny one.

Here's the worst of Pete. Incredibly mean. A complete inability to empathise with other people. A lousy drunk. Mean and aggressive in ways you wouldn't believe. Inappropriately sexual in public. Could dish it out, but couldn't take it.

This is really scratching the surface. Pete deserves his own book.

I met him in my first week in adult publishing. He was upstairs on the American mags, I was downstairs on the British ones. He'd been employed because his editor wanted to meet a *Countdown* champion to see what one was like and liked his confidence. He was not the kind of man to wear that shit lightly. We soon heard tell of each other as hip-hop fans, and he came downstairs to tell me he'd read my stuff in *Hip-Hop Connection*. A friendship began, albeit one tinged with an element of rivalry right from the off.

We eventually shared an office in that same building, but Pete also started to write for *Hip-Hop Connection* after I put him in touch with the editor. I then invited him to write for *Fat Lace*. He became a major contributor – as detailed earlier, we went to New York and shared a room together with Mike and Dan. He stood his ground at the Big L memorial tribute concert when ego trip decided to lose it over a font. He could have just legged it.

Again, however, the Merlot.

Pete's filter was often broken, and he often didn't care what it meant for other people. There were the everyday slights, the way he'd be talking to someone in the pub while glancing over their shoulder constantly, looking for someone else to talk to. Something he did with absolutely no degree of subtlety. He'd always be perched at the fruit machine wherever we went, trying to work out its shortcuts and systems, always with a glass of wine, no matter how terrible the pub's vinous offering. If you tried to engage him when he was on the fruities, you'd get monosyl-labic Pete, phoning in the conversation. But this kind of slightly dickish behaviour is not in and of itself unusual in men who work in the media. Or men, generally. Or, you know, humans.

Our office local, The Lyric in Soho, was not just the scene of many a long lunch, it was also the scene of many of Pete's lows. With its tiny ground floor, even smaller upstairs and Dickensian basement loo plumbing, it was a hub for Soho workers, arty types, actors and the-atre-goers. You might see Pete Postlethwaite there. You might see David 'Bumble' Lloyd do a quick pint before moving on. You might almost throw punches with Woody Harrelson. All under the protection of the rosy-faced Irish landlord, Richard, a Soho character through and through. At that time, let's say the late 90's through to the early 2000's, it was unspoiled. There were no £7 craft beers. You couldn't get any-thing with sriracha smeared on it. What you could get was a pint of Guinness and a sausage and cheese toastie made with bread as thick as a concrete slab. You would leave smelling of cigarettes, even if none of you smoked.

For Pete, it was a place of lunchtimes and ignominy galore. The peo-ple he fell out with. The arguments he started. That time a bunch of graduates from a local theatre school were in there celebrating with their parents and Pete made one cry. He befriended her, invited her to play pool upstairs with us, started getting cheeky, and when it turned out she could give it back, he threw a glass of red wine in her face. Graduation day ruined. We spent the afternoon apologising for him and buying her mum and aunt drinks, Pete long gone to stew in his own funk of feelings.

It wasn't an isolated event, however. A glass of red in Peter's hand wasn't just a drink, it was also a time bomb and a grenade. He'd get more aggressive, and eventually he'd throw it somewhere, at someone. I went to an office party once, hosted by a print company who we used and who were graciously funding the drinks all night. It was in a private room at the Pitcher & Piano in Dean Street, London. I'd arrived late as I'd gone to an optician's to get my first ever pair of glasses. I wasn't happy about being shortsighted, so I went a bit all out and spent £400 on some Gucci frames. I'd been at the party five minutes when Pete spotted me, said 'nice glasses', took them off me and then snapped them. He was already in his cups.

That wasn't the end. My friend Suszi berated him for what he'd done. His response? Throw a full glass of red wine in her face. Her husband Nat, one of my best friends, responded by fronting up to Pete, who promptly hit him. In front of colleagues, they started to scuffle, and I joined in trying to split them up. While I was doing so, Pete saw his opportunity and took a cheap shot at me. Next thing, there are three of us brawling, a scene much uglier than in cartoons where you just see a big ball of dust rolling along the floor and the occasional limb emerging from the melee. This was three out-of-shape men throwing ineffectual blows at each other.

Eventually, others intervened and Pete was bundled out of the party and told not to come back. We apologised to our hosts, who knew of Pete's reputation and didn't blame Nat or me for what had happened. Pete, however, wasn't taking his eviction lying down. He waited outside for a couple of hours, until the party wound down and everyone was making their way home. He tried to start the fight again, and was stopped by a colleague of ours who had the unfortunate nickname of 'Wanker Nick'[2]. Pete then started to shout to everyone on Dean Street at 11pm on a Friday – i.e. a shit-ton of people – that Nick had AIDS.

---

2 Wanker Nick was given the nickname Wanker Nick very, very early in his PRO career. A couple of years later, Nat was showing a new colleague around the office, introducing him to various members of staff. When he stopped by Wanker Nick's area, Wanker Nick introduced himself as 'Wanker Nick'. Until then, we'd never realised Wanker Nick knew his nickname was Wanker Nick.

He screamed it until someone else decided to give him a smack, and he scuttled off. I returned home to find eight messages on my answer phone[3], which started out with him swearing at me, telling me I hit like a girl and on and on until at about message six his tenor changed. At that point, he apologised and offered to pay for my glasses. Pete remains the only adult I've ever exchanged blows with, which seems somehow very fitting.

We remained friends. We worked together on various pieces, and then Pete left for publisher IPC Media, working for the likes of *Loaded* and *Nuts*. He kept up his tradition of having a tattoo inked on his body for every magazine he worked on, a walking LinkedIn profile, and he even sent some work my way. But now he was getting into scrapes with a different crew, and some of my friends who worked for the same publisher would keep me updated on what he'd been up to, who he'd upset, which model he'd been lecherous towards.

We saw each other more sporadically, but we kept in touch. I invited him along to my regular 5-a-side game, made up of some of the nicest people I've ever known – Sean, Pete, other Pete, Kieran, Matt, Ollie, Joe, Viv – and he became the first player ever to start celebrating 5-a-side goals like he'd won the World Cup. In the 20 years the lads have been playing pretty much every single Wednesday night and then going to the pub afterwards, he was also the first – and indeed the last – person to almost get us all into a fight, with a recently released ex-convict and his friends, no less. We spent the evening diffusing that one, buying the drinks once more.

There was a *Countdown* reunion, with former champions taking each other on. Pete was invited. We put together a little crew of colleagues and made a road trip up to Leeds to support him. I enjoyed

---

3 This is back when people used to use their landline phones. I loved to get rappers to record answerphone messages for me, and I had a great one from Lauryn Hill.

being able to take us all to some of my favourite pubs in Leeds. Pete lost, however, and didn't cover himself in glory. He flirted shamelessly with Carol Vorderman, and he submitted some questionable words when better answers presented themselves not only to his mates, but to 95% of the *Call The Midwife* viewing crew in the house. When he gave the word 'rapist' as an answer, when there was a blatant seven word answer for the taking – I say this as someone who is useless at *Countdown* – it was clear he was just being provocative. He prefaced it with, "Not a very nice word this, Carol."

Afterwards, we went backstage to collect him. His parents, who he hadn't seen for months, joined us. They met him with no hugs, no kisses. Just a very frosty, 'Well, Pete, that was disappointing'. You could hear all of our eyes swivelling to look at each other, our looks communicating 'right, that explains a lot of Pete'. Unfair, perhaps, but it's human nature to look for an explanation for someone's personality, a root cause that would make an easy win for any therapist. My one meeting with Pete's mum and dad had me and the several other friends present going, 'Ah, that says it all.' Perhaps they were just reserved, and not all families are the same, but I know my mum would have given me a hug and a kiss before commiserating with me. She wouldn't have gone straight for the disappointment. Keeping it strictly Swiss, I also don't want to blame his parents for what Pete was. We've all had our moments.

Our proper fall out, when it came, was so banal I still can't believe it. We were swapping jokes over text, and I made one about yes, Carol Vorderman. It wasn't very funny, but it wasn't offensive either. Just a silly joke. In 2014, she won 'Rear of the Year' for the second time[4] and I broke the news to Pete. 'Your mate Carol has won,' or something equally bland, I texted. Later on, I followed up with something like

---

4 Harmless fun? Or is the very existence of such a prize a sign of what a truly stupid, cretinous and embarrassing country we really are?

'I'm surprised, as I thought she was like you and her best years were BEHIND her'. Just a stupid pun. Within minutes, Pete had blocked me on every form of social media we'd been friends on. Over that. A man who'd punched me, broke my glasses, embarrassed me countless times, a man for whom I'd spent a decade apologising, He unfriended me over a bum pun.

In *Wiggaz With Attitude*, Pete got a footnote as a 'moronic former friend'. Regardless of that swipe – clearly we weren't on good terms at that particular moment in time – he really liked the book and thawed our detente by dropping me an email about it. We swapped a few more although, like many others, I'd been too burned by friendship with Pete to contemplate ever going further, to try to rekindle what we once had. Pete's approach to bridges was usually not just to burn them, but to act like a retreating army and mine them, before salting the land and slaughtering the cattle.

That was it for quite a long time. Pete was no longer writing about hip-hop. He was having treatment for mental health issues[5]. He was living back in his native Wolverhampton with his parents and writing a column for a local newspaper. He was also, strangely, a battle rapper.

He'd always loved concocting disses – we'd email them to each other at work – and we ended up doing a little battle rap thing in an issue of *Fat Lace* where all the team took a pop at each other. But then he started to do it in real life, and was apparently good at it. But I'm going to have to caveat this.

The kind of battle rapping he was doing – a very popular kind – is one where people battle each other with mostly pre-written lyrics, but

---

5 In retrospect, it was clear he had numerous mental health problems and they were probably the cause of and an explanation for many of his outbursts and less lovely aspects. While mental health wasn't completely ignored in the 1990s and early 2000s, when most of this stuff was going on, it wasn't as mainstream and commonly discussed as it is now.

without music. For me, personally, I don't regard that as really rapping. It's a performance, sure, but one of the great skills of true battle rappers is to tailor their lyrics to the music while reacting in real time to what the other person has just said about them. Calling each other names acapella? It might be very funny at times, but it's too stagy for me to really consider it as hip-hop. That whole thing of delivering a couple of bars then pausing for the laugh or the 'ooooooh' from the crowd makes it more a form of poetry than of rap for me. But then I'm a fussy, contentious bastard. Either way, Pete was made for this stuff, his sharp verbal wit at home in this world. It was a good fit for the fact that he was usually too clever for his own good. It also let him continue to say the unsayable, as he always had, but now with added applause rather than revulsion.

Pete was an excellent writer, an ever-interesting friend and an absolute fucking mess. He was passionate about hip-hop without ever knowing all that much about it, save for some minutiae that he'd use to fuel his funnier pieces. As a hip-hop writer, I never really rated him. As a comedy hip-hop writer, I loved him. He wasn't the man you'd go to for some fresh insight into this music we adore, but if you wanted something controversial, scurrilous and wonderfully crafted with a laugh out loud moment or two, he was your man.

Pete's dead now. He killed himself. Like many friends of his, former and current, I wasn't all that surprised. He'd taken to dramatic pronouncements on Twitter/X, more bridge burning with former colleagues, picking fights with writers – usually female – who worked for outlets he didn't respect, such as *Buzzfeed*. This from an ex-pornographer with a *Nuts* tattoo on his back, which was a bit rich. He'd disappear off that particular forum for a while, then reemerge in fine form, then spiral again and start cursing out people who'd given him support throughout his career. Then it went quiet. The longueurs grew longer. He once spent an entire bank holiday weekend posting abusive messages about Terri White, his former editor at IPC, just because she'd – correctly – advised him to wind his neck in when he was piling in on some young female writer.

I was surprised how much his death affected me because Pete had become a punchline for many of us. A source of 'classic Pete' stories, filed away with former colleagues like Smudge, Badger, Windows 95, Screeny McClean, Cadfael, Ruprecht. And Wanker Nick, obviously. Trotted out at boozy reunions as a source of anecdote. But then the memories came back, the years we spent intertwined. The reality that a peer felt so hopeless he ended his own life. The emptiness he must have felt. Messages flooded in. 'Can you believe it?' 'That's so miserably sad.' 'About fucking time'. 'Whoda thunk it?' Time had not dulled people's opinions about ol' divisive Pete.

I wrote some words in *The Guardian* with some other people who knew him, because we'd both contributed a bit to it in our time, and our old editor, the lovely Malik Meer, thought I'd be able to give an insight into Pete that perhaps other people couldn't. Not half. Writing that piece about Pete reopened some old wounds, but also let me reflect on his friendship – a more combative and spiky one I couldn't imagine. I also didn't hold back, and they printed most of it – just taking out the above anecdote about him sucking a sex worker's toes at a hip-hop party in New York. To be fair, it was a sensitive touch on the editor's part.

One of the lasting mysteries of Pete is that my friend Justin Quirk never met him. They both lived in the same London media bubble, wrote for intersecting magazines and knew mutual friends and colleagues. I'd become friends with Justin through writing for *Arena*, where he was a staffer, and I often regaled him with Pete's latest antics. He'd heard them from other people as well, and lived in equal bafflement that they'd never once run into each other. It's probably for the best – they couldn't be more temperamentally different. Justin has a sincerity that would have felt false if Pete had ever tried it on for size.

He's one of life's good guys, always thoughtful and interesting. He likes to scratch beneath the surface of stuff, to understand it. True to his nature, I showed him an early draft of this chapter – figuring he knew of Pete, but didn't know him personally so would have some distance – and rather than a message saying 'great stuff thumbs up emoji' he came back with some incredibly pertinent and incisive feedback.

He also made me think about something I hadn't faced up to before. I always thought Pete killed himself because he constantly fought everything in life. That he'd backed himself into one corner too many, and found that the only person left there was himself. I didn't know he'd been sectioned before his death but that, too, wasn't a shock to the system. But something Justin said in his feedback really resonated with me.

Pete was very much a product and inhabitant of a world that had disappeared. While he straddled both the middle shelf and the top shelf in his writing career, he lived long enough to see both go the way of the dinosaurs. The career that he'd dreamed of and worked hard to achieve was taken from him by the evolving market. The magazines he read and longed to work for were no more. This is the truth of why he'd rail at young women on Twitter – they were forging a new kind of career in a new kind of media. He was standing still, maybe even moving backwards. That's a big loss to take on the chin.

You've spent your teenage years reading every page of the music magazines, dreaming of emulating your writing heroes. You've seen the arrival of the lad's mags, with their casually sarcastic journalists doing a modern gonzo thing, and you know you've got what it takes to do that. You've then worked your way there, via a stint in porn publishing, climbed the ladder and then… poof, it's gone. The trend has died, the magazines have closed or the budgets have been slashed.

How you respond to that upheaval very much depends on your personality. You can lick your wounds, retrain, segue into a marketing career where your journalism smarts and ability to tell a story that resonates will stand you in good stead. Many writers I've admired have done exactly that. Equally, many of the best writers have disappeared altogether, unable to adapt or, in cases like Pete's, unable to compromise, to smooth off the rough edges that will let you make it a wholly different environment. The behaviour and attitudes that worked in a Soho pub in the 90's and a Hoxton bar in the 2000's don't translate to the here and now, and that's lesson hard learned for many.

As a writer of a certain age, you can either accept that things have moved on or aggressively resent and target the new generation doing things in the new landscape. This is why Pete was bullying women – and it was always women – on Twitter. They had what he'd lost: a future in writing. He couldn't simply be happy for them, to accept that things change, he wanted his old life back. The old certainties that had died out for good reason. I wish he'd been able to turn that anger, that fiercely burning talent of his, in another direction. Ultimately he turned it on himself.

I have numerous friends, who I won't name, who simply couldn't bear Pete. I've got others who could, but they also knew how to deflect his bullshit whenever it reared its head. I've got a friend who wasn't gleeful when Pete committed suicide, but would brook no sympathy for a man he thought of as a bully. It's probably a position Pete himself would have taken. Never compromise. It's easy to reach for the nice words, to gloss over the reality of the person, once they're gone. It would feel dishonest to do that about Pete.

I didn't get invited to the wake. In fact, none of my friends or former colleagues, all of them with their dozens of Pete Cashmore stories, did. It was all people from IPC, with a few mates from the battle rap scene thrown in. Not even a ghost of the past that had formed so much of his life. No pornographers, no hip-hop writers, no Carol Vorderman. Pete had reinvented himself, but he'd stayed pretty much the same. Classic Pete.

20: THE FINISH LINE

We started sketching out issue six of *Fat Lace*. I've still got the flat plan, half completed, with Barrie's addition of a Weetabix breakdancer as a possible logo. We may have had copyright issues to contend with, but it felt right. I've got a printout full of ideas too, based on me brainstorming, sounding out the other writers. I've clearly run this printout past Dan, as he's scribbled on some helpful feedback: "Rubbish. Andy is gay."

To be fair, if half the stuff we had planned had come off, it would have been a cracker. We were going to expand to 64 pages, with Robin becoming the music editor. We had pieces lined up from regulars DJ Yoda, Rat Saunders and Phillip Mlynar, with Stu Egan set to make his debut. The ideas fill three sides of paper, and while I can't even remember what some of them were supposed to be – 'Who wants to be a Chamillionaire?' – but even in its early stages, it was going to be a blast to put together.

After the reception that *Cover Me Badd* got, we had another photo shoot lined up, this time with us recreating the brilliant video for Public Enemy's *Night of the Living Baseheads*. We also talked about recreating Jay-Z and Beyonce's wedding day. We were going to get a psychiatrist to analyse Elliott Wilson's unhinged editorials in *XXL* magazine, in a clear sign we were still happy to beef with *ego trip* alumni. Dan had interviews in the can with Busta Rhymes and Pharoahe Monch, and teased me with these gems:

"I have an article on the terminology for getting shot, an article on Freeway's beard and an idea whereby we select three well-known rappers to be an agony aunt for the Fat Lace Crew. Each one of us gives him or her a personal issue to address."

These all ended up on the flat plan, the latter under the title *Dear Yvette*. He also had a Dilla interview in the bag that was a potential cover story[1], and wanted to write about Cutmaster DC. One of us was going to write a diary about wearing gold fronts[2] for 24 hours. I was going to compile a list of the worst hip-hop reggae tracks ever – shout out The Fat Boys for *Hard Core Reggae* – and do a Rap-A-Lot retrospective, which I remember being very excited about. After our look at UK rapper's rides and day jobs in previous issues, we were hoping to do some interviews with their partners for a feature titled *Rags – Rapper's Girlfriends.*

We were aiming to write some spoof classified ads, conduct a spoof interview with MF Doom where he talked about projects with Status Quo and Barbra Streisand, and include erotic fiction as if written by rappers. Phillip was down to do a piece called *It Must be the Shoes* about famous shoes in rap history. I thought Robin would be the ideal person to do create a 'frustrated wedding DJ' character for a new column, while he and I were going to launch a made-up rap consultancy service to advise people on good rap names:

---

1 We'd sketched out some new and old combinations for the cover. I think my preferred one of Lil' Wayne and Melle Mel would have set the cat amongst the pigeons at Boom Bap Dad's Towers.

2 Gold fronts, also known as grills, are basically pieces of jewellery for teeth. They're largely temporary, although some people have been known to have them fitted permanently. Well-known wearers of fronts include The Rza, Paul Wall and Lil' Wayne. They basically make you look like Jaws off of *Moonraker.*

*Been hoodwinked into calling yourself Guilty Simpson in the last
five years? You could be owed £1,000's. Let our experts guide you
through the mess of Big Poohs, Red Cafes and Gravys into rap
name nirvana.*

Everything else is a bit more sketchy. Many just names we liked in
search of an idea to match. Crap Graf Stencils. Dead Rapper's Seance.
'William Ill – the odds on the next rapper to die'. Hip-Hop record catalogue number sudoku. Keeping up with the Mike Jones'. Sway meets
Suggs (that would have been great). Righteous But Toothless. Only Built
for Cuban Lunks / Ba-dunk-a-lunk: the role of lunks in hip-hop from
Suge Knight to Eric B by way of Lonzo from World Class Wreckin' Kru.

So, I've written this far based on what I thought was the only *Fat Lace 6*
plan. I had this chapter earmarked right at the start, when I was planning
stuff out with index cards, shuffling endless HHC cuttings into chrono-
logical folders. And then just now, looking for another article, I found a
separate plan for *Fat Lace 6* that's almost entirely different. Possibly even
better. I don't even remember doing this one, but it's such a contrast to the
other one there must have been a year between preparing them.

There are still photo shoots planned, but now one of them is us recreating the old Sleeping Bag Records merchandise adverts, the other a reimag-
ination of the Jay-Z and Nas beef. God knows how that would have panned
out. There's the *Fat Lace Beef Generator*, while Lo-Life Thirstin Howl III
was going to deliver a guide to his favourite Brooklyn boosting spots. I've
earmarked four pages for a Big Daddy Kane piece, another two for something called the *Greg Nice Appreciation Society*. Nat is doing *Hip Hop Mysteries of the Paranormal* and Yoda is down for *Neptunes Sheet Music*. My
friend Chris Hayward has had his arm twisted to do a comic strip based on
Slick Rick's *Children's Story*. We hoped to get a make-up artist and someone from the world of fashion to give some UK rappers makeovers. Mike
wishes to explore defunct rap fan clubs. You want more? No? Tough.

For *Dante Up*, we were going to ask Dante Ross to ascend some tall buildings. If that doesn't sell magazines, what will? Apparently we contemplated melting some particularly rare records for a feature that seems somewhat inspired by The KLF. One double page spread offered up the enticing one-two punch of 'What old rappers look like now' and 'What old rappers do now'. Again, other ideas are lost in time, only their names remaining: Misadventures of Talib Kweli. Learn how to scratch with Eric B. God Body. We dress Edan. Westwood Graph. Fay Ripley's Believe it or not. A fake advert for a fake DVD called *Hip-Hop Slags*, taking the mickey out of the *Hip-Hop Honeys* series. Most triumphantly, there's an idea that I still feel could get traction – Where were you when you found out Magoo was a man? RIP Magoo.

The main event was going to be six pages dedicated to a parody of *The Guardian's The Editor*[3] supplement, where we'd do our versions of pieces by other hip-hop magazines. We were going to a page of *HHC* Connections, a *Fatboss* conspiracy piece about Dickie Davies. An article from *The Source* about Made Men. *ego trip's* top ten top tens. *Big Daddy*, *XXL* and *Vibe* were all lined up for mockery too, which I imagine would have ranged from affectionate to quite bitter.

If I combined the two plans, I've no doubt that *Fat Lace 6* would have been the finest issue of a rap magazine ever. Honestly, I have no doubt about this. It would only have sold 2,000 copies, but it would have been wonderful. I'd be reading it back now and thinking 'Ooh, we could get cancelled for that in 2024' about six times per page. Instead, I only have these ghosts of magazines, these foetal ideas. What happened?

Nothing happened, is what. Or, to be more accurate, life happened to all of us. Dan was married, children on the way, trying to make working

---

3 *The Editor* acted a bit like the magazine *The Week*, picking up the most interesting or pertinent stories from around the world and a huge range of publications over the last seven days. They featured *Fat Lace* once, and I also had a review of a Queen Latifah book mentioned as well.

in the UK rap industry work. I was juggling jobs with freelance, commuting all the time. Yoda had gone from being a little-known mixtape DJ when he first met the *Fat Lace* bunch to being one of the most in-demand and brilliant live DJs around. Rob was running his Hip Hop Karaoke night and he too was married, starting a family. Barrie had kids, and had left PRO for a proper job. Mike was running his own record label, having lunch at the House of Lords and still signing everything in block lettering with a purple felt tip. Everyone had bills to pay and people to look after, and earmarking time for a cult hip-hop magazine, dedicating days to silly photoshoots, was no longer a priority.

And I'm totally fine with that, even though I was probably the last person to realise it was no more. I was in denial. I hoped, hopelessly, that everything would click into place and everyone would suddenly free up some time and want to spend it writing comedy columns about rap. In reality, everything else that everyone had to do was more important than making an article called *An ordnance survey map of Jay-Z's face* a reality, as it should be.

Fat Lace didn't die entirely, not for a while. Our old friends[4] from Rawkus Records, Brian and Jarret, had launched a platform called Uproxx

---

4 Dan and I had kept up a cordial relationship with both Brian and Jarret for years after Rawkus, and we even went for dinner with them in London once. Another time, we were invited to Brian's house after a dinner in New York. But let's say I saw them once every six years. When all the Rupert Murdoch / News International stuff was blowing up in the UK media in 2011, *The Guardian* invited me to write a tiny piece about James Murdoch's connection with Rawkus Records, which they titled *When James Murdoch Was a Hip-Hop Mogul*. It's still online if you want to read it, but suffice to say it did not go down well with Brian, who fired off quite a strong and angry email to me. There was nothing in the piece that wasn't already in the public domain, although the sell *The Guardian* added is misleading – I never knew James Murdoch. I could have added some personal details I knew for a fact to be true, but that would certainly have excited News Corp's lawyers, so I left out anything scurrilous. Brian wrote to me that he was surprised I'd sold out a friendship for £500. That was not only a slight overreaction, but also a huge overestimation of how much *The Guardian* paid me for 350 words.

and we transferred the old fat-lace.com site over to there. We kept up the blog for a few years, putting quite a lot of time and effort into it. There was the odd interview, an exhaustive – and exhausting – trawl through all the Roxanne Wars records, some old magazine ideas reheated, photos of glamour models wearing rap promo T-shirts for a regular feature called *Freaky Fridays*. We put audio of some rare and exclusive stuff up there. But we didn't get paid, despite frequent promises, and we probably weren't delivering the numbers that some of Uproxx's other blogs were. And once you know you're not doing another issue and no-one is going to stump up a load of money and no-one has any time left in their lives for a hobby, your heart goes out of it.

And so that was *Fat Lace*. The most fun I ever had. I miss it.

21: GUESS WHO'S COMIN' TO DINNER?

When I first imagined being a writer, I thought I'd be one of those journos joining the press scrum, holding out my dictaphone beseechingly and trying to shout my question the loudest. When I became a music writer, I reckoned that most of my interviews would be deep dives where I got to know an artist over several meetings, like they seem to do in *New Yorker* pieces. They accompany them here, they go with them there. They speak to plenty of friends, peers and colleagues to round out the piece.

This was all highly unrealistic. The vast majority of writers get just about enough money to justify spending a few hours on a piece. Maybe a day or two if it's a feature. The idea that most of us will get to do those eight-page assessments of a career is a joke. If you get more than 30 minutes in a busy hotel lobby while the next writer taps their foot, awaiting their turn, you're lucky. Yet I did get to do one thing I'd never expected, quite often. I got to dine with rappers.

Watching rappers eat is one thing. I've sat in interviews countless times looking on as rappers tucked into a plate of hotel food, a cheeseburger delivered beneath a cloche. If you were extremely lucky, they'd offer you a chip. But dining with them is a whole different matter. It can not only feel like a privilege, or like you're their mate for one night (you're not), but it changes the standard interview scenario.

Artists are less guarded over dinner or drinks. A bunch of people sitting around a table sharing wine or beers and food is much more convivial, and breaks down that interviewer/subject relationship to a degree that makes things markedly easier. Interviews can sometimes be almost adversarial, but rappers tend to relax more over a bite to eat.

Of course, not every meal with a rapper is an interview. Sometimes it's just dinner. Mike, Dan and I were once passing through the Garment District in New York and walked past someone having a smoke outside a building. We all did a double take – it was Godfather Don[1]. We doubled back. Hello, are you Godfather Don? Lovely to meet you, we're a bunch of hip-hop journalists from the UK and we're fans of all the records that we've just mentioned in that footnote. Could we interview you for *HHC*? Yes, why not, shall we do it over dinner tonight?

It turned out that Godfather Don paid the bills not by being a talented rapper and producer, but by designing children's clothes as a day job. He invited us out for some dinner, and told us to meet him when he clocked off. His friend Lance (aka Big Lance) would be joining us. And what a charming evening it was. It wasn't really an interview at all, but just five people hitting it off really well, with Dan and I having to occasionally slow things down to let Don and Lance work out what we were saying in our northern accents. We also got to witness Don being an incredible flirt with several women, both in the street and in the restaurant.

We ate a few times with The High & Mighty[2] – also known as DJ Mighty Mi and Mr Eon – in New York. This was both business and

1 Godfather Don released his debut LP, *Hazardous*, in 1991, and was always a double threat, as good a producer as he was an MC. He later recorded with the Ultramagnetic MC's, put out the superb *Cenobites* EP on Fondle 'Em with Kool Keith and helped outfit countless American children.

2 The Philly duo of Mr Eon and Mighty Mi released their debut LP on Rawkus Records in 1999. *Home Field Advantage* is a veritable who's who of the indie rap scene at the time, with guest appearances from Mos Def, Evidence, Defari, Mad Skillz, Eminem, Cage, Thirstin Howl III, What What, Pharoahe Monch and more.

pleasure. We interviewed them for a *Fat Lace* piece – Mr Eon running through some films for our regular *Movie On Em* feature, as well as grabbing some content for *HHC*. It all went so well we arranged a breakfast date, and then met them again for lunch later in the week. We were fans of their work, but also them. After the group called it a day, Milo (Mighty Mi) moved out to Las Vegas to DJ there, and very kindly let Dan and I live in his Manhattan apartment on one of our trips to New York. In addition to being in a brilliant location, just a block or two from Bloomingdales, it was also the 'Muthafuckin' Spot on Lexington', the place credited on many of their records. The bedroom Dan and I shared had a small booth for recording just off it, the very same place Milo and Eric made many an indie gem, and also where Eminem recorded his vocals for his guest appearance on their 1999 track *The Last Hit*.

My dinner with Dilla – well, with all of the original line-up of Slum Village, to be fair – was more of an interview, but also a whole lot of fun. It was 1999 and despite the fact that their debut album *Fan-Tas-Tic Volume One* hadn't had a proper release, the group already had a cult following. Anticipation was already growing for their much-touted second album, *Fantastic Volume Two*, although this wouldn't see the light of day until 2000. Dilla, then known as Jay Dee, had built a production reputation with work for The Pharcyde, De La Soul, Janet Jackson and A Tribe Called Quest, but he wasn't yet the man who would go on to inspire 'J Dilla Changed My Life' T-shirts.

Instead, he was just a humble and funny dude, making music with his Detroit friends T3 and Baatin. Over an Italian meal that mostly saw three of us chatting while T3 ate all the food, they were comfortable in each other's company, as befits high school friends. They talked about how indie rap has opened rap music up again, about their dream of working with Prince and, because I was conscious that it was the last interview on a long day of doing press, I asked them to tell me five things they hadn't told any of their other interviewers. Their five were:

1. *We haven't told anybody that Baatin's sister sang on the album. She's on Climax which might be the single[3].*

2. *We just did a song on Common's new album[4].*

3. *We're here to do a remix of Jamiroquai's Supersonic. It's gonna be different but we're ready for it[5].*

4. *Q-Tip is doing a solo album and a movie with Danny Glover. Tip scripted it. He's got Mary J. Blige and Eric Clapton in the movie[6].*

5. *Phife just locked down a major label deal[7].*

The other sidebar I did for the piece represented both the highpoint of the evening – and the riskiest gambit of all. The press officer, who dined with us, dropped into conversation the tidbit that my day job could occasionally involve naked women. We ended up, somehow, discussing porn stars and then making porn puns about rap stars. Between us, we came up with Bang Starr, Psycho Lesbian and managed to crowbar in both original BDP members Assmaster KRS One and Scott La Cock. All good fun, until a certain journalist, a few Chianti's in, gets carried away and says to Dilla – then known, to reiterate, as Jay Dee – "If you were a gay porn star, you could be Gay Dee." Tumbleweed.

I don't contend that rap stars are more homophobic than the aver-

---

3 It was the third single from the album.

4 That would be *Thelonius* from 2000's *Like Water For Chocolate*.

5 In fact, the track they remixed was *Black Capricorn Day*. They may have done a *Supersonic* remix, but it hasn't seen the light of day.

6 Q-Tip did indeed release his solo debut *Amplified* later that year, with the first single *Vivrant Thing* dropping only weeks after I met Slum Village. Of the film, which frankly does not sound good, there is nothing.

7 I'm not sure Germany's Groove Attack label was a major, but it did release Phife Dawg of A Tribe Called Quest's *Ventilation* LP in 2000.

age person or artist. You'll know it if they are, because of the nature of rap and how very little goes unsaid, however. Some artists – pieces of shit like Lord Jamar from Brand Nubian – are deeply homophobic and happy to rap and opine about it[8]. I didn't know if the members of Slum Village were, but there was definitely a sudden lull in the chat which had been all bonhomie and good vibes a second earlier. "Erm, how about 'Jizz Markie?" I added hastily, and we were back on track. Phew. Note to self: not everyone thinks you can make jokes about absolutely everything.

The last time I broke bread with a rapper in a professional sense, where I'm actually writing something about the encounter, is with Bubba Sparxxx in the spring of 2004. Bubba (I was going to make this a footnote but then realised I've already done a load in what is a relatively short chapter and frankly that would be taking the piss) had achieved a crossover hit in 2001 with *Ugly*, produced by the one and only Timbaland – who oversaw most of his first album. He'd been unfairly labelled as a stereotypical southern white rapper and, while there are certainly elements of the iconography of his videos – men riding pigs, say – and press shots that play into that, he was also bloody good.

I regard his second album, 2003's *Deliverance*, as an actual classic, which I thought put me in limited, but very good, company. However, I've just Googled it and it turns out critical opinion is in step with me. The usually spot-on Dorian Lynskey gave it a thumbs up in *The Guardian*. Nathan Rabin, who wrote for the website The A.V. Club back when it was an absolute must-read, raved about it. In fact, the only real mixed review I can find is from some guy called 'Andrew Emery' in an obscure magazine called *Hip-Hop Connection*, but we've already covered that.

---

8 Jamar also contends that the holocaust was exaggerated by a factor of 12 because he believes there weren't close to six million Jews living in Europe. He's an idiot.

Suffice to say, I've changed my tune. I love that album. It treads a fine line between inventive hip-hop genius – thanks to production from Timbaland and Organized Noize – and slightly overegging the southern archetypes. But it got away with it because the songs were great, the hooks endless and Bubba brought his very best stuff to the party. In the process, he proved he's no one-hit wonder.

I myself fed into the southern stereotyping, by inviting Bubba to one of London's finest purveyors of down-home cooking, the venerable Bodean's. The idea was to get a man from one of the barbecue capitals of the world to pass judgement on how we get down in the Big Smoke when it comes to smoking meat. At a basement booth, we shared ribs, and Bubba was in his element. He also made a compelling case for the splendour of his second album. Well, after one of my typically wordy preambles:

First albums, given a long genesis, are usually personal outpour-ings of emotion, Bubba saved it all for his second. It's where he gets it off his chest and also digs deep into his background. Is that a fair perception?

"Absolutely," he concurs, reaching for the fifteenth moist towelette to clean up some barbecue sauce. "On the first album, with the Ugly video, the songs were marketed more than I was. With that video I left a lot of questions unanswered because the song and video don't necessarily match. A lot of people yelled 'gimmick' at it and I didn't do a good enough job of elaborating and explaining what it was about. Obviously, anybody with a fucking brain knew that we did some of the things in the video for theatrical effect, to entertain, and that's the whole point. At the same time, there was a real culture represented. Those were real people. I just wanted to go back on this album and fill in the blanks. Paint a more vivid picture of where I come from."

Mission accomplished, as far as anybody who heard it was concerned. It's why many regard it as the first successful fusion of country and hip-hop – sorry, Sir Mix-A-Lot's *Square Dance Rap*. Bubba served up lyrics that talked about the same heartaches and troubles as country musicians, and challenged the men behind the board to find the music to match. They rose to the occasion. And the food? He approved. He confessed that on tour he'd been hitting Pizza Express and Nando's, rather than traditional British food, but also that he enjoyed fish and chips. He'd demolished an order of ribs and burnt ends but made it very clear that, "the best place in the world to get barbecued food is Memphis, Tennessee. That's just a southern tradition." I'm still waiting for the return invitation.

22: THE ART OF STORYTELLING

Way before – almost two decades before – I decided to be a writer, I wanted to be an author. Football players aside, all my early heroes were writers. Before Dickens, there was Douglas Adams. Before Douglas Adams, there was whoever the hell wrote about Chicken Licken and Henny Penny. I can't imagine a life without books and a reading pile that is constantly growing. Fiction, non-fiction, comics – I'm one of the many people who've amassed more of all those than they could hope to devour in a lifetime.

And there's one thing that reading all this stuff has taught me – I can't write it. Well, I can write non-fiction, I'm doing it right now, but I'm one of those readers who is resigned to the fact that I simply don't have a good novel in me.

Ideas for novels? Quite a few. My graveyard of notebooks is full of scrawled ideas, titles, plot synopsis after plot synopsis. But the few attempts at opening chapters I've written are painful to read back. Mangled metaphors, strangled similes, all of it straining for gravitas, instead of just being some writing. I simply don't know what voice to do it in. I've read the 'how-to' guides, the essentials books about plotting, arcs, the stories that all others are variations on, it didn't help one bit.

So if I was going to be an author, there was only one thing for it – I was going to have to do a picture book.

One of the benefits of being a committed record collector – other than having constant amazing music on tap, obviously – is having shelves and racks full of incredible artwork at your fingertips. Hip-hop albums and 12"s with iconic photography by the likes of George Dubose, Janette Beckman and Glen E. Friedman. Indelible logos, stunning graffiti pieces and more. Design work that made the art just as important as the records within – and often much better.

That's the good ones, of course. There were also many that were awful. Hideous afterthoughts, sexist concepts, stuff that showed about as much ability with design software as my work on *Fat Lace* issue one. I chronicled a lot of these in a piece for *HHC* in 1999 called *Deep Cover*[1].

Every time you buy a record you're buying a work of art, and what it comes wrapped in is an important element of the whole product. Of course, many classic LPs have been housed in what looks like cardboard decorated by someone with a splatter gun arse, and some of these great records have been slightly enhanced by the very naffness of the visual element. A great LP is never undermined by the cover, only rendered slightly more human and fallible.

As evidence, I cited my personal pick of the 10 worst rap covers of all time. Well, 10 that I could lay my hands on in my record collection. They included such art abominations as The Dismasters *Black and Proud*, Chill Rob G's *Ride the Rhythm* and Stezo's *Crazy Noise*. Don't get it twisted – I absolutely love all these records. They just have shit covers. My caption for Chill Rob G sums it up pretty well, I think:

> *You are Chill Rob G. You are skill, and have the world at your feet. You have an album tentatively titled Hit the Ground Running, which in 1989 is a spankingly good title. Someone makes you change it to Ride the Rhythm and have some crap pictures*

---

1 *Deep Cover* is the go-to title anytime a hip-hop publication does something about cover art, based on the 1992 Bill Duke movie of the same name. I made a conscious effort not to call this chapter that.

on your LP cover. You spend the rest of your life picking fights
with Snap's Turbo B.

While I had lots of fun making jokes about rubbish cover art, delving deep into symbolic artwork, drawings and serial offenders, it wasn't all negative. For a sidebar, I did a dozen great covers that took in hall-of-fame stuff like King Tee's *Act a Fool*, Biz Markie's *The Biz Never Sleeps* and Ice-T's *Power*. It must have put a seed in my mind. Maybe this was the book? Not shit covers, as much as that would be joyful to put together. No, amazing covers.

Just like Chill Rob G, I failed to hit the ground running. I sat on the idea for a few years, not sure what to do with it. What I should have done, of course, is sit down, write a pitch and approach publishers, but for some reason I put it off. And then, in 2002, I went to Turkey on my own for a week to get over the break up of a relationship, do some reading and work up a pitch for what I was calling *The Book of Hip-Hop Cover Art*.

Kalkan turned out to be just what I needed. I got sunshine, I got time to think after a couple of full-on years in terms of work and my personal life and, unlike the mob-happy trips to New York, I got a bed to myself. I ended up making a bunch of friends out there, a crew of Brits and Danes who I got chatting to round the pool and who I ended up eating and drinking with, before we eventually hired a boat and went out to sea for a party. Among all this fun and gluttony, I planned out my book. What would be in it. What I'd leave out. What I'd write. Who I wanted to interview for it.

Back in London, I put my pitch together, not really expecting anyone in the UK to take a punt on a book about hip-hop, and sent it out to a handful of publishers who put out art, design and music books. Within a couple of weeks, I had some interest, and was invited to a meeting in Canary Wharf at Octopus Publishing.

I couldn't have been more nervous. "Don't cock this up," was the mantra on repeat in my brain. Luckily, the editor I was meeting, Hannah Barnes-Murphy, put me at my ease. She had some important questions for me, but they were very interested in publishing my book. It was early stages, but I almost did a little wee. I'd moved a few inches closer to my dream.

What would the actual structure be? Good question. How certain was I that I could access the interviewees I wanted in there? Pretty certain, with *HHC* on my side. Would I be able to help with the marketing? Most definitely, as by then I was writing for quite a few music magazines, and hoped they'd be interesting in features about the book, or reviews at the very least. Would I help get the rights to the artwork? Oh balls, I hadn't thought about that at all.

That really brought me up short. I could see the book disappearing. Major labels might be relatively easy to contact, but would they give permission? Would they require editorial approval of what I wrote? Would money have to change hands? All the books I'd cited as successful examples of the kind of thing I wanted to do were single-label things like *The Cover Art of Blue Note Records* where the label's imprimatur was a given. What would be really hard is contacting all the defunct labels – and this being hip-hop, that would be most of them. It would be a nightmare to track these people down, and I knew that in many cases it would be hopeless.

Basically, whether or not the book happened was going to come down to rights. Get permission from all the labels and, in some cases the recording artists or the designer or photographer, or wave the whole thing goodbye. This sounded like a lot of legwork, and I'd have to do it. Was this writing or was this spending hundreds of nights trying to get hold of the guy who used to run Urban Rock Records, a label who hadn't put out a record since 1989, to ask if I could use that very same Dismasters cover?

I knew immediately that I could do the book if I confined the book to the major labels who'd probably give permission. I assumed, as did Hannah, that they'd be flattered to be included. But that would severely restrict the book. It would cut the heart out of it, in fact. For me, it was essential that it included not just famous artists from big labels, but also those tiny indie concerns who were the lifeblood of rap. Some of the finest covers were put out by labels with only a few releases, imprints that were never heard of again but whose records were cherished by hip-hop fans. In order to make it definitive, I wanted it all in there.

I sought advice, far and wide, and ultimately found a solution: Fair use. This isn't a book of legal advice, and I'm no hotshot city lawyer – no, really – but fair use saved the book. For the purposes of criticism, I could use whatever artwork I wanted. After all, did *HHC* seek permission when we were scanning covers for my *Deep Cover* piece? No, it didn't. In the same way that countless magazines and newspapers printed pictures of albums, books, paintings, both new and old, often without permission. It would have to go to the publisher's legal team for final judgement, but Hannah and I put our case strongly. I'd be talking about the art, putting it into context, discussing the designers and photographers, the labels, the artists. This should be enough for fair use. It was. The book was back on.

Putting *The Book of Hip-Hop Cover Art* together was, after that, relatively simple. I plundered my own collection, but also borrowed heavily from other friends, mainly Dan. I decided to follow a common-sense chronology, which would allow me to discuss the art in the context of different rap eras, to show how the covers often – but not always – reflected the shifts in rap itself. I wanted to do a chapter dedicated to 'cover versions', the rap covers that were direct spoofs or tributes to earlier covers from other genres. And I wanted to talk about the power of musical art not only with designers and photographers, but with a man I considered to be key to it all. Chuck D of Public Enemy.

Chuck D is my hero, and has been for decades. I'm old and ugly enough to be able to caveat my hero worship, and I've criticised Chuck and Public Enemy in print almost as often as I've praised them. I even put one of their album covers in that *Deep Cover* piece for *HHC*[2]. But before that, Chuck, his crew, the label and the photographers and designers they collaborated with were the absolute masters of hip-hop branding.

The contrast between Chuck's black-Wranglered austerity and Flavor Flav's clock-adorned clowning. That powerful sniper sight logo. The S1W's marching in military formation on stage and in videos, at a time when other rappers had day-glo dancers. It was all of a piece with their music which was challenging, righteous and often contradictory in fascinating ways.

They made great music, they accompanied their singles with thrilling videos, and their covers were the icing on the cake. Chuck D and Flavor Flav standing resolute behind prison bars on the front of *It Takes a Nation of Millions to Hold us Back* is an exercise in powerful simplicity. The cover of *Yo! Bum Rush the Show* is a beautiful symphony conducted by Chuck along with Eric Haze and Glen E. Friedman. The strength of the cuttings collage for the *Black Steel in the Hour of Chaos* single, positioning the group as provocateurs. Hell, even the array of cars on the front of the *You're Gonna Get Yours* 12" made this full-time *Top Gear*-hater want to drive. It all added an extra element to the music, which was already revolutionary.

Chuck, a former graphic design student, really understood what it meant to shape and guide a group's visual identity. The look might not have been quite as important as the content of the records or the powerful vocals he committed to wax, but he retained control of it nonetheless, and used it to enhance the group's marketing. From 1987 to

---

2 It was the cover of *Apocalypse 91*. I stand by that.

1989, no-one used imagery, logos and artwork with the brilliance and cohesion that Public Enemy did. I had to speak to Chuck.

Reader, he said yes.

His ever-so-helpful press representatives explained the project to him, and he was in. The only problem was scheduling. Public Enemy were touring at the exact time I needed to speak to him. Was there a London show? There was. And thus it was that I waited backstage at one of their legendary performances to meet Chuck as he came off stage, pouring with sweat. I assumed we'd do the interview in the dressing room, but he wanted to head back to his hotel to freshen up, and invited me along. He also had a haircut scheduled and so, as he sat getting a fix up in a chair in his hotel room at around 2am, we started the interview.

It wasn't the greatest set up for what I hoped would be a vital part of the book, but Chuck didn't disappoint. He was patient, interesting and thoughtful, giving me exactly what I needed. Unsurprisingly, he also agreed with me in my assessment of the importance of image and record covers to getting Public Enemy's message across.

"You read through a book and it freezes that time. When you see a picture, it brings up the sounds in your head. If you're talking about cover art, you're talking about something that feeds the imagination because your imagination takes it three steps further than the photo itself. A picture can tell a thousand words."

While he didn't regret any of Public Enemy's covers, he did talk candidly about 'terrible covers' and did include his own *Muse Sick N Hour Mess Age* in there.

"You have to understand art is what relates also. The terrible covers of Doggy Style and Muse Sick... relate more now. Doggy Style

is a very profound piece of artwork by dumbing itself down to simplicity where it actually speaks volumes. I've looked at Doggy Style in the years since it came out and thought that shit was a fucking stain. It's a stain that signified a great piece of a period, which is good art, great art. What we talked about earlier, about intentionally trying to do something as opposed to accidental art, the latter happened with Doggy Style."

As I climbed into a cab home at 4am, I was buzzing. I'd met my hero, and I couldn't have wished for a better interviewee. A few nights later, I was invited to a launch of something or other in London by Chuck's press people, who said he'd be there. I walked into a room full of partygoers at 8pm, and caught Chuck's eye across the room. He broke off his conversation and shouted, "Andrew, my man," beckoning me over. To be honest, I would have been fine with dying the same night. I didn't need anything else. My hero acknowledged me. Was I dreaming?

My other interviewees for the book were also brilliant. Jeff Jank broke down the inspiration behind his marvellous artwork and covers for Quasimoto. George Dubose gave up brilliant stories about his time working for the Cold Chillin' roster, putting together visual masterpieces for Kool G Rap and Biz Markie.

To be honest, did this book really need my contextualising and my mini essays about the Golden Age and the indie era? Most books of cover art are just that. However, writers have to write, and I wasn't content just to curate a book of pictures. I wanted it to present my central thesis – an obvious one, really – that cover art reflected the tenor of the times.

Publication was set for 2004. The label appointed a press person to work on the book, while I put feelers out to my contacts at the magazines I wrote for. I was enormously lucky. *The Guardian* dedicated a double-page spread to the book. *Q* invited me to pick my favourite covers for a feature and *HHC* earmarked several pages for a preview. All told, the book got preview coverage and reviews in over 30 magazines and newspapers, from *Entertainment Weekly* in the US to *Big Issue* in the UK. I was interviewed for German fanzines and even got a good notice in *The Source*. I felt very lucky indeed.

Hannah invited me to a party held by the publishers at the Royal Courts of Justice, and told me I could have a launch party for my book. In the end, I called on some favours myself to get the location – the clothes shop Boxfresh on Seven Dials in Covent Garden – and the DJs for the evening. Friends and family piled in, and I wore my left wrist out signing copies of the book. It was all a thrill, although the real thrill had arrived a week or two earlier.

Hannah had called me in for a final meeting at the publishers to hand me my personal copies of the book, hot off the press, to choose just one overused cliche. I'd seen the book proofs, but to hold a finished copy in my hand was something else entirely. I felt like I'd arrived as a writer – like this was the culmination of all my childhood hopes and dreams of being an actual author. Okay, it was largely pictures, but still. To weigh the heft of it in my palms felt incredible. It's a feeling I wish I could bottle.

The weird thing about writing a book is how weirdly disconnected you can become from the process once it's out there. After years of dreaming about it, pitching it, writing it, lying awake at night worrying over the finer details, it's out there in the world and there's not much you can do about it. The reviews were positive, the sales were good but, the odd interview or feature aside, there's nothing else for the writer to busy themselves with.

I tried to get some other projects off the ground with the same publisher, but nothing really stuck, and Hannah left the world of publishing afterwards to make cakes and raise a family. So it was that I didn't come to realise my book was out there in different forms. A European edition was identical, except that it lost the Slick Rick image from the cover and replaced it with Public Enemy's *Yo! Bum Rush the Show*, which was a fitting choice. However, I never got sent one, so I had to buy that one on eBay myself a few years later. It was at least 10 years after publication that I discovered a Japanese edition, with yet another cover. Dan found that one, and gifted it to me. I haven't seen another one since.

I also tried, years later, to revert the rights of the book back to me but, since all the people who'd worked on the book had left the publisher by then, that proved a Kafkaesque task of talking to people in various legal departments and getting nowhere. I was then told that all the proofs would have been destroyed anyway, so I'd have to recreate the book from scratch anyway, scanning every cover all over again. It wasn't worth pursuing. Who's for a part two[3]?

---

3 As is the way of such things, by the time the book went to press I'd either been told about or discovered a load more covers that warranted inclusion. In the years to come, I'd find way more. I'd covered all the great stuff from well-known labels, but one of the joys of hip-hop is that you've never, ever seen or heard everything. 25 years after a record came out and sold three copies in a forgotten corner of the US, it will appear on a blog and you'll fall in love with a record that's going to cost you an arm and leg to buy, if you can even track one down.

23: THE QUESTIONS

Interviewing rappers can be a joy. It can also be a pain. With apologies to Frankie Beverly, it's rarely sunshine and rain. We've covered some triumphs and some horror stories already, so let's take the subject out of the equation and consider the absolute basics of interviewing.

What do you want to cover? What can't you leave the encounter without? It all depends on why you're interviewing them. Most interviews take place to promote something, whether that's a new single, album or tour. No matter what you want to talk about – let's say the subject has said something controversial elsewhere – their PR people will attempt to steer you away from that line of questioning and towards just asking them about the thing they're promoting. You have to play the game, but only to a degree, because that generally makes for a boring chat and a boring piece afterwards.

Don't get me wrong. Readers like to know about an artist's new release or what they've got planned for their live shows and you want to cover those things in full. You just don't want the whole thing to be about that. You want some stuff that provides context, you want the subject to open up and be honest, to perhaps give you a juicy quote to build a piece around. Ideally they'll take shots at someone, which gives you a headline or at the very least a pull quote.

When I interviewed Sadat X, he had a pop at Diddy over an unreleased track that Sadat had recorded with Biggie. As previously mentioned, I chatted with Houston legend and Geto Boy Scarface and he was tearing a strip off his record label for suggesting he needed Jay-Z on a track. Both of those things happened without a PR in sight, as they'd likely have asked for those remarks to be off the record. It's when things deviate from the plan that your interview takes off.

You also want some 'extras' or 'overs'. There are several reasons for this. Firstly, the more material you have, the more you can tailor and hone the piece. You can leave out the dull stuff if you've got lots of gold. You also might need to do a couple of sidebars or box-outs on the page. These are good places for some of the better quotes, or questions that perhaps don't fit in with the overall piece. This is where you can do a box called something like 'Jay-Z on deep-sea fishing' should that have come up in conversation. Your sidebar is also a good place to do an old music journalist standby – the track-by-track breakdown of a new album.

Your track-by-track run through can sometimes be little more than space filler, especially when the artist has nothing to say. "What's the track *Maintain* about?" "That's just about me maintaining, nahmsayin'?" Note – this is a real exchange. If the artist is more revealing, it can be a highlight of the article. Those people who'll talk you through the inspiration for the tracks, the samples they've flipped, the producer they collaborated with. But that's rare.

Another reason for getting some overs is that, as a freelancer, you might be able to use some of it elsewhere. Once we'd launched *Fat Lace*, I didn't do a single interview for any publication without throwing in a few questions that could work in my magazine. As *Fat Lace* was largely a comedy mag, that gave me the opportunity to ask the kind of questions rappers weren't really used to being asked when they did their press junkets. Hey, Jay-Z, what do you like most about deep sea fishing? Note – this is not a real exchange.

So those are your basics of interviewing rappers. Ask them what they're doing, talk about the new album/tour/single, talk about the guests and producers who are on there and try and get in some other stuff to make the piece less dull. The problem is, most of them are exactly that. It's an issue that very few writers are able to overcome.

Let's say that an interview goes very badly. The artist might be uncommunicative or just boring. They may be like the world-famous chef who can't talk about his food, but can conjure up unforgettable tastes on the plate. The rapper might come alive in the booth and on the track, but can't string a sentence together in real life. If your editor has just given you a Q and A format for your piece, there's not much you can do with what you have from your interview. But if you've been given a feature to write, a bad interview can sometimes be more valuable than a good one.

Some of the best pieces I've ever read are where the interview went dreadfully, for any number of reasons. The people who don't understand why they have to answer any questions. The ones who decide it would be fun to interview you instead. The ones who bristle at your line of questioning and become petulant or aggressive. Writers love doing a stitch-up job when someone has been a complete prick. They're lovely to write, just as much fun to read.

When it comes to hip-hop, it's something that British writers have been better at doing than their US counterparts. Maybe it's because we're just horrible people, but I think it's largely because we always had that geographic distance from our subjects. A prominent New York or LA-based writer always runs the risk of bumping into the artist they've just spent a thousand words dissecting in print. That doesn't mean such pieces don't happen, just not with the frequency that they do in the UK.

One thing you really need to make sure you do is record the interview. In my earliest days as a rap journalist, I was trying all kinds of paraphernalia to capture my chats with rappers. I'd be at my mum's house, on the kind of phone you had in the 1990s. That meant no speakerphone, no intrinsic recording device, no smart capability of any kind. Some people swore by a sucker that attached to the back of the earpiece section of the phone and amplified the call through to your recording device. Others relied on cables. I was down at Tandy[1] in Leeds city centre buying everything I could get my hands on, all with the aim of boosting the signal enough to capture the call on my Dictaphone. Again, this was pre-Internet and even pre-digital recording devices.

As a result of this makeshift approach, I botched a fair few early interviews. I interviewed Nine a couple of times, the second time made necessary by the first, which my equipment totally failed to record. I used to get so nervous about one kind of recorder not working that I'd have a back-up. Once digital recorders arrived, I bought one but still had my creaky old Dictaphone as a fall back. A couple of times, I tested my recorder, found it working, then played it back later. After my 'testing 1-2, testing 1-2' there was nothing but static. Great.

When working from home, this wasn't usually the end of the world. As with Nine, you could hopefully reschedule, or if it was a small piece I could often remember enough to fashion an article. But what happens when you're halfway across the world?

As chronicled earlier, free trips to interview rappers were few and far between in my career. I usually paid my own way. But in 2002, Malik Meer – now *The Guardian*'s West Coast Editor in the US – was editing *Muzik* magazine, and he had a couple of assignments for me. The first involved me entering a battle rap competition. I'm still slightly haunted by that night so you'll have to pick up a copy of *Wiggaz With Attitude* to read all about that Guinness-fuelled calamity. The second involved me flying to Puerto Rico to speak to Missy Elliott.

I'd gone from being initially sceptical about Missy – something by which I'm frankly baffled now, and one of the reasons there's a whole

---

1 For younger readers, Tandy was a chain of shops that sold electrical equipment and cables. It is no longer with us, like other things from the 80s such as video shops, Thatcher and racism. That's gone, right?

chapter about getting stuff wrong earlier in this book – to adoring her. She was set to release her *Under Construction* album, which is a marvellous thing, and I'd been invited along with a handful of other UK journalists to meet her at The Ritz Carlton in San Juan. We'd not only get generous interview time, we'd get a day to explore the old town, rooms for two nights at the same hotel, and time to relax in the pools and spa. Yeah, I could get with that.

I flew out in the company of Sandra from the record label, and writers including Hattie Collins (who went on to edit *RWD* and was a great chronicler of the early grime scene, among many other talents) and Lulu Le Vay (DJ, writer, academic and all-round darling), and they were just as excited as me. This kind of trip rarely came around.

We flew from London, changed planes in Miami, then landed in Puerto Rico. After checking into our rooms – obligatory trying on of the fluffy robes after a reviving shower – we had an album listening party to attend.

Missy's just a few hours late – a mere blink of an eye by hip-hop standards, rap time usually being GMT plus two hours, plus a couple more hours to keep the journalists on their toes[2]. She slides into the room, apologises for being late and slips her new album into the CD player.

"Y'all getting this album raw," Missy tells us. "Timbaland hasn't even mixed these tracks down yet, and a couple still need guest vocals." After all the waiting, the CD screws up on the first track and, while they clean it off, Missy jokingly chides the record label

---

2 This sentence, written in 2002, is very similar to one written by Andy Cowan in his generous foreword. Considering he hadn't had sight of this book before very kindly contributing to it, that's either proof of the uncanny or just emphasises the malleable nature of hip-hop time we operated in.

guys for eating doughnuts and handling the CD. No storming
out? No dispatching of minions? Missy doesn't play like that.

We got to spend the promised day in the old town, shown around by the delightful Sandra, and then went back to the hotel for our allotted interview time. Missy was just as charming one-on-one as she was playing to the assembled press corps. I was wearing some sneakers that I was particularly proud of and Missy was very taken with them. They'd literally just dropped and, as she was and is a passionate sneakerhead, she wanted to know all about them. That broke the ice. The rest of the interview? Who knows. It didn't record. Even worse, I didn't realise it hadn't been recorded until I decided to check my device on the plane back to the UK the next day. I looked out the window and wished the plane would just plummet into the ocean. With obvious apologies to my fellow passengers.

You can't arrive home from what is basically a jolly with nothing to show for it. This was a cover story for a successful dance music magazine. The editor had put his trust in me. It wasn't the kind of piece you could blag, glueing together quotes from memory. I didn't think the record label would be too happy about scheduling another interview when they've just picked up the tab for my transatlantic flight, accommodation in a 5-star hotel, along with drinks tab and food.

Would male journalists have come to the rescue in the way that Hattie and Lulu did? Maybe. I'm not sure. But, before we were halfway back across the ocean, those two had talked me out of my panic and had promised to provide their interview transcripts to me. They'd take out the bits they were using, as they didn't want those to be repeated elsewhere, understandably, but I could have everything else. With that and my memory I could fulfil my brief. In the unlikely event either of you is reading this, thank you both. I loved meeting Missy, I loved the interview, it's just lost in the void, so I won't quote any of the things she said – mostly because she didn't say them to me.

24: FRESH IS THE WORD

I thought the New York trips to interview my heroes had gone. For a few years, I'd been somewhat on the sidelines at *HHC*. Not that I'd been sidelined, per se – it was more a matter of me choosing to concentrate on my increasingly busy day job, with all its attendant battles against management and redundancy, with a little bit of freelancing here and there. I'd also grown older, and didn't always have the spare time and energy I'd once kept reserved for writing about rappers into the early hours, no matter what the next day had in store.

I was still writing more than I had in 2001, however, and in 2006 I had regular columns and features galore. I was cooking DMX's hot dogs for *Def Chef* (not the most taxing of recipes), collaborating with Dan on a look back at the '50 Essential Indie Rap Records' and was happily still provoking letters to the editor from readers. But I'd almost stopped interviewing people.

Part of that is that I wasn't as available then as I'd once been. The days when I'd have jumped on a National Express coach for four hours to do a 1/2 page piece on a rap-adjacent jungle artist were long gone. But perhaps I also wasn't as engaged as I'd once been. Andy Cowan had other, younger writers champing at the bit to get on the phone to the latest breakthrough rappers. Was I, after 10 years writing for *Hip-Hop Connection*, putting myself out to pasture?

Not just yet. *HHC* reached its 200th issue in May of 2006, and celebrated with a 204-page special. It's a gem of an issue, and Def Chef cooked a birthday cake to celebrate. The editor had chosen some classic pieces to re-run, along with commentary from the original writers, and I was honoured to have my Oscars evening with RA the Rugged Man included. I contributed a new piece on hip-hop journalism through the ages, and also revisited the Cool C/Steady B bank robbery in a some-what more sober vein than I'd managed in *Fat Lace*.

> *Cool C might have been a victim of sorts – there are whisperings that he and Steady B weren't entirely happy with their manage-ment and they didn't recoup the monies they felt they were owed throughout their career – but tell that to the children of a woman killed doing her job because three men wanted to get other peo-ple's money out of a bank.*
>
> *Cool C's impending death is a sad one – sad that it should come to this; sad that he felt the need to act as he did; sad that he's tarnished the memory of his classic recordings. Sadder still, of course, that it's another senseless death on top of that of Lauretha Vaird, and that it's doubtful that it will lead anyone in hip-hop to question their blind, unreciprocated love for murder and murderers.[1]*

I spoke to DJ Tat Money for that issue, a man who became Steady B's DJ once Grand Dragon KD moved on. He also worked with Cool C before moving on from the Hilltop Hustlers to further success with Kwame. He'd maintained his career while Steady and Cool's took a slide, and he described not only his reaction to his old friend's fall from grace, but why they might have done it:

---

1 This was accompanied by yet another mea culpa, about the *Fat Lace* 'Free Steady B' T-shirts that we produced a limited run of. As I explained then, we didn't really want to free Steady B, we just wanted something silly to put on a promo T-shirt.

"I don't think it would have happened had they gotten their fair share of monies. As an artist you get to a point where you have to continue to look good and if you don't people talk about you. If you have no plan on releasing songs to the public, then you better have a back-up plan if you plan on looking your best in the public eye. And when you're on videos and having money and cars and jewellery, well, it's tough when that money stops. Then you end up selling everything. Thank god for being a deejay, you have nine lives like a cat. Once an emcee is over, it's usually the end."

In October, I started writing the monthly *The Andrew Emery Column*. I am still at a loss as to where the inspiration for the title came from. I got to express my opinions about all manner of stuff in the hip-hop world, and the collective readership probably sighed and thought, 'he's doing that already'. I also started getting the itch to do interviews again.

Never underestimate the power of music to give you energy. At the lowest moments, when you're feeling uninspired, it can still give you a jolt. I got the bus into town to sit in my favourite pub in Leeds and write this chapter. On the way in, I discovered a new track on Spotify, played it three times, shared it with some friends I thought would like it, and now that's a new artist on my radar. 39 years into my hip-hop fandom at the time of writing, this music still gives me joy in spades.

In 2006, I'm taken with a lot of the music coming out by a collective called Justus League. The de facto leaders of the League, Little Brother, had released their second album *The Minstrel Show* in 2006, but were part of a crew that included people like Cesar Comanche, Chaundon, Median and singer Darien Brockington. I interviewed them all for a chunky feature. Few of them are remembered now, Little Brother aside, but it was a passion project, and hip-hop has been full of these cliques that burn briefly but brightly.

Now New York was back on the agenda. Clipse[2] were releasing their second album, *Hell Hath No Fury*, after multiple problems with their label Jive had delayed it repeatedly. *HHC* were invited to the listening party, and I was itching to go. Flights were covered by the label – a rare joy – but we had to sort out our own accommodation. This is when we stayed in Mighty Mi's Manhattan apartment. Big up Milo.

Of course, you don't just get to go to New York to hear an album played in a venue that isn't entirely suitable or built for audio fidelity. I was doing an interview too. I loved Clipse, their rich voices, their swagger, their way of making a tale about selling drugs simultaneously boastful, wistful and regretful. I loved the production from The Neptunes that underpinned it, their collaborations with label-mate Kelis. After their debut *Lord Willin'* came out in 2002, I'd occasionally DJ at a night called *Spread Love* at The Social, just off Oxford Street in London. Clipse's *When The Last Time* was a permanent fixture in my record bag whenever I did my amateurish slot.

Dan accompanied me, and we sauntered into a midtown hotel to listen to the album. In attendance: numerous record label people, some friends of the artists, lots of journalists, and the group themselves. This is the main problem with listening parties – the artists are often there.

This is a double-edged sword. Often, you're told that the group will be present, and you may get a chance to have a drink and chat with them, but then they don't show up at all. You feel short-changed. Realistically, you've missed out on nothing at all as they'd be surrounded by security or shielded by the record label or in some unreachable VIP

---

2 Clipse are brothers Pusha T and Malice – latterly No Malice after he found God – from Virgina. Their early records, mostly produced by Pharrell Williams, are wonderful things, especially the *Lord Willin'* album. Their specialty was in a kind of cold-hearted, numbed look at the world of cocaine selling, and they turned coke raps into an artform. They later split up, with Pusha T enjoying significant solo success, although the duo have started to record together again.

section, but still. Yet it's even worse when they do turn up. Because that's when you've got to show that you like what you're hearing.

If there's no artist there, and you don't like the stuff that's being played, then you've only got the PR people to worry about. You don't want to give the game away that you're about to go back to your room and write something unpleasant. They don't invite you along and give you free drinks so that you can be all honest and scrupulous, after all. But if the artist is in attendance at the unveiling of the new music they've been sweating over for a couple of years, it's a bit trickier. Let's say you're sitting where they can see you. Do you look away as a new track starts, or do you dutifully nod your head. Do you do the screwed up head-nod face that in hip-hop is shorthand for 'this is a banger?' I went to the launch of Eminem's debut album in New York with Dan, and we were spared having to do a facial performance because they didn't actually play any of the album. I've also been at album launches where I've hated what I've heard, and I've either had to fake it, put on an enigmatic face that could mean anything, or just hide near the bar to mop up the free booze.

I really loved Clipse's second album, which made things somewhat easier. There was plenty to nod our heads and screw our faces up to. Good job, as not only were Pusha T and Malice sitting about five metres from us, we were due to join them at their record label offices for an interview the following lunchtime.

I had my questions ready. I had my digital voice recorder and backup Dictaphone ready. Dan was coming as he liked Clipse too. But first, a shopping trip. We headed to the BAPE shop in Downtown New York, and I treated myself to a black and white varsity jacket. It was not a cheap purchase, but I hadn't been to New York for a few years – not since BAPE became a thing – and I felt like treating myself. We went straight from the BAPE store to the offices of Jive Records… and were greeted by one of the Clipse brothers wearing the exact same jacket.

This is not in the same category as saying, "If you were a gay porn star you could be Gay Dee" to J Dilla, but I still felt pretty stupid. Pusha T – for he was my jacket twin – did a double take, then just laughed about it. I should have known better. Clipse were poster boys for BAPE. They wore it, they rapped about it, they appeared in fashion shoots rocking it. That jacket had come out in the shop that very day – but they already had it, because of course they did. If I was trying to one-up them (I wasn't), I'd failed. If I was trying to impress them (I wasn't), that was just a bit sad. I quickly took the jacket off, hung it over the back of a chair, and got on with the interview.

The feature was published in the April 2007 edition of *HHC* and, in times past, would have been accompanied by seven other pieces that month, with a load more in the next couple of issues, all gleaned from the same trip. But times had changed. Instead, Dan and I had spent the remainder of that short trip actually doing some socialising, dining and acting like two old friends in a city that they loved. No more breathlessly tearing from one part of town to the other, no more chasing the story.

I mean, we didn't just meet Clipse. That would have been ridiculously lazy. We also went out for dinner with Brian Brater of Rawkus Records, sitting on a sidewalk table at a charming place in his neighbourhood, before we went back to his place for drinks. Rawkus has tried to transform itself following the implosion of its original model and roster. It was searching for new artists, and had moderate success with the likes of Kidz In The Hall. They'd also pivoted into digital media, and were hosting several blogs and platforms across music and sports. They invited *Fat Lace* to be part of it, which was flattering, even though it was strictly a hosting offer, there was no cash involved. Nor would there ever be. But the meeting led to a 'Rawkus the Inside Story' feature for *HHC*, along with a look back at their original roster. Had it been so long already? It felt like the end of an era. Was my time writing about new hip-hop ending too?

Yes, it pretty much was. There'd be more interviews to come – some of my very favourite ones – but I no longer had the desire to pursue what was new, to go and meet or speak on the phone to the next new star on the block. This didn't reflect a disaffection with contemporary hip-hop. To this day, my go-to playlist on Spotify is *Release Radar*, with a selection of the week's new tracks. Every single week I discover a new artist I really like or someone who completely passed me by when they dropped a few years ago. Me and my friends Rob and Rix share stuff we like on WhatsApp all the time. I've never fallen out of love with hip-hop, although many of my generation have.

I've written about this before, but I think it bears repeating. The Internet, rap forums, Facebook groups, your local record shop – they're all full of music 'fans', mostly men, who hate new hip-hop. They might say they hate 'mumble rap' or 'trap', but they can never really define what these genres are. They still love all their old records, but have fallen into the trap – no pun intended – of thinking that hip-hop should have stopped when they did.

It is, obviously, okay to not like new rap. There's lots of stuff I don't like, and I'm not backwards in coming forwards about it. Equally obviously, there's a huge difference between not liking something and saying it's de facto shit, or saying everything now is rubbish. That's not being critical about music – that's being your parents. They scoffed about hip-hop when you got into it back in the 80's or 90's, and now you're passing on that same small-minded rubbish to the next generation.

If you're happy just playing the same segment of records, going along to the few hip-hop nights where you're guaranteed to hear Gang Starr's *Full Clip* single played, that's good. But don't even attempt to deny that hip-hop is still vibrant, varied and essential. The music didn't grow old, you did. Don't try to wither everyone else's soul. I'm delighted, 39 years after discovering this endlessly entertaining music, to be alive at a time when I can hear fresh tracks from Kendrick Lamar, Rich the Factor,

Devin the Dude, LaRussell, Larry June, Armand Hammer, Curren$y, Step Brothers, Conway and countless more.

I'm just as happy that the UK rap scene has grown and evolved to such an extent that Knucks can release a masterpiece then record a track with US slow-flow don Larry June, that people like Central Cee and Giggs are just as exciting as Demon Boyz and Hijack were when I was growing up. That the British underground thrives, and my man Whirlwind D, a teacher and family man, can still be on stage support-ing the Jungle Brothers, releasing new albums, while in middle age. I couldn't be happier that this music remains thrilling, important and global. Why do a bunch of people want it to die with them?

What has certainly changed, for me, is my inquisitiveness about the artists themselves. I just no longer have it in the way I used to. Again, I don't think this is being tired with rap or rappers, it's just that I've done it an awful lot. A good decade of being on call day or night to speak to someone for a piece. Turning poor interviews into read-able pieces. Being left hanging by rappers who don't turn up for the allotted time. As you get older, and you get a clearer picture of time's finite nature, you don't want to put aside a portion of what's left to do a phone interview with someone whose music might be good, but you don't really care about.

It was at this stage that I realised I just wanted to interview heroes and legends. And this coincided with *HHC* realising they wanted to do a fair bit of this too. At last, the nostalgia scene in rap was strong enough to sustain a section in the world's first rap monthly – and thus *The Original* was born. It was a shot in my arm.

It took me and Dan back to New York, together in the hip-hop city for the very last time. It was late 2007, bitterly cold, and we had a full agenda. So full, in fact, that we had to split up and conduct our inter-views separately. By now, Dan had his own record label career, so he's got some meetings. We'd get back together for dinner, for drinks, and for a visit to Katz's Deli with Bob Perry[3]. On my slate? Doug E. Fresh, Mr Magic and LA Sunshine.

I met the first of these at Five Pointz in Queens. It was a derelict building that had been turned over to graffiti artists, at a spot close to where the five boroughs of New York interconnected. Even for a graf sceptic like myself it was an awesome sight, sprawling, towering and kaleidoscopic. On the day in question it was getting a new piece, in honour of a special guest. No, not me, but the one and only Douglas E. Fresh. It felt somewhat fitting, because Doug had been a fixture in the hip-hop record racks since the days when graf and rap were intertwined. He made his name as a human beatbox, released key early rap records mixing that artform with rap, and then had a worldwide hit with *The Show*.

There's a nice link between my first and second interviews on that day. In the seminal rap film *Beat Street*, Doug pops his head out of a hole in a backdrop to deliver a beatbox solo in the middle of the wonderful Christmas rap performed by The Treacherous Three. I'd be meeting one third of that trio, LA Sunshine, right after I'd finished with Doug. In fact, he'd drive me there. Unfortunately, he had a prior engagement that evening, and so I was unable to affect a mini reunion.

Doug had stories, as you might imagine. This was an artist who'd grown up inspired by the early hip-hop tapes passed around his school. As a man who rapped under the aliases Kool Kid and Melody Ski before settling on Scam, I loved his tales of his constant name changing in his early rap groups:

---

3 Bob ran Landspeed Records, a label and distributor, that put out numerous indie rap gems in the 1990s and 2000s. Their compilations of Cold Chillin' Records classics are absolute essentials. Bob himself is a good man to share a mountainous pastrami sandwich with as a) he knows how to negotiate Katz's often confusing ordering system and b) he's a great source of scurrilous stories about many of the rappers he's dealt with.

*"I was Dougie Doug, I was Dougie D, I was Law-D. I was playing
with all kinds of names – Dougie Doug the Prince of Love. I used to
sit and just think of names – Christian D and the Criss Cross Crew."*

After settling on Doug E. Fresh, he later added the sobriquet 'The
World's Greatest Entertainer', given to him by that inveterate donor of
names, Chuck D, when they were touring together. He had tales about
the countless labels that had tried to jerk him, about the firsts in his rap
career, about meeting Slick Rick and about such obscurities as his work
with The PC Crew and Boodah Bliss Crew. This is the stuff that made
me want to fly thousands of miles across the world and, later, carry out
the usually tedious task of transcribing the interview.

I'd recently bought a stack of original promo posters for Doug E.
Fresh & The Get Fresh Crew's second album, *The World's Greatest
Entertainer*. I had these with me and, after the interview was finished,
we returned to Doug's car so he could graciously sign all 10 of them for
me. He asked where I was heading next, and I told him I was going to
Harlem to speak to LA Sunshine. I was planning on getting a cab, as I
was cutting it close. He wouldn't hear of it – he was heading past there
to check on one of his restaurants – he's one of those artists who put his
money to work – so he offered me a lift.

Doug was driving an Escalade, and I was sitting in the back. That felt
a little bit weird – it's like he was my taxi driver – but if I can recall he
had a lot of stuff in the front passenger seat. But I wasn't going to look
a gift horse in the mouth – a cab from Queens to Harlem would not be
a bargain, and the editor wouldn't want that particular expense receipt.
And it's not every day you get driven around by a genuine rap legend.
One that's been on *Top of the Pops* and everything. What really stood
out from this journey, however, was the phone call he took.

His phone rang, and he answered it hands-free. It took me a few seconds to tune into what they were talking about – I was initially trying

not to pry, looking out the window and being nonchalant – and who he was talking to. But eventually that voice started to sound very familiar. Who was it? The penny dropped when Doug mentioned his name. Tom. It was Tom Cruise.

Would it have been rude to record the conversation on my digital voice recorder? Yes, it really would. I could imagine Doug pressing an ejector seat button and sending me flying off into the New York sky. So I just sat back on the luxury upholstery and took stock of what was happening. One of my musical heroes was driving me to meet another of my musical heroes while taking a call from Tom Cruise. Tom was asking him if he was able to DJ at a film premiere or a birthday party, I can't remember which. I was wondering how they know each other as they're on first-name terms and both asking after family members. The showbiz scene? Do they share an agent? And then it hit me – Scientology.

Tom Cruise is the world's most famous Scientologist, but Doug had come out as a member of the bonkers church too[4]. In fact, he'd even recorded tracks for a Scientology album that featured other members of L. Ron Hubbard's made-up scam including Chick Corea and Isaac Hayes. As fellow showbiz Thetans, it made sense that they'd know each other. And that is why Cruise was calling up Doug E. Fresh to DJ at his events, rather than calling on, say, DJ Greenpeace or Rob Pursey. And Doug being a Scientologist made a kind of sense too. This is, after all, a rapper who dedicated his albums to god, who once went by the short-lived name Christian D, and who recorded *Abortion*, an anti-abortion track on his debut album. I felt I was in on L. Ron Hubbard's inner circle, but then we reached our destination and I had to miss the bit where

---

4 I'm sticking with 'bonkers church' as my description of Scientology. My friend DJ Yoda would later interview Doug E Fresh at London's Church of Scientology, which must have been weird.

they talked about locking people in trailers if they wanted to leave the church, or whatever they were on about next.

That would normally be quite enough fun for one day, but I had that appointment with LA Sunshine at the Moca Bar & Grill on Harlem's Frederick Douglass Boulevard. It was clearly the day for generous rap legends, as LA brought me something no rapper had ever done before. A present. He gifted me three different Treacherous Three T-shirts, with each one sporting a different likeness of each member – Kool Moe Dee, Special K, and LA himself. It was a lovely gesture. It was a lovely evening.

We sat downstairs with drinks and he told me about a career that started even before Doug E. Fresh's did. He could even date his life in rap back to when MCs weren't the stars of the show, and DJs were.

> *"The first gig we had – I'm not gonna say it was a show – was during rap's conception, really, and it was more about the deejay than the emcee. You were hired to deejay the party rather than to put on a performance for the party. Within our deejay set we would do some beats and rhymes and a coordinated set. We got paid in pizza. We just wanted to get on the mic, say our names a couple of times – that was a level of prestige that other cats weren't reaching. To be able to go behind the deejay booth and pick up the mic at will – that was prestige."*

LA, along with his partners in rhyme, was one of the generation who shifted the power balance in rap. The Three had a DJ – Easy Lee – but their emphasis on performance, lyrics and memorable hooks flipped the dynamic. It wasn't immediately lucrative – they released the seminal and influential *The New Rap Language* single in 1980, and came out with around $300 paid to them in a brown paper bag. They'd go on to have their contract sold to Sugarhill, where they emerged as rivals for Grandmaster Flash and his Furious Five and, when label owner Sylvia Robinson wasn't paying him properly, LA Sunshine walked away from rap.

Well, almost. He kept working in the background with Kool Moe Dee as he pursued a successful solo career, doing his choreography and helping out on his videos. A reunion album in 1994 was warmly received, but it's strange to think that's pretty much that for a rapper and a group that was genuinely groundbreaking. As LA himself put it:

> "Our very first record was *The New Rap Language* and that was the fast rhyme. Cats are doing that now and thinking that they're being innovative. Chuck D said that when he heard it he had to change his thought process as far as becoming an emcee. He didn't want to be run of the mill, and he thought that if that was the level, he had to do something else. Go be a deejay or something. Coming from Chuck D, that's big."

Outside, night has fallen and the cars that streaked past now had their lights on. I'd lost track of time entirely, blissfully listening to stories of the old school from one of its finest practitioners. Tales that might have been told before, but never to me, and never there.

There was one more stop for me on this trip, and it took me to Brooklyn. I headed into a music school that housed a studio where the man I was meeting, John Rivas, was helping to tutor the next generation of local musicians. It's something he knew plenty about, having become the first man to play hip-hop on the radio at the end of the 1970's. Better known as Mr Magic – AKA Sir Juice – Rivas played a fundamental role not just in expanding hip-hop's reach, but as a key figure in such pieces of hip-hop history such as the Bridge Wars, nurturing the Cold Chillin' roster of artists and, oh, so much more.

For many of us in the UK, Mr Magic, along with his rival DJ Red Alert, were almost mythical figures. Between them, they ruled the rap airwaves in New York. If we could get a dub of a tape of one of their shows, we felt like we'd found the Holy Grail. Magic was on air on WHBI in 1979, before most people in the UK had even heard of rap music, before being poached by Frankie Crocker to move to WBLS, the station with which he's synonymous. There, he launched the *Rap Attack* show, co-produced by Tyrone 'Fly Ty' Williams – the co-founder of Cold Chillin' Records, and assisted by rising star Marley Marl[5], who would go on to be one of the most important producers in hip-hop, period.

Magic may have only hosted the show for six years, but you could make a case for those six years being the ones that really cemented hip-hop as a global genre. It encapsulated the beginnings of the Golden Era, and Magic was playing the first songs that were becoming commercial hits[6]. One of those, that I first heard on a compilation my sister owned, was *Magic's Wand* by Whodini, a track dedicated to the man himself.

His career was storied beyond the radio shows he hosted with Marley Marl and, later, Mr Cee. He helped discover groups like The Force MD's as well as Cold Chillin' artists like Roxanne Shante and MC Shan. I saw Mr Magic in the flesh when, as a 15-year-old, I went to the Cold Chillin' Tour show at Rock City in Nottingham. I'd been to hip-hop all-dayers and jams before, but this was my very first proper rap concert. And what a line up. Biz Markie, MC Shan, Kool G Rap & Polo, TJ Swan, Roxanne Shante, Big Daddy Kane. All in their prime. It was

---

5 Marlon 'Marley Marl' Williams is an absolute rap hall-of-famer. He was mixing and producing electro classics as far back as 1983, working with CDIII, Captain Rock and Dimples D. By the mid 80's he was already approaching legend status for his work behind the boards on Roxanne Shante's *Roxanne's Revenge* and his own *Marley Marl Scratch* single. He'd go on to be the sound of the Juice Crew, providing gem after gem for MC Shan, Biz Markie, Kool G Rap & DJ Polo, Big Daddy Kane and more. He was, at the same time, hosting radio shows with Mr Magic. I can't think of many other producers who've been as important and influential in hip-hop as Marley.

6 To get a flavour of Magic's magic, listen to Will C's excellent mix *Down The Dial*, a loving tribute to both Magic and that era of rap radio.

the crew's first tour outside of the US and, as Magic told it, it went how you'd expect it to go:

> "One time we were in Liverpool... I don't know if I should go
> there. Well, we had tried to get some 'ladies of the night', let's say.
> Being that I'm the oldest, me and Ty went and scooped a couple
> of the girls and brought 'em back. I think they were charging,
> like, £20. So we were in the hotel and I don't remember who went
> first. Me and Ty, we did our thing separately. It might have been
> that Kane went first and he gave her the £20 note, but when he
> went in, he took the same £20 note and passed it to the next kid.
> So she went through the whole Juice Crew and by the end had the
> same £20 she started with."

It was the 1980s, kids. Dodgy dealings with Liverpudlian ladies aside, Magic still had a twinkle in his eye as I left him in the studio with a bunch of kids a third of his age, all eager to learn how to sing, rap and produce from this man who had been around the block and back again. He died just two years later, at the ridiculously young age of 53[7]. But then, barely a week goes by without some hero of mine passing away or being murdered in what is barely middle age these days. MF Doom, Biz Markie, J Dilla, The Jacka. It's why it's so important to speak to them when they're alive. To tell their story. To not save the flowers for after they're gone.

---

7 I wrote about it for *The Guardian*, attempting to capture his importance, how it
  spread through generations and how you could even hear Magic on the game *Grand
  Theft Auto: Vice City*. Super Rockin' Mr Magic always stayed true to his motto: No
  more music by the suckers.

25: BUGGIN' ON OLD TV

If you flick through Netflix, iPlayer and Amazon Prime today, you'll find hip-hop content galore. Dramas inspired by rap moguls. Tales of aspiring teen rap stars from all parts of the world. You'll come across rap reality shows, documentaries, retrospectives and more. Add in films starring rappers – T.I. popping up in *Ant Man*, Ludacris heading up a new twinkly Christmas film – and you'd be forgiven for thinking it was always like this.

It really wasn't. As an 11-year-old rap fan, back in 1984, hip-hop on TV was a true rarity. There would be the odd *Top of the Pops* appearance from a rapper who broke the top 40, and patronising little news segments about breakdancing. It wasn't until the late 80's, with BBC2's *Def II* strand, that we got regular rap content on television. Even then, it was so rare you'd set your VHS to record it. At school and in record shops we traded recordings of *Yo! MTV Raps*[1], long before YouTube became the repository of rap video history. What films we had – cash-

---

1 When Yo! *MTV Raps* first debuted on MTV in the US, it was hosted by Fab 5 Freddy, a man whose enthusiasm almost – almost, mind you – made up for his terrible presenting skills. The show got much better when Dr Dre (not that one) and Ed Lover took over. That was the definitive version, with the studio performances and antics as essential watching as the rao videos they presented. We got a different version in Europe, with French photographer Sophie Bramly fronting it. It was endearingly amateurish compared to the US version, but started earlier, in 1987. Bramly would go on to be a notable cultural figure in France, producing a series of feminist erotic films and hosting sex-positive websites for women.

ins like *Breakdance* and *Krush Groove* – had their moments, but weren't anyone's idea of serious films. We adored the breaking battles and rap performances in *Beat Street*, but they were shoehorned in with a pretty dismal plot that doesn't bear close attention.

Perhaps the main reason I was so ambivalent about hip-hop on TV is that I was a relentless nerd. I wanted every rap 12" ever, and I wanted to understand in my mind the links between this producer and that artist, who else they'd worked with. I was the kind of fan who wrote to fan clubs, who compiled personal 'best-ofs' in a notebook, who read every single liner note and dedication on the back of a record. When TV finally gave rap some attention, I felt it did it in the most cursory way possible. It was about exploiting this growing medium, not really trying to understand it in any but the most shallow way.

I think, until recently, all the documentaries made about rap kept up that approach. Even the well-meaning ones, the multi-part extravaganzas, relied on the same stories, the same footage. I can imagine the production meetings where they're making sure they've ticked the Bambaataa box, the Kool Herc box, the Grandmaster Flash Box. Let's get Sugarhill Gang in there, then Run DMC doing *Walk This Way* and Public Enemy's *Fight The Power* is a must. I found this broad brush approach frustrating. I wasn't just being a purist – although of course there was a bit of that – but I felt this was all paper thin. Not because it wasn't a real narrative, which it very much was, but because I really thought this story had been told again and again. Do we have to revisit the same anecdotes repeatedly? What about all the other stories?

It's not like those tales weren't out there for everyone to find. They were in the pages of all the rap magazines. They were in *HHC* and *Fatboss* and *Complex* and *Fat Lace* and *ego trip*. They were on blogs, on message boards. A whole citizen army had done the work of speaking to hip-hop's other founders, forgotten heroes, nearly men and women. And yet we got the same clips of Flash in his tracksuit, the oft retold tale of Bam and the gangs, the tired simplistic leaps from NWA to the Daisy Age to the East-West coast rivalry. It's like picking up an Antony Beevor book about World War II and, instead of his usual deep dive, he skips from Munich to the invasion of France then cuts right to the liberation of same. Where was all the detail? The nuance? Why weren't they talking about Captain Rock? Where were the fans in all this? Hadn't they heard of DJ Doc or Mark the 45 King?

I always swore that if I ever got to be on television, it would be entirely different. That I'd cut through the same old tropes and shine a light on the forgotten and fabulous. This never happened. The TV bit happened, just not the game-changing approach to hip-hop history. Instead, I popped up and did some gags about rappers and tried not to get too red-faced from nerves.

My debut was on the ITV2 show *Bedrock*, a daily live culture show that boasted a very fresh-faced Ben Shephard among its presenting team. It was the kind of show where you'd have a boy band on, some funny business between the co-hosts, Tess Daly would drop in to present a bit and then Dave Prowse from *Star Wars* would be interviewed. I was invited to be on it on the strength of *Fat Lace 2*, which was doing the rounds in limited media circles. They thought it would be a good idea to get a hip-hop pundit on who might potentially be funny.

I don't think I've ever been more nervous, except for when I've had to give best man speeches. But with those I could self-medicate with copious glasses of wine. This time, I had to be sober. Waiting in the wings for my cue to join presenter Neil Cole on set, I was chewing gum to calm my nerves. A producer put her mouth close to my ear. "Is that gum in your mouth? Lose it."

There are a few VHS tapes stored away in the loft, awaiting the probably never going to come day when I digitise them. This is one of them. I remember watching it back when the production company sent me a copy and was struck by the beetroot hue my face had taken on, and the fact that I was talking at 200 words per second. It could have gone worse, but talent agents were not going to be circling me like sharks.

In the same year I was on an obscure tech channel high up in the Sky programme guide numbers. It was a show called *The Lounge*[2] and involved a pretty in-depth interview all about *Fat Lace* with a man I'd never met before called Hari Kunzru. My more literary readers may recognise that name as belonging to a man who, only a few years later, got a £1m+ advance for his debut novel. It was fully deserved for taking my silly little hip-hop fanzine seriously for half an hour. Rather wonderfully, Hari was later awarded the prestigious John Llewellyn Rhys prize for literature, something won in previous years by V.S. Naipaul, Angela Carter and David Mitchell. That's not the wonderful bit, though. It's that he turned it down because it was sponsored by the Mail on Sunday, releasing a statement castigating that paper's history of hostility and prejudice towards immigrants.

The short-lived prominence of *Fat Lace* – we were featured in *The Face*, interviewed and then photographed on top of a London building, which made us feel like pop stars – got Dan and I on to Channel 4 too. They were doing a hip-hop list program, and invited us on as pundits. We took different approaches. Dan turned up sober, I was tipsy. I'd been out for lunch with colleagues, which had turned into an all-afternoon session in The Lyric. I actually felt I'd probably be funnier with a few drinks inside me – the bravado of all drinkers – and it turned out that I was. When it was eventually screened, I got a lot more prominence than Dan, which was a rare occurrence in our shared music industry careers. He's the man who goes on to release music and do a high-profile rap radio show with Zane Lowe. I was just slightly better at telly.

That snowballed – largely due to my friend Anna Abenson, a TV

---

2 With thanks to my friend Robin Delbourgo – better known to attendees of Hip-Hop Karaoke events as host Bobby Champagne Jr. – who worked on it.

producer I knew from various London hip-hop evenings – into regular appearances on TV list shows. Every few months I'd get an email saying something like, "We're doing *TV's 100 Sexiest Moments*, fancy it?" I always said yes. I did several of these, covering music, sport, horror and, yes, sexy moments. They were staples of Channel 5 and ITV in the early noughties, and I was flattered to be invited on, as I was one of the few non-famous faces on there. I'd get a list of everything they were going to feature and I'd get to cherry-pick the things I knew and wanted to talk about. This helped me skip my main objection to some of these programmes – that many of the guests were too young to remember the things they were talking about, and were being spoon fed what they were saying. I felt insulated from this, thanks to Anna, but once she moved companies, I experienced it first hand.

I was invited to do another list show, which turned out to be my last. Instead of getting to choose my topics, I was given five or six things they wanted me to talk about. I went back to them to say that I didn't really know anything about a couple of them, and I didn't like to talk about things I didn't know about. They told me it didn't matter. They then said they wanted me to talk about Jamie Lee Curtis. Great, I replied, I'm a big fan. Specifically, they said, about the rumours that she's actually a man. What rumours are these? I asked. Oh, they're all over the Internet, they informed me. Can you talk about it? Why would I do that? I replied. And just like that, my TV list show punditry career is over. I was happy to appear on any old crap, but I wouldn't have words put in my mouth.

I did miss these little assignations. I'd go to some Soho bar the production company had hired out for the day, sit in some plush chair and do my bit for the camera. It never took long. I'd get £200 and be on my way. At one point Anna and I met for drinks in The Soho bar The Player and she told me I should consider getting an agent, as I was good at it. That was flattering, but it wasn't for me. I wasn't desperate to be on television. In fact, I only had two reasons for doing it. One, it was quite good fun. Two, I thought my mum would like it. And she did. She was very happy telling her friends at the club that I was on telly again. It's not like she had any interest in rap music, she couldn't show anyone my fine work in the top shelf arena. But she could settle down to watch me on Channel 5.

There was just one moment where I might have broken out into doing something else on TV, and that was again through Anna. Vanessa Feltz was hosting a new panel discussion show, and they wanted a male guest as a counterbalance to an otherwise all-female line-up. The set and mood were designed to give the feel of a late night, after-hours chat. Low lighting, a table full of wine, olives to nibble on. However, it was filmed first thing in the morning. Of course, that didn't stop me, and soon a runner was coming over to top my red wine up. And then my neighbour at the table, Big Brother psychologist Dr. Linda Papodopou-los, was offering me her glass, as I'd emptied that one. These were not good signs. Was I only going to be able to do telly half-cut? I enjoyed the day, it felt easy and natural. I had a chat with Vanessa afterwards, as we'd both shared a mutual boss in our publishing work. She was lovely. But I wasn't desperate to do it again.

Ultimately, it's nice to do a bit of TV. Good for the ego. Nice for your family, as long as you don't make a tit of yourself. But I wasn't really telling a new story about hip-hop, was I? I wasn't shining a light on the forgotten artists or saying anything interesting about the ones we all know. I was talking about dating etiquette with Vanessa Feltz. I was chatting about the time Derek Redmond was helped over the finishing line by his father at the 1992 Olympic Games for a three-hour long list show. I was drinking red wine and eating tinned olives at 9am in a TV studio in the arse-end of nowhere. Back to the day job.

26: WHO'S YOUR RHYMIN' HERO?

'Never meet your heroes' is a spectacularly bad bit of advice. Who wants to live their life dodging meetings with the people they admire? Then again, 'meet your heroes, but be prepared for the fact that they might be a bit of a knob,' isn't perhaps as catchy.

My biggest musical hero, Chuck D, was bloody lovely. Schoolly D? Brilliant fun, but I've done those two stories already. And, of course, there are the difficult ones. Method Man. Jay-Z, The Beastie Boys (for me, the most disappointing encounter of my career). The ones who were far from my heroes but got nice write-ups from me and then later slagged me off to someone else because I hadn't written enough about them. Many rappers are humble, many are entitled.

Sometimes you know in advance that a meeting with one of your heroes is destined to go well. You've heard enough about them from other interviewers to feel that it's a sure thing. And so it proved with RZA of Wu-Tang Clan. I'd chatted to him briefly on the phone for my Gravediggaz story in 1997, but had my first in-the-flesh meeting with him in 2002 in the run-up to his *Digital Bullet* solo album, released under his alter ego Bobby Digital. I didn't have long with him, as the previous writer overran by so much, so it was ultimately a bit rushed. I had to wait until late 2007 to get the real deal.

Wu-Tang Clan released *8 Diagrams*, their first album since the death of Ol' Dirty Bastard, in December of that year. *HHC* already had its interview in the bag, so I got to chat to him on behalf of the *Guardian*

Guide, with a meeting set up at his London hotel room. It ended up being one of those interviews where you wish you had 5,000 words to play with, rather than just 800. We started the chat on sofas opposite each other. Then he told me that he'd be more comfortable talking if he could also walk. Would I be happy for him to carry my digital recorder as he paced around the hotel room? More than happy. So it was that I sat on the upholstery yelling out the occasional question – loud enough for my recorder to capture it – and then RZA would wear a groove in the carpet answering it. He waxed long. He waxed interesting.

I'd love to quote at length from it, but *The Guardian* decided back then that it would retain all your rights when you wrote for them, so I can't. Suffice to say the meat of the interview was about the internecine battles in the Wu-Tang at the time. Raekwon had come out in advance of the release of *8 Diagrams* to say it didn't sound like a Wu album. He labelled RZA a 'hip-hop hippy'. Many artists would quickly dodge questions around issues like this, or segue elsewhere, but RZA was more than happy to front up. He explained his reasoning for the different production style, and he pointed out that while Wu-Tang was a democracy, it was a 'George Bush democracy'. In other words, he was content to play the role of dictator to a degree. He didn't say this explicitly, but it was implied that he'd got them to where they were, and they needed to fall in line. As a writer, if you leave a room with a big fat long interview and it's got some juicy beef in the mix, you're golden.

There were no fallouts or disputes to sift through when I met another hero, Jazzy Jeff. This was also in late 2007 and Jeff gave me so much in a 90-minute interview that the piece ended up running for two consecutive issues – a first for me after 10 years at *HHC*. The occasion was the release of his *Return of the Magnificent* album but, by the time this dropped, I'd been listening to Jazzy Jeff – often in the company of The Fresh Prince – for 20 years. The first time I heard them was in 1986, when their single *Girls Ain't Nothing But Trouble* charted in the UK.

It set the blueprint for their approach to rap – cheeky, self-effacing, but with some serious musical and lyrical chops on display. Jazzy Jeff's reputation was further established by *Live at Union Square, November 1986*, a live show recorded for posterity where Will Smith exhorted his DJ to perform incredible acts of turntable trickery. It was that performance that fuelled the legend that Jeffrey Townes invented the 'Transformer Scratch' although he, with typical modesty, said that he just put it on record first – he cited DJ Spinbad as the person he saw perform it first, and credited DJ Cash Money too.

By the time we met in – yes – a London hotel, Jazzy Jeff had gone from breakthrough Philadelphian star to hall of famer. A run of albums that mixed wit with skills, commercial hits with genuine bangers beloved by hip-hop purists is one thing, although the musical accomplishments had, by the time of our meeting, been overshadowed by two things. One of those was *The Fresh Prince of Bel Air*, where Jeff often cropped us as a guest star. The second was Will Smith's Hollywood career. Smith had become an actor who occasionally rapped. Jeff was somewhat side-lined. At least, that's one way to see it. In reality, Jeff never stopped making music, and had never stopped being delighted for his friend and partner. As their best album puts it, *He's the DJ, I'm the Rapper*.

The time he gave me allowed us the latitude to cover that stuff, but also dial right back to the beginning. I always liked hearing about how artists first discovered the music in which they'd made their name. The early rap names, the groups that never were. Jeff was happy to oblige:

"Yeah, I had Mixmaster J. We used to go to this store called The Balcony where you'd get shirts made. You'd buy the shirt and pick your letters out and they'd iron the letters on. Mixmaster J was really expensive. Jazzy Jeff came about because of financial necessity – I could be that in one swoop."

He told me about the Network Crew, about scratching for local groups like Cazal Boys and The Korner Boyz[1], about forming Jazzy Jeff & The New Look Four with MC Rockwell and MC Ice before he even met Will Smith. In fact, if Ice hadn't failed to turn up for a house party he was supposed to be playing with Jeff, chances are there would never have been a DJ Jazzy Jeff & The Fresh Prince. Later on, we touched on the Fresh Prince TV show, how it affected their group dynamic, and how Jeff used the money from it to build and fund his 'A Touch of Jazz' studios. It was wide ranging, it was full of big chunky answers and stuff he hasn't shared before. This is why you need to meet your heroes. He was also erudite on something that was bothering a lot of people at the time – why New York had lost its hip-hop mojo. As a Philly artist coming through when everyone genuflected to New York, he saw it all:

> "It took New York a long time to get out of that 'we are the
> mecca, we are the one, we created everything'. That has been one
> of the reasons other territories have come and staked a claim
> in the business. You can't ever think that you own it – you're
> not humble, you're not learning. You act like the teacher, but in
> music you're a student forever."

The launch of the *The Original* section in *HHC* was perfect for someone like me, someone who'd grown tired of asking the same promotional questions again and again. It gave me the freedom and space to nerd out. So, while we'd interviewed Milk Dee for a *Fat Lace* cover, that had only been a brief chat, conducted by Dan. For *HHC*, I got to dig a lot deeper for a five-page feature on one half of Audio Two in 2008.

---

1 On a song with the none-more 1985 name of *Bust a Move*.

Milk was always a standout artist, from the days of his mega-hit *Top Billin'* all the way through to the brace of Audio Two albums[2] and his solo work on Rick Rubin's American Recordings. In recent years he has embraced his role as a hip-hop elder statesman, happy to turn up and perform the iconic lyrics to *Top Billin'* wherever it's needed. He told me the story of producing the track in his basement, on his own, and the stunned reaction of his mentor, Stetsasonic's Daddy-O, when he played it to him. He also told me about working with Rick Rubin, about label dramas, about enjoying a second career because of the sheer weight of artists who've sampled the song with which he's synonymous.

He skirted around the subject of the split with the other half of Audio Two. Giz wasn't just his DJ, he was also his brother. It's a split that time hasn't healed. Most importantly, he revealed to me that, had there existed a way for me to get $100 to the First Priority Music Fan Club in 1988, I could have been a proud owner of one of their amazing varsity jackets, which would undoubtedly have been the pride of my collection. I'd written to the Fan Club address on the back of an early First Priority release, and had received a bulging envelope advertising T-shirts, badges and jackets for all of the label's artists. But I was 15. I didn't have dollars. I didn't even have a bank account. I had to content myself with looking repeatedly at the folded, black and white pages they'd sent me, dreaming.

In November 2008, I got a dozen pages to explore the history of Trenton, the New Jersey city that birthed or hosted some of the most influential rap artists of the 80's and 90's. I can still remember piecing this together, scheduling interviews from my Soho office, often late at

---

2 There is a third Audio Two album that remains stubbornly unreleased to this day. At one point I was trying to strike a deal with Milk Dee and his father, the label owner Nat Robinson, for a vinyl release of said album, *First Dead Indian*. While that never happened, they did give us an unreleased collaboration between Milk and his sister MC Lyte, taken from that album. We put the track in question, *Jeep Voices* on the *Fat Lace* website.

night[3]. I'd work until 6, nip over the road for a couple of pints with colleagues, then back to the office to double-check my questions. For this piece, I'd lined up three interviews, with Tony D, YZ and Wise Intelligent of Poor Righteous Teachers. What made it especially exciting for me was that, not only did I have deep affection for all three artists and their music, they'd intersected in numerous ways. Tony D produced music for both YZ and PRT. PRT and YZ made diss records about each other. And, years later, they've got words to say about Tony D that are both salutary and barbed. Throw Aaron Fuchs of Tuff City into the mix – YZ was signed to the label at one time – and you've got a heady mix.

> *The Lower Free Bridge which spans the Delaware river is famed for its slogan 'Trenton Makes, The World Takes', first installed in 1935 and now picked out in waterproof neon. The slogan took on new meaning in the mid-to-late 80s when this city of less than 100,000 residents spat out some of the finest east coast hip-hop ever witnessed.*

YZ is actually from Paterson, a nearby New Jersey city, but it's fair to say that his story is indelibly linked with Trenton. He met Tony D while doing talent shows in The Capital City – as hardly anyone calls it – and recorded a quick demo with him called *I'm Bad*. That led to an independent deal and more studio time with Antony Depula. Wise Intelligent, meanwhile, had left his early crew Magnetic Building Factors – "Damn, that's a wack name," – and had formed Poor Righteous Teachers with Culture Freedom and Father Shaheed. Both PRT and

---

3 On one particular night of contrasts, I recorded the interview with Wise Intelligent, then hung around for a phone chat with supermodel Heidi Klum for an *Arena* cover story. There was no recycling of questions on that particular night.

Tony Y were at the Trenton War Memorial show where the local crowd booed and threw coins at Eric B & Rakim. As Wise tells it:

"I remember when Rakim was challenged by The Chief MCs at the War Memorial. They did a recording called We Got Your Melody. It was also next to impossible for other artists to perform on a ticket with Poor Righteous Teachers. Trenton is notorious for booing and throwing pocket change at artists. You had to really be on point."

PRT were supposed to sign to the same label as YZ, and when that fell through, with Tony D somewhere in the middle, two artists who might have become great label mates ended up becoming rivals. It was a rare opportunity for a writer to get three different perspectives on the same 'he said, she said' story, although YZ's take was perhaps the clearest and most honest.

"What ended up happening was Tony was an agitator. He was an agitator before I met him and he was an agitator when we were business partners in Two Tone Productions. We signed PRT to Diversity Records and then Tony caused friction between Wise and myself because he knew that they were green and he was putting shit in their ear about this, that and the other, about how Diversity was going to fuck them. Just basically straight lying to these kids which led to them having beef with me because I'm part-owner of the label."

The respective artists took to the recording studio to capture their unhappiness. While PRT recorded some lines about the Diversity situation, YZ fully went for PRT with his ferocious *Crocodile Dundee* track. Tony D was smack in the middle, producing both. Or, as Wise Intelligent put it with customary style, "Tony D was selling weapons to the Hutus and the Tutsis regardless of if they killed one another."

Happily, they didn't, even if the artists did end up meeting in an abandoned house for YZ to play them his diss track, packing a weapon in case things went sideways. Years later, they do shows together and are gracious about each other's talent and records. Wise told me how much he likes *Crocodile Dundee* to this day. Where YZ And Tony D could agree was on Aaron Fuchs, Tuff City label head. YZ's first album and subsequent EP came out on Tuff City, and while Tony D found Fuchs not entirely honest financially, he was still dealing with him. YZ was less forgiving.

> *"Tuff City could have easily become that label like Def Jam, but instead he let his simple-ass greed get in the way of him becoming a powerhouse in this business. What major will want to fuck with you when you fuck all your artists over?"*

I had loads more stuff like this planned. A who's who of Philly hip-hop. A look at long-lost labels. I wanted to speak to the Dismasters, Sir Ibu, Funkmaster Wizard Wiz. I dreamed of doing a deep dive on the careers of Roxanne Shante and MC Lyte. I planned on charting the evolution of Greg Nice from beatbox to rap legend[4]. But it wasn't to be. The world's first ever rap monthly was about to shudder to a halt.

---

4 I did get to spend some time with Greg Nice in New York, but it's not among my fondest memories. He picked Dan and I up from outside Mighty Mi's apartment. His car was a battered old thing and despite being the tallest of the three of us, I got into the back seat. I was seated behind Greg, who had his seat pushed right back. He was playing us some new music, and literally jumping up and down in his seat to the beat. I couldn't take in what the music sounded like as I was basically being kneecapped by the man who thought Dizzy Gillespie played the sax. We spent most of the next two hours driving from bodega to bodega in search of exactly the right flavour of Snapple for Greg. This is not what I had envisioned.

27: THE START OF YOUR ENDING

The strange thing about the end of *Hip-Hop Connection* is that it was absolutely brilliant as the curtain fell. I suppose this is true of many things, but it still felt like a real kick in the teeth. It had been very good for a very long time, but those last few issues had the perfect formula, a beautiful mix of content, brilliant writers, photographers and design. US artists didn't just want to be interviewed for it, some of them wanted to write for it. It was a magazine that still mattered.

But was it a magazine that still sold? Well, yes. But sales were far from the main income source for music magazines, which is why many great and acclaimed magazines – *The Word*, for example – still folded. Magazine economics are a complicated mix of staff expenditure, printing costs, distribution deals, freelance bills, advances, returns, advertising and more. Did you know, for example, that many shops don't stock magazines because they want to sell them, but because they're paid by the publisher to do so? These deals can be huge. Equally, even on a small-scale magazine like *Fat Lace*, we could sell a single full-page advert to a record label that would net us more money than all the sales to readers combined.

The days of peak magazine sales had long gone before time was called on *Hip-Hop Connection* as a monthly. We were firmly in the blog era, which had an impact. You could tap into brilliant interviews online from independent writers, while many of the mainstream mags also uploaded plenty of material for free as well. But no website, for me, has ever conjured up the joy of a physical magazine. The range of voices over a double-page spread. I am unrepentantly dewy-eyed about the age of physical magazines, which is why I still subscribe to a bunch of the remaining ones now[1].

It's not the magazines that changed, it's us. We disappeared. The shelf space shrank. More importantly, budgets were squeezed, pagination and paper quality dropping as advertisers disappeared. Where the hell did they go?

Well, many of them went online. They chased the clicks, they reapportioned their budgets. And some of those budgets shrank too – as a result of downloading and music piracy, we were told. As CD sales fell, so did ad spend. Of course, let me inform you that the wasteful lifestyles of record label marketing departments barely missed a beat. The same useless middle-class divs and nepo babies still failed to do their jobs even close to well.

Real life example no. 1

"Hi, this is Andrew Emery from HHC. Yeah, I'm fine, you? We're doing X artist as lead album review this month, can you bung the promo CD in the post for us?"

"We've only got a few left in the office, if any. Can you not go and buy one?"

"It's not out yet."

---

1 Fair enough, you can head into WH Smith at a train station and see magazines galore. But it's the ones that have disappeared that I mourn. Hats off to the ones still going.

Real life example no. 2

"Hi mate, it's Andrew from Hip-Hop Connection. How are you? Yeah, me too. Could you pop so-and-so in the post, as we're running a feature on it in the March issue?"

"Sorry, Andrew, you'll have to go and buy one, we're short of copies."

"This is the same CD I did the liner notes for free as a favour to you, you remember?"

"Sorry mate, my hands are tied."

Honestly, RA the Rugged Man's statement that 'every record label sucks dick' isn't far from the truth at all. Artists would be horrified to learn that their marketing budget was being spunked on wasters who couldn't get a CD transported a few miles to a magazine that was promising to review it. Even the ones who played ball often did so to excess.

Soho in the 90's was drowning in bikes taking things from one building to another. In the pre-Deliveroo days, bike couriers were transporting photos, CDs and more between offices at great expense, even when you were just 100 yards away. I'd offer to nip round to a label office during my lunch break to pick up a CD I was reviewing. They'd insist on sending it by bike.

A publisher I worked for in London had an office just round the corner from Joe's Basement, one of the main photo-developing hubs in Soho. It was like *BMX Bandits* with the amount of bikes going back and forth between the two. Did everyone have no legs? Of course, the bikes were also a handy way for an editor or two I knew to get their weed or coke delivered straight to the office on their publisher's dime.

So, I take the claims of record label penury with a pinch of salt bigger than that prick Salt Bae could deliver. Yet still, the cold hard fact is that advertising spend fell off a cliff, and magazines like *HHC* bore the brunt of it. A niche magazine with quite high production values could only survive for so long, and one of the reasons for *HHC*'s longevity was that the writing staff were prepared to write for very little. For many of us, writing about the music we adored was part of it, but the rest was writing for a magazine that supported you, let you explore ideas, and put you in the company of other writers who knew their subjects inside out.

That final writing lineup at *HHC*? Easily the best it had ever had, and one of the best seen by a hip-hop magazine anywhere, ever. Wily veterans writing columns, hip-hop theorists dazzling with their acumen, comedians, nerds, rabble rousers – all passionate about at least some part of hip-hop, and able to bring that to life vividly in words. And that's not easy. Most people can't articulate their musical passion – and they don't have to. But a music writer has to, and the *HHC* crew did.

David Sadeghi and Rob Pursey were fierce in their championing of scenes and sounds that many of us more close-minded writers were slow to embrace. The modern hip-hop world closely reflects what they told us it would. Again, Andy Cowan didn't stand in their way.

At the same time, Dan Greenpeace and I continued our proselytising on behalf of artists both underground, mainstream, old and overlooked. DJ Yoda and Mike Lewis, the superb deputy Phillip Mlynar, Richard Watson, Tom Dartnell, Angus Batey, Ryan Proctor, Hugh Leask, James McNally, old hand Stephen Worthy, and others I've doubtless forgotten and to whom I apologise – it may have been a writing staff of largely white males, but between us we wrote about every damn aspect of hip-hop, R'n'B and more. Hats off to the photographers as well, including the legendary Paul H.

The diversity of those later issues – in a world that was already seeing a boom-bap backlash of the irreparably old school – captured both the underground and coming overground in a fascinating way. It's a magazine that did a deep dive on MF Doom, ate ribs with Bubba Sparxx, adored Paul Wall and Rodney P and gave YZ a 2,500-word interview a good 20 years after his last notable record. In other words, it's a magazine that loved hip-hop.

The day it died, a tiny bit of me was sad that I wouldn't be able to write for it anymore. A little bit rued the loss of the few hundred quid that arrived every month. But mostly, I was gutted that one of the things that had long been part of the hip-hop landscape for me had gone. The first ever hip-hop monthly in the world. The best one. The magazine that had given room to everyone from Kista to 50 Cent, Nobby Nutsta to Jay-Z. That had charted the rise and fall of the greats, but also found space for blink-and-you'll-miss-them one offs and no marks. A magazine that had let me cook rapper's recipes, slag off heroes, write appreciations of forgotten obscurities, that had propelled me to New York again and again. It was gone.

The final issue was the first – and last one – with a brand new look. A really fresh, modern redesign that was set to take the magazine into the future. But the sums didn't add up for Andy any more, and he had to pull the plug. He didn't know that last one was it, so there's no blaze of glory. No look back in anger, no hidden acrostics spelling out 'Fuck You, Ministry'. Yet there's glory in the issue itself. The rich editorial mix. Writers who can really write doing their best work about the best music this world of ours has ever created or heard.

Alongside those legends, I was still ploughing my little furrow. Being a little pompous in my self-titled column, a quick interview with DJ Mike Nice for my new *Crate Expectations* column – one and done – and, for the thousandth time, revelling in the minutiae of largely forgotten hip-hop. My piece on Witchdoctor & The Dominating Three MC's *Kickin' it Live* album, some 31 years after it came out[2], contains my final

---

2 For a monthly column called *Weep Cover – Shining a Less Than Flattering Light on Rap's Worst Artwork*. I told you *Deep Cover* and variations thereof are always the go-to for pieces about hip-hop record art.

words for *Hip-Hop Connection*. Fittingly, they bring me full circle back
to when I was a kid in Nottingham, buying my first rap records.

> *I first saw this album in Arcade Records in Nottingham on its*
> *release. I didn't buy it as I was scared off by what my adolescent*
> *mind interpreted as scary voodoo. With the benefit of over 20*
> *years hindsight, it turns out that the crew of Mellow Nate Dee,*
> *Mr Count Cool Out, Rock Master J and Witchdoctor himself*
> *were only bugging. It's a mighty fine record, but worse than the*
> *hokey cover is the group blurb on the back. Mellow Nate Dee is,*
> *apparently, 'Relaxed and Mellow and 'Loud and Crazy". Which is*
> *it to be? Count Cool Out is the, 'Love of all Loves'. What does that*
> *mean? Rock Master J claims, 'His blood is always warm." These*
> *dudes aren't House M.D. As for Witchdoctor, 'Funny as it may*
> *seem, as fast as he slices a record, he's faster than a head sliced on*
> *a guillotine'. Yes, that does seem funny. Maybe the cover isn't the*
> *reason why I didn't buy this until 2008 – it was the laughing at*
> *guillotines. This wasn't big in France for the same reason.*

Niche jokes about an old rap record's artwork? I'll proudly take that
as my *HHC* epitaph.

In the wake of *HHC*'s demise, what was the hip-hop magazine landscape like? In the UK, there weren't any. We'd already called it a day at
Fat Lace. *Fat Boss*, *Big Daddy* – later called *Grand Slam* – had done the
same. There remained a hip-hop presence in *Echoes* and *Blues & Soul*,
but that was only a small part of the black music picture they chronicled. No, you had to go to the Internet or the US for your hip-hop
reading pleasure – and that wasn't always rewarding.

The blog era threw up plenty of talent, and I'd even written a blog
world cup feature just before *HHC* folded – turkeys voting for Christmas, perhaps. But you only ever got a singular voice when you went to

one. In some ways, that reflected the nature of browsing the web – it was second nature to gravitate from one blog bookmark to another, from *Unkut* to *So Many Shrimp* via *The Martorialist*, so you'd get different voices that ways – but it still didn't replicate the feel of a magazine. Those trusty columns you knew would be there. How you'd know exactly where to flick with your thumbs every month to get to the single reviews. Blogs didn't replace hip-hop mags, they were something entirely different. They felt more ephemeral, but at the same time profited from their own immediacy. The comments underneath, say, an interview with Chill Rob G on Robbie Ettelson's *Unkut*, would be a great place to pick up further nuggets of information, for the artist to respond to the piece. But this is an outlier – this is the good stuff.

Many of the blogs were just aggregators of content, places to hear new songs with maybe a paragraph of context or information. They'd encourage frequent visits, but often you'd be going just to download an MP3 or follow a link to YouTube. It was a different mode of consumption to a magazine and, for an old schooler like me – didn't come with the pleasures of flicking through the pages, earmarking and saving the juiciest piece to read last.

Yet this was still preferable to the remaining mainstream rap magazines. *Rap Pages* had shuttered in 2000. *Rap Sheet* was gone. *XXL* was still there – as it is now – but reflected a narrow, popular part of hip-hop and had, by then, nothing special editorially to distinguish it from anything else. *The Source* had lost all its lustre, turned by rapper-turned-publisher Benzino in the early 2000's into a vehicle for personal beefs. It famously gave great reviews to his own music, while disparaging his enemies, such as Eminem. No one took it seriously anymore. If it felt like hip-hop publishing had died, well, it had.

15 years later, it has never returned. The old guard have gone on to work in marketing, TV, to publish their retrospectives, their books. The stars of the blog era have done the same. There are still pockets of joy to

be found – Jeff Weiss' *Passion of the Weiss* blog, Andrew Barber's *Fake Shore Drive* – but many of the most passionate writers and chroniclers of hip-hop have moved on to podcasts or given up altogether. Books about hip-hop? Loads of them. Monthly digests of the latest music, the latest artists, looks back at legends, opinion, news – why is that not a thing anymore[3]?

---

3 I realise there are a handful of fine music mags still plugging away, but there's a real paucity of choice. The last one I really loved was *The Word*, which seemed to spring from a starting point of 'let's write about stuff we like, not just stuff that's new'. It felt enthusiastic and it felt like it understood how people actually listened to music. So you'd get an in-depth interview with, say, Nick Cave, but then a column about how to transfer MP3s. I did a few pieces for them, including a look at hip-hop skits and an interview with the excellent music writer Dave Tompkins about his *How to Wreck a Nice Beach* book – which is basically an eccentric and singular history of the vocoder. I highly recommend it.

28: X VERSUS THE WORLD

Where do all the great hip-hop journalists go when the magazines die? The 1990s and 2000s truly look like a Golden Age for hip-hop magazines now. The shelves were thickly stacked with *The Source, Vibe, Hip-Hop Connection, Rap Pages, Rap Sheet, URB, Murder Dog* and *XXL*. Dig a little deeper and you'd turn up independent publications such as *ego trip, Fatboss, Fat Lace* and *Big Daddy*. If you were a writer with an idea to pitch, there was no shortage of potential marketplaces.

If you were lucky, you'd parlay the ability to write and some knowledge into covering hip-hop for bigger publications. That might be *The New Yorker* or the *Village Voice*, say, or perhaps *The Guardian, The Face* or *Q*. Most of these magazines and many of the newspapers have now gone.

As print died, the rush online sparked a new era. The tired old behemoths of print tried to replicate online what they did on the newsstand and found that it didn't work. The pop-ups and ads distracted people, while the endless polls and needless interactivity felt like taking a personality test when you simply wanted to find out who Kanye West had produced a new track for.

At the same time, the record labels were finding their old models couldn't stand up in the face of illegal downloading and decided that they were going to be content creators too. I remember Universal Music throwing an obscene amount of money at a 'content portal' that barely went live. They hired a music journalist I knew to head it up, paid me six times the going rate to contribute and told me I could pretty much retread previously published material of mine that they liked. This was not waving, but drowning.

It took a good while for hip-hop on the internet to settle down, but once it did, the stuff that flourished wasn't coming from the big brands. It was coming from individuals with original takes and niche tastes that could develop a core audience and, just occasionally, make a bigger splash. The likes of Byron Crawford, Robbie Ettelson and others made their names in the internet era – they weren't magazine transplants. Robbie's *Unkut* was so good precisely because it interviewed rappers that no other magazine (especially once *HHC* died) would pay you to interview. Other blogs were bleeding edge on new music, others controversial in opinion, others addicted to memes. All were bookmarked.

Unsurprisingly, the remaining old media publications, newly on the internet, tried to cannibalise many of the internet's blog stars. It was a good way for them to get paid, but rarely did the material match what they produced on their own. However, it was still Dostoevsky compared to the Dan Brown that is hip-hop Twitter.

Let's make it clear, I'm no luddite when it comes to new media. I was a late adopter of smartphones, Twitter[1] and more, sure – mostly out of laziness – but have always known their power. Before I'd even installed Twitter on my own phone, I was contributing content to it for one of the world's largest news companies. Anyway, enough caveating – hip-hop Twitter sucks.

The good thing about Twitter is you can just follow the people you like and admire, and block out the rest… right up until they like or retweet something you don't want to see. Then you're down the rabbit

---

1 Halfway through writing this book, Elon Musk decided to change the name of Twitter to X, in a baffling piece of brand management.

hole. A world away from a blogger asking Lord Alibaski[2] the questions I'd always wanted to hear him answer, rap on Twitter is, with precious few exceptions, moronic, simple-minded and circular.

There are people worth following. Those with an ear for new music or a nose for digging up the old. All hail those marvels digitising lost radio tapes and sharing them with us. Those with a turn of phrase who can express a musical opinion with the elan of a true writer. But that's the exception rather than the rule.

The rule is: Which is better, *Illmatic* or *Reasonable Doubt*? The rule is: Four classic albums – lose one. The rule is: Four classic albums – rank them. The rule is: Four classic albums – lose three. The rule is: *Reasonable Doubt* or *Illmatic* – which is better?[3]

The rule is also: Do we all agree that this is a classic album? It's: "None of you have heard of this album, and it shows." It's: "This is so underrated." It's an endless cavalcade of empty or thin content masquerading as something of substance. Many of us are guilty of indulging in the endless quest for clicks and likes, but what is the point of this stuff?

Let's be fair – some accounts do this to spark debate that ties in with their podcast. They go somewhere with their online poll. But numerous accounts just churn out this lowest denominator bullshit without any aim – it exists purely to exist. And what is the aggregate of information at the end of it? 58% of people on one account prefer *Reasonable Doubt*

---

2 Lord Alibaski only released one single, but as it was the DJ Mark the 45 King-produced *Lyrics in Motion*, he warrants a footnote. He was cousin to fellow Flavor Unit members Latee and Apache, and contributed four tracks to the *The 45 King Presents The Flavor Unit album*, in addition to an absolutely sensational verse on *Flavor Unit Assassination Squad*, which for me is an all-time top ten posse cut.

3 The answers: a) *Illmatic*. 2) No, I don't have to. 3) Can't be arsed, and it changes on a weekly basis. 4) Again, I don't have to. You can't make me because I'm allowed to have them all. 5) *Illmatic*.

to *Illmatic*, but an entirely different account with different followers finds that Nas made the better album. Who. The. Fuck. Cares?

A poll for the sake of it is one thing, but people deciding what's 'underrated'[4] is another entirely. I once saw someone post that the Ultramagnetic MC's incredible *Critical Beatdown* album is underrated. Nothing could be further from the truth. For hip-hop fans from a certain era, it has been and always will be a top ten album of all time. It has been analysed, discussed and celebrated at length. Everyone who heard it on release loved and still loves it. But 'underrated' isn't what the tweeter means.

No, that tweet (and oh so many like it) has a number of not very well hidden meanings. First among these is: look at my exceptional taste. I adore this album so I'm going to tell the world (well, my 46 followers) that it's underrated, even though it's always high up in any hip-hop poll that matters and online message boards are full of it. Second: I don't like the other hip-hop that people are talking about on here.

The same goes for people telling us that Main Source's *Breaking Atoms* is underrated, or *Madvillainy* is underrated, or countless others. No. Again, no. These albums are what is known in music circles as 'correctly rated'. They are loved, but they did not sell 10 million copies.

If you had the chance to shine light on a little known or ignored album, what would it be? That Priority One album with the terrible artwork but amazing production on Tuff City? Would you tell the world that both the Boogiemonsters albums have aged so well that they actually sound better now than they did on release? Perhaps you'd want to talk about how brilliantly Positively Black sampled Bill Withers' *Can*

---

4 I say this as someone who came up with a *Fat Lace* column called 'Underrated' and 'Underhated'. It really existed for us to use the latter to pour scorn on albums we saw as sacred cows that needed taking down a notch or two. However, the former involved us writing about actually obscure and underrated albums rather than established classics.

We Pretend on their one and only self-titled album from 1989? Don't bother. To capture the spirit of Twitter, just go on there and tell people why Nas' second album, *It Was Written*, is so misunderstood and over-looked that it only sold two million copies in the US.

Hip-hop Twitter is like the hip-hop Internet in the bad old days of the big magazines flooding it with crap content and polls. Only it's getting worse, not better. I've just come off Twitter/X. No matter how hard I tried to curate my timeline so I only followed interesting people, a deluge of crap was still filtering through. But those comments, those polls, those endlessly recycled questions are not the worst thing about the bird app.

No, that's being cancelled on Twitter, especially when it's by a bunch of clowns. I've seen many friends almost purposely misunderstood by people who've then gone out of their way to organise a pile-on. I've seen people with large accounts tell lies in public and then stifle all debate. One notable tweeter, who also masquerades as a hip-hop writer without having written one interesting or elegant sentence in their life, once started a niche hip-hop debate. They argued strongly for a particular viewpoint. I could remember them arguing the exact opposite only months ago. When I pointed this out, I was blocked. Friends then told me that the same person was writing insulting tweets about me. They then did the same to other people. What a child.

I was the victim of a Twitter pile-on myself. A woman who had known MF Doom in the latter part of his career has tweeted that she wished he'd done more interviews in his life, but only with black journalists. I had the temerity to reply by saying I wish I'd got to interview him. The original poster and her friends then started to call me a white gatekeeper. They told me I couldn't understand the black experience in any way. That I was stealing their music and identity. They called me a culture vulture. Any attempts at a rational reply – I was a rap writer of long standing who'd followed Doom's career since his very first recordings as KMD, that he had a huge fanbase in the UK and Europe – consisting largely of white people – and that he actually died in my city, Leeds[5] – fell on deaf ears. People who hadn't read the original back and forth just joined in as it allowed them to be awful to someone behind the cloak of anonymity. Friends were messaging me to say they couldn't believe what they were seeing. The unfairness of it. Hey, when it comes to Twitter bullying, I got off lightly. I've got thick skin. I was never going to be dissuaded by a bunch of people who've been into hip-hop for five minutes. People who think rap should still be just the preserve of black people from New York. That ship has sailed, everyone.

Rap awfulness on Twitter. No hip-hop magazines left. Most of the great bloggers retired. In 2024, you can either launch a podcast, or just write the damn stuff yourself.

---

5 How Daniel Dumile, man of many aliases, ended up living in Leeds at the end of his life is in itself a fascinating story. He was, technically, British, which may have had something to do with it. Leeds Hospital Trust even issued an apology about the standard of care it provided to Doom. The best telling of Doom's time in Leeds can be found on The Square Ball's website, in an excellent piece by Rob Conlon. My friend Ash Kollakowski, who featured in *Wiggaz* as rapper Horny Baker, has a mural of MF Doom on the side of one of his bars.

29: OFF THE BOOKS

Hip-Hop Connection disconnected. *Fat Lace* untied. And, one by one, the lights have gone out on all the other magazines I've made a living from, and that spoke to their audience in a way that had them coming back month after month. Until they didn't, or there was nothing to come back to. *The Face* was now faceless. *Vox* no longer had a voice. *Select* hadn't been chosen to survive. *The Word* had printed its last ones.

There was the odd bone from *The Guardian* to chew on. A meeting with Donald Glover in London where the artist also known as Childish Gambino told me he got his name from the online Wu-Tang Name Generator. I told him that they ripped off *Fat Lace*. I'm not sure he believed me. Then they killed off *The Guide*, and that was another outlet for my writing gone. I did a back and forth on Chris Brown with another writer for *The Observer*, me making the case for the defence. I'm at pains to point out that it was just an exercise in debate for me, I had no real case to make for Chris Brown, either the man or his music. After that, all my encounters with rappers were purely as a fan, or as a bystander while Dan did business with them. I did get to go quad biking with Diamond D, however[1].

Marketing is now populated by ex-music writers, jostling for elbow room at the table with all the refugees from local newspapers and press

---

1 Quad Biking with Diamond D sounds like an Alan Partridge pitch, if Alan Partridge knew about the man who gave us the incredible *Stunts, Blunts & Hip-Hop* album.

agencies. As the world of print has contracted, the world of content has come calling. I made that switch too, leaving behind the days of dreaming up questions for Necro and Frankenstein for coming up with campaigns for car hire companies and building societies. If you knew how to make things engaging, you could take that skill anywhere, was the thinking. And, if you've spent a good chunk of your life interviewing rappers, you've got some good stories to tell on 'cocktail club Fridays'.

Yet… It's not enough. If you're a writer in love with music in general, or with one genre in particular, you might still have something to say. Unfinished business. A story or five still itching to burst out of you. The problem is, you just might not have anywhere to say it.

Even if the middle shelf was spilling over with music magazines, even if there was a thriving hip-hop press in the UK, that still might not be the place for what you want to do. It's a story you don't think anyone has told before. All the hip-hop books are about rappers, about stars, about the business, the origins in New York. There's hardly a word about the fans, the failures, the ones plugging away at the margins. There's nothing that captures what it felt like to have your life turned upside down by hearing a record in 1984, at a time when hip-hop was still in its relative infancy. Maybe that's a story I could write, but who's going to read it, and who's going to publish it?

Getting a book published about rap is, despite the huge number of them out there on Amazon and on the shelves of bookshops both real and virtual, still quite difficult. You largely need to get an agent before you can get a publisher. UK publishers and agents, in particular, are not generally drawn from the demographic that understands how important hip-hop is or how big the potential market there is. Instead, you tend to get a book deal if you've got a large social media following or a significant public profile from a radio or TV show. That gives a publisher an established market to sell to. This is the same reason that you could be forgiven for thinking that celebrities are the best people to write children's books, instead of a load of hacks who largely have them ghostwritten while full-time writers starve.

Sending letters to agents and publishers is dispiriting. They have exacting submission guidelines, which I suppose you would have too, as lots of people think they've got a book in them, and you've got to filter out the complete timewasters somehow. But nine times out of ten you don't get an acknowledgement or even a rejection. You're talking to ghosts.

Things are somewhat easier in the US, as publishers are more willing to take on hip-hop books due to the much larger market there. That's why there's simultaneously a healthy library of books about rap written by genuinely gifted writers, and also a whole host of them by people who have no business writing a book. It's much easier to do a footnote about the worst rap books than about the best ones, but I'm going to resist the temptation[2].

When I was pitching *Wiggaz* round, I got lots of lovely feedback, but no offers. Somebody at Faber said they loved what I'd written so far, and could I please send the rest as they wanted to finish reading the story, but they wouldn't be publishing it as it was too niche. I approached Unbound, who take a crowd-funding approach to publishing, and they turned me down. Once it came out, a publisher I'd got to know there said they should have done it after all[3].

So, the story I wanted to tell was bubbling over inside me, and my friend Justin Quirk, who gave me the seed of the idea, published an extract from it in *Soho House* magazine, which he was then editing.

---

2 Someone will only go and put mine in a similar list.

3 They did take on two projects of mine, both of which failed to get anywhere near their funding target. What's annoying is that, after the projects closed, people were messaging me asking 'what happened to your book, I was looking forward to that?'. Yes, but you didn't back it, did you? THAT'S LITERALLY HOW IT WORKS!

Off the back of that, I heard from a couple of publishers and a team of filmmakers. Nothing came of it. I put the book on the backburner and got on with life.

I moved back up north, I took the obligatory job in marketing, I jettisoned the Jordans for work-appropriate footwear. The rap T-shirts were boxed up in the attic, along with all the years and years of cuttings. I was done with all that.

But I wasn't. Not really. The book still worried away at me. I'd lie awake in bed thinking of things I wanted to talk about. Those early jams in Nottingham. Choosing which record to buy when you could only afford one. The cringe of breakdancing in front of the school. I'd open up the same file that had been sitting on my hard drive for years, and add another paragraph or two. But it was disjointed, a mess of fragments. At that pace, it would never see the light of day.

A crisis of confidence saved the book. I found myself working long hours for not very much money at a digital agency in Leeds. The people were largely lovely, but the company was in the midst of a takeover and the owner, who'd launched the company way before Google was even a thing, was keeping costs down to make the company more attractive to its suitors. That meant hardly anyone was being hired, and wages stifled. I would be in the office at 8.30 at night putting together content calendars for clients I couldn't bear, with a feeling that life was passing me by entirely.

I'm generally pretty contemptuous of digital agency culture. They often offer low pay to good people, having realised that snazzily coloured break-out areas and a foosball table offers a patina of good employee relations. It's much cheaper to have Friday night cocktails than to give everyone a pay rise. As I write this, many of them – including my former employers – have realised this isn't really good enough any more. There's no point in a ping-pong table if your staff are working so hard they never get to play ping-pong.

I just timed my arrival into that world badly. I met some wonderful people, many of whom I'm still in touch with, picked up some vital new skills, and made myself thoroughly miserable. At the same time, my marriage was in trouble. I started taking prescription anti-depressants. I drank too much. Something had to give.

Encouraged by friends and family, I packed in the day job. I decided to take three months off. I cleaned out the dusty summer house that sat at the end of the garden of the house I'd bought, and I put a desk in it. A room with no Internet, no distractions, but with about 18,000 spiders for company. It was time to write.

As the book took shape, and the rejections rolled in, I decided to do what some of my all-time favourite rappers once did when hip-hop shifted gears: Go independent. If it was good enough for Lord Finesse, for The High & Mighty, hell, even for old shit-name himself, Kukoo Da Baga Bonez, it was good enough for me.

A quick distinction between self-publishing and vanity publishing, before we proceed further. Vanity publishing is where you pay someone to put out a book for you, even if no-one anywhere wants to read it. You supply the words, they do the rest. Self-publishing is very different. You write it, you typeset it, you publish it, you market it. Although one similarity, I suppose, is that no-one may want to read it either.

With my *Fat Lace* history, I knew some of the ropes when it came to independent publishing. How proactive you have to be to get out there. The importance of rereading and rereading and rereading and then rewriting your work until you are happy with it. No cutting corners. No expecting a leg up from anyone. Getting good people on your side. On the latter front, it was having readers who would give me worthwhile, honest, actionable feedback, and I got that from Justin, from Dan and Susie, from Rob and Susan. They helped me fix things I'd missed. Stories I'd misremembered. Justin told me, at an early stage, that I was still writing like a magazine journalist with only 1,500 words to get my story across. I needed to let the words breathe, to slow the pace right down. It was tough to change how I'd always worked – I'd forever been someone who wrote in short, sharp bursts.

I had my friend Rich Firth on my side too, who provided the cover for *Wiggaz With Attitude*, as well as for this book. But, once the book was ready, written, proofed and typeset, I thought I'd be on my own. So it was that I threw myself into learning the ropes of being a self-published author, how to upload ebooks to Amazon, how to do an author profile, which self-publishing prizes it was worth submitting my book to and finding out whatever the hell Goodreads was.

Reviews would be tricky too. All the magazines I'd once written for and which lavished generous inches upon *The Book of Hip-Hop Cover Art* were long gone. I didn't have *HHC* on my side any more. Even though I was still doing the odd bit for *The Guardian*, several of my contacts there said they wouldn't review my book – they didn't cover independently published stuff as a policy. I was one more writer facing up against a world of indifference.

The main obstacle, in my mind, was that I'd written a memoir despite the fact that, the few *HHC* or *Fat Lace* readers who remembered me aside, I was famous to zero extent. No social media following. No TV or radio show to keep my name alive. I was at a standing start. I contacted Joanna Penn, a significant figure in self-publishing, and wrote a piece for her blog, The Creative Penn. Titled *5 Ways to Market a Memoir When No-One Knows Who You Are*, it starts:

> *The chances are, you've never heard of me. In fact, not many*
> *people have. Okay, I had a book out a decade ago, I've written for*
> *plenty of magazines and newspapers, but I'm barely a household*
> *name in my own house. And yet I've just released my memoir.*

Ultimately, I realised that to trade on what little name I had made no sense. That would give you a core of readers, your friends and family included, but at that point you might as well just stick to vanity publishing and send them all a copy for Christmas. Instead, I had to try and emphasise what I thought the book did well – tell other people's stories as well as mine. Capture something of a generation, in my limited way. And I think that's why the book did very well for a self-published memoir. It did connect, and the early feedback on it helped to propel the book further. People said it was funny and they saw themselves in it. For me, that's all I wanted.

Harold Heath, my 'labelmate' at Velocity Press, author of the excellent *Long Relationships: My Incredible Journey From Unknown DJ to Small-Time DJ*, wrote a piece for the Innate website where he cited my memoir as one of the inspirations for his:

> *"One of the problems with writing a memoir when you're not well known is you can't help but wonder if your story is too pedestrian, if anyone will actually be interested in it. The truth is of course, that humans absolutely love stories, regardless of the fame of the protagonist. This book – the very funny story of an unsuccessful UK rapper – helped me realise that perhaps I could write a memoir too."*

Very kind words, but also further proof that other kinds of stories need and deserve to be told, and there are people like Harold[4] who can tell them. They can't all be about success. They can't all be about the grand moments of history. There's truth and beauty in the minutiae of

---

4 And fellow labelmate and early *Fat Lace* correspondent Paul Terzulli whose *Who Say Reload: The Stories Behind the Classic Drum & Bass Records of the 90s* is another Velocity Press sureshot.

musical life too. The near misses, the never-wasses, the people whose toil and passion underpins these genres.

Wiggaz almost blew up. Romesh Ranganathan generously invited me onto his *Hip-Hop Saved My Life Podcast*. Sales of the book spiked. Rupert Majendie, his producer, liked the book and passed it round to a few friends and colleagues. That led to me heading down to London for a lunch at BAFTA with Rupert and Tom Davis[5]. They wanted to option the book for TV. A story I almost never told now had a sniff of a chance of being a TV sitcom.

Several writers took a run at it, including Andy Milligan, who writes the great *Man Like Mobeen* and pretty much every funny word that comes out of Ant & Dec's mouth – he used to be a *Fat Lace* reader. Lloyd Elliott, who had an MOP-inspired script called *Kidnap That Fool* doing the rounds, also had a go. I've still got all the draft scripts – the show had the working title *Can I Kick It?* – and they're generally excellent. Dave, the channel, was strongly interested. We talked about sonorous rap voices for the voiceover, with the very real possibility that Snoop Dogg or Ice-T would be approached to work on a TV show about my pathetic, failed rap career. 2018 turned into 2019. The option ran out, the show wasn't getting made. Maybe there just wasn't any actor handsome or charismatic enough to play me, at 11 years old, with spots, bumfluff and bad sneakers.

Luckily, I'd harboured very little hope that it actually would, so it's not like my expectations were dashed. I'd watched my friend and colleague Nat Saunders move from publishing into comedy writing and, while very successful with several shows you might even have watched, seen how some of his best scripts never went anywhere. The endless back and forth with TV executives. Being told, with the first set of notes, to take out certain jokes or plot elements and then, ten revisions

---

5 Of *Murder in Successville*, *King Gary* and lots more.

later, being asked to put them back in. Getting a TV show to pilot stage is like pulling teeth. Getting your show actually on TV is like having all your teeth pulled. I'm still grateful to Tom and Rupert for even trying to get it there.

What the experience did make me realise is that there is room for these stories. It's never going to do Richard Osman numbers, but there exists an audience ready to laugh at plucky failure, at tales of the hip-hop world both tiny and somewhat notable. Well, at least I hope so anyway, because I've just given you a bunch more.

They're all I've got. Stories I've told in pubs. In articles. Over meals. If there's nothing left for me to do but tell stories, to lift the veil on this little career in the hope of entertaining a scattering of readers, then I'm perfectly happy with that. When everything and anything I once wrote for is no more, that seems a nice way to spend my time. Thank you for listening to them.

ACKNOWLEDGEMENTS

Andy Cowan for pretty much everything, Colin Steven, Paul Terzulli and Harold Heath. I owe you all bottles of something nice. The Fat Lace Crew: Dan Greenpeace, Mikey Mike, Barrie Bee, DJ Yoda, Rob Pursey. Rich 'Superix' Firth, for more than just the cover art. Tom Davis & Romesh Ranganathan. Rupert Majendie. Nat Saunders. Justin Quirk. Chris Read. Samilton the Musical and Floppy for putting up with me bellowing at them when they come to ask me a question that doesn't need asking while I'm trying to write. And for being lovely. Lucy, Martha and Alex. Everyone who supported *Wiggaz* in one way or another. All the editors and magazines who have given me work over the last 30 years. Ash Kollakowski, Ollie 'O-Real' Scull, Stephen Worthy, James McNally, Phillip Mlynar. All the HHC writers I grew up admiring and the ones I was proud to work with. The landlords and landladies of all the Leeds pubs and bars I wrote this in, in particular North Bar Social, The Rawdon Moustache, The Woolpack and The Turk's Head. All Leeds crew, London crew, Nottingham Crew, Otley crew, Yeadon and Rawdon crew. My family. Busby, Lord of dogs, forever with his head on my knee while I'm writing. Thanks to hip-hop music, for giving my life a purpose. Most of all, thank you to Emma, my incredible wife, for her unfailing support, love and patience.

Thanks to everyone who pre-ordered the book: Tim Aldous, Michael Ashiru, Toby Baldwin, Benny Ben, Paul Berryman, Susan Brown,

Simon Charvet, James Clarke, Charlotte Clayton, Daniel Cocker, Simon Coles, Neil Craven, Tom Dartnell, Ross Denoon, Matthew Eley, Andy Ellis, Holly Elsworth, Jennifer Elsworth, Morten Flobakk, Tim Forrester, Adam Gow, Thorsten Haag, Martin Haddock, Calum Haswell, Timothy Hocks, Ben Isaacs, Simone Ivatts, Dudley Jaynes, Krispijn Ju, Philipp Killmann, Sean Kirkegaard, Ash Kollakowski, Vincent Krasauskas, Daniel Ladd, Peter Lamb, Dan La Soul, Andrew Lawson, Hugh Leask, James Lebens, Ben Lewis, Alexandra Lynch, DJ Madnice, Phil Martin, Paul Mayman, Iain McNee, Alan McVeigh, Charlie Minnis, Alex Moitt, Kieron Molloy, Roger Mumby, Leon Nockolds, Phil Oliver, Adam Ormerod, Nick Oshikanlu, Paleface, Duncan Peetoom, Nika Peters, Claire Porter, Emma Porter-Emery, Florence Porter-Stephenson, Sammy Porter-Stephenson, Peter Rayner, Paul Sagar, Andrew Sanders, Oliver Scull, Christopher Sharp, Jonathan Shaw, David Smith, Matt Smith, Jack Southon, Antoni Spencer, Jamie Stephens, Kevin Strachan, Raine Supreme, PQuest, Atilla Tasdogen, Dave Taylor, Paul Terzulli, John Thompson, James Trice, Bryn Tyson-Diggle, Jussi Vesikansa, Richard Warren, Michael Wheeler, Joshua White, Daniel Whittle, Jamie Williamson, Simon Winfield, Marc Wood, Demyon Wright, Matt Yates, Daniel Young

CHAPTER CREDITS

1: The Saga Begins (Rakim, Universal Records, 1997)

2: Writing Slaps (The Jacka, Sumo Records, 2007)

3: God Connections (Al' Tariq, Correct Records, 1996)

4: Sleeping With the NME (Paris, Scarface Records, 1992)

5: My Writes (De La Soul, Tommy Boy, 2000)

6: Travel Jam (Brand Nubian, Elektra, 1993)

7: Appointment at the Fat Clinic (Digable Planets, Pendulum Records, 1993)

8: I'm Not a Player (Big Pun, Loud Records, 1997)

9: Straight Jacket (The Beatnuts, Relativity, 1994)

10: The Fine Print (King Geedorah, Big Dada Recordings, 2003)

11: How's Life in London? (London Posse, Bullett Records, 1993)

12: Write My Wrongs (The Jacka & Freeway, Golden Mean Music, 2013)

13: And The Winner Is (Chubb Rock with Howie Tee, Select Records, 1989)

14: Live on Stage (Roxanne Shante, Cold Chillin', 1989)

15: Destination Earth (1999) (Newcleus, Sunnyview, 1985)

16: Independent Leaders (The New Style, MCA Records, 1989)

17: Critical Beatdown (Ultramagnetic MC's, Next Plateau Records, 1988)

18: Breakdown New York Style (Rusty P the Toe Jammer & The Sure-shot 3, Critique, 1984)

19: For Pete's Sake (Pete Rock & CL Smooth, Elektra, 1992)

20: The Finish Line (Busta Rhymes, Elektra, 1996)

21: Guess Who's Comin' to Dinner (DJ Cash Money, Spoiled Brat Recordings, 1996)

22: The Art of Storytelling (Slick Rick, Def Jam Recordings, 1999)

23: The Questions (Audio Two, First Priority Music, 1988)

24: Fresh is the Word (Mantronix with MC Tee, Sleeping Bag Records, 1985)

25: Buggin' On Old TV (Crusaders for Real Hip-Hop, Profile Records, 1992)

26: Who's Your Rhymin' Hero (The Genius, Cold Chillin', 1991)

27: The Start of Your Ending (Mobb Deep, Loud Records, 1995)

28: X Versus The World (Overlord X, Mango, 1990)

29: Off The Books (The Beatnuts, Relativity, 1997)